BRITISH AND IRISH POLITICAL DRAMA IN THE TWENTIETH CENTURY

BRITISH AND IRISH POLITICAL DRAMA IN THE TWENTIETH CENTURY

Implicating the Audience

David Ian Rabey

The play's the thing
Wherein I'll catch the conscience of the King.
Hamlet

I want to bite the hand that feeds me
I want to bite that hand so badly
I want to make them wish THEY'D NEVER SEEN ME
Elvis Costello, 'Radio Radio'

MACMILLAN

First published 1986

Published by
THE MACMILLAN PRESS LTD
Houndmills, Basingstoke, Hampshire RG21 2XS
and London
Companies and representatives
throughout the world

Typeset by Wessex Typesetters
(Division of The Eastern Press Ltd)
Frome, Somerset

Printed in Hong Kong

British Library Cataloguing in Publication Data
Rabey, David Ian
British and Irish political drama in the
twentieth century: implacating the audience.
1. Political plays—History and criticism
2. English drama—20th century—History
and criticism
I. Title
822'.912'09258   PN1643
ISBN 0–333–38707–4

Dedicated to
Ken & Roma Rabey, my parents,
Robert Wilcher
and
John O'Brien
with thanks for their support and encouragement

Contents

Preface

In writing this book my intention is to examine the interaction of preconceptions, attitudes and consequent dramatic tensions between the audience and the author (via the actors and production team) when a play is presented in a theatre. I do not aim at providing a detailed critical analysis of individual plays – although some plays will be considered in more depth than others – but at providing a view of the developing trends and various strategies that British and Irish dramatists have adopted to express political dissatisfaction.

I will mainly restrict myself to the analysis of political drama in the legitimate, established theatre. This choice is in no way meant to disparage the work accomplished by the political theatre of fringe groups or touring companies; in their cases, it would probably be difficult to improve upon Catherine Itzin's survey of post-1968 developments, *Stages in the Revolution* (London, 1980), or Sandy Craig's collection of essays on recent or contemporary alternative theatre, *Dreams and Deconstructions* (London, 1980). Instead, I will discuss the often paradoxical position of a playwright who seeks to promote his or her views although (or because) they are opposed to the values represented by his or her audience (or even his or her medium), and the most notable attempts of this kind, successful or not, that have been made on the legitimate British and Irish stages in the twentieth century, along with some of the more profound influences upon their development from abroad.

D.I.R.

Acknowledgements

The author and publishers wish to thank the following who have kindly given permission for the use of copyright material: The Society of Authors, on behalf of the Bernard Shaw Estate, for the extracts from the plays and prefaces of Shaw; Judy Daish Associates Ltd, for the extracts from the works of Howard Barker; and Methuen, London and Random House, New York, on behalf of Bertolt Brecht, for the extracts from the plays of Brecht, and to the translators of the plays involved: Eric Bentley (*Mother Courage and her Children*), Howard Brenton (*The Life of Galileo*), Gerhard Nellhaus (*In the Jungle of Cities, Man equals Man*), Ralph Manheim (*The Exception and the Rule, The Resistible Rise of Arturo Ui*), Carl R. Mueller (*The Measures Taken*) and John Willett (*Drums in the Night, The Good Person of Szechwan, Mr Puntila and his Man Matti, The Messingkauf Dialogues, Brecht on Theatre*).

I would like to pay particular thanks to the following people: Susan MacMillan for her painstaking annotations, Stephen Booth for his moral support, and the friends, staff and students who made my time as a lecturer in English at Trinity College, Dublin, 1982–84, so enjoyably memorable, especially Geraldine Mangan, Christina Bauman, Brendan Kennelly, Terence Brown, Nicholas Grene, the participants in my Brenton and Edgar seminars, and Matthew Campbell, Damien Magee and Declan McCavann for introducing me to the plays of Martin Lynch. I am very grateful to all of the above for their encouragement and advice, though the main debts are recorded in the dedication.

D.I.R.

Introduction

The important thing
is to pull yourself up with your own hair
to turn yourself inside out
and see the whole world with fresh eyes

Peter Weiss,
Marat/Sade[1]

All theatre is political; such is the persuasive claim of George H. Szanto in *Theater and Propaganda*.[2] All dramatic presentations are propagandistic, presenting 'partial information (the play's aesthetic perspective) and [taking] an ideological position in relation to that information'.[3] In the words of Roger Hudson, if a play 'doesn't criticize the political and social system of the country it is in fact supporting it and indirectly (or directly) propagandizing for its continued acceptance as the way things should be'.[4] This constitutes what Szanto terms 'integration propaganda', and is characterized by its very refusal to acknowledge its own political bias or provoke any suggestion that it might contain one, thereby disqualifying its purported claims to objectivity, impartiality or verisimilitude. Correspondingly, Roland Barthes claims in *Mythologies* that 'The bourgeoisie hides the fact that it is the bourgeoisie and thereby produces myth' – myth being a latent affirmation of the status quo based on the removal or subordination of historical determinants from the image in question. Revolution, on the other hand, he says, 'announces itself openly as revolution and thereby abolishes myth'.[5]

If this is true, then what is special about overtly 'political drama'? Perhaps, following Barthes's theory, the label itself. *'Political* drama' emphasizes the directness of its address to problematic social matters, and its attempt to interpret these problems in political terms. Political drama communicates its sense of these problems' avoidability, with implicit or explicit condemnation of the political circumstances that have allowed

1

them to rise and continue to exist (just as Brecht identifies *The Rise of Arturo Ui* as *Resistible*). In perceiving social problems as avoidable, political drama is necessarily diverging from the worldview that the agents of the status quo would seek to impose for the continued smooth running of society in its present form.

The merging of social drama into political drama is an easy transition and may cause problems of classification (as in the work of Osborne and Wesker), but for the purposes of this study I will take *social* drama as that which purports to act as an impartial report on social relations, or to focus on specific social abuses, without stepping over into an attack on the fundamentals of the society in question; in contrast, I will take *political* drama as that which views specific social abuses as symptomatic of a deeper illness, namely injustice and anomalies at the heart of society's basic power structure.

So how does political drama achieve its ends? By what means does it convincingly illustrate the avoidability of social problems, or expose the contradictions inherent in the values of the established order? By being *dramatic*. Peter Brook has warned those who attempt to use a play as a bearer of a political message that 'Whatever the value of the message, in the end it only works according to values that belong to the stage itself'.[6] But when successfully realized, this qualification becomes a strength. When a play works 'according to the values that belong to the stage itself', it places itself beyond the values of the social, or even theatrical, institutions that produced it. Drama, the most public of art forms, seeks to unite its audience in a common charge of feeling. This may take the form of an emotional catharsis, as advocated by Antonin Artaud's Theatre of Cruelty, illustrating the dark, amoral urges within man and his position of powerlessness before the dark, amoral forces which govern his world; or it may take the form of a more intellectually based response such as Brecht's objectives in theatre provide, namely 'the pleasure we feel when we discover new truths, the exhilaration we experience when we enlarge our understanding'.[7] In both cases, the unifying charge of feeling produced by successful drama works by means of an expansion of consciousness. Tragedy and comedy are not catered for in our sense of the norm, and the emotional response they elicit stems from their violation of propriety. This power of violation stems from the tension between two value systems, neither of which can be denied; moreover, neither can one establish a prior claim or be identified as the interloper; they are simply coexistent. For example, in *Macbeth* the audience oscillates between the human viewpoint of Macbeth and the cosmic viewpoint of the witches; in *The Comedy of Errors* the audience is sole party to discrepant (and apparently mutually exclusive) viewpoints of both the natives of Ephesus and the natives of Syracuse; and in Samuel Beckett's *Waiting for Godot*, the play capitalizes on the delicate balance it is likely to set in the audience's minds between the existential dignity salvaged by the tramps by their continued existence and the frustrations involved in their clinging so squalidly to a hostile, absurd universe.

I contend that political drama is successful when the audience's morality is poised against contemporary society, so that the enforced fluctuation between two ostensibly congruent sets of norms reveals a contradiction. Having exposed this contradiction as being forced by the social status quo, the drama will espouse a general moral, which the audience would support, but in a way which conflicts with conventional social edict – which the audience would normally assume to be the practical embodiment and enforcement of this moral. The thrust of the drama seeks to demonstrate that society's embodiment of this moral is only ostensible – or perhaps, from an alienated viewpoint, inimical to it. A fruitful comparison is the dramatically attractive figure of the Jacobean malcontent who becomes disillusioned with social corruption to the point of acting as an agent of a super-social morality. In *The Revenger's Tragedy*, Vindice's defeat arrives when the forces of the supposedly logical and just social mechanism are once more in the ascendancy, and his sense of super-social ethics is condemned, but it is a rare audience who will exult in hearing his sentence. Many political dramatists endeavour to invest their protagonists with a similar dramatic power at the expense of the forces of conventional society, so that the audience is caught in a disturbing conflict between submission to the dictates of society and sympathy for the hero's charismatic appeal to some higher moral law which contradicts these dictates.[8] In the words of Edward Bond, 'They judge and in judging extend their self-consciousness because they have not merely responded to a situation in the socially prescribed way (as conditioned by institutions and tacitly accepted mores) but have been made to see aspects of the situation or character which the socially prescribed response blots out'.[9]

Alternatively, rather than elect to use a dramatically powerful spokesman, a dramatist may choose to provide a satirical anatomy of society, like Wesker's *The Kitchen* or Brenton and Hare's *Brassneck*, which is organized to prove Marx's theory that by intensifying a situation it becomes a revolutionary one.[10] The very absence of an overt expression of morality may become a characteristic of a society's degenerate state, and clever rogues may prove the only dramatically attractive alternative to dull rogues, as in Jacobean city comedy. Satirical anatomies work by referring to a latent sense of morality, all the more striking by its absence from a play's heightened image of our society engaged in its characteristic processes. Hegel and Marx, profound influences on Brecht's theory, both discussed the nature of alienation (*Entfremdung*) in the dialectical process of thought. Hegel claimed that only when an object is alienated can it be known, that is, no longer taken for granted, but seen in a new light; whereas Marx uses the term 'alienation' to discuss the separation of modern man from his total human nature, proposing that the more extreme the process of alienation becomes, the more urgent the contradictory pressure to reverse it.[11] By presenting an alarming image of modern society, the satirical anatomist correspondingly can provoke a revulsion which depends on a sense of discrepancy between moral idealism and social reality. As Sartre claims:

> If society sees itself and, in particular, sees itself as *seen*, there is, by virtue of this very fact, a contesting of the established values of the regime. The writer presents it with its image; he calls upon it to assume it or change itself. At any rate, it changes; it loses the equilibrium which its ignorance had given it; it wavers between shame and cynicism; it practises dishonesty; thus the writer gives society a *guilty conscience*; he is thereby in a state of perpetual antagonism towards the conservative forces which are maintaining the balance he tends to upset.[12]

What is the usual response to political drama? In his 'Short Organum', Brecht claimed that the pleasure derived from a perfect representation of social life 'must be converted into the higher pleasure felt when the rules emerging from this social life are treated as imperfect and provisional. With this the theatre will leave its spectators fruitfully disposed, even after the spectacle is over'.[13] However, audiences are rarely so co-operative. Indeed, political drama that is widely applauded or even placidly accepted requires close attention. If a political playwright articulates unexpressed feeling of a minority which is nevertheless large enough to form a sizeable proportion of his audience, or better yet wins new support for the minority's viewpoint, he deserves critical and commercial success. But there are dangers that popular political plays may have tackled subjects too petty to create any radical changes in consciousness, so that the plays are dismissed (like Osborne's *The World of Paul Slickey*) or readily assimilated by a majority or are addressing the very section of society for whom the playwright is trying to speak, and end up preaching to the converted. In so far as the playwright's audience is representative of society in general, he must oppose their values. As Robert Brustein claims in *The Theatre of Revolt*, rather than be the spokesman of an audience, the rebel dramatist will most likely become its adversary, and the audience may find itself assailed directly or represented on stage by a satirical figure.[14] However, political drama that can only repulse its audience commits artistic (and commercial) suicide, because it hinders the acceptance of its viewpoint. The playwright must seek subtle means of communication rather than simply abuse contemporary norms, yet he must not compromise his message so much that it is lost. Bernard Shaw found success through the manipulation of conventional dramatic forms, using them as a palliative to his political message. This technique of evoking a stock response in order to subvert it is a frequent characteristic of successful political drama. Ronald Ayling has described this effect as manifested in the work of Sean O'Casey:

> by encouraging stock reactions . . . at what prove to be wholly inappropriate moments in the dramatic action, O'Casey sets in motion a series of emotional and intellectual collisions with which to disturb the minds of the spectators, to challenge and subvert the conventional moral and social attitudes of native audiences. He wanted to startle, shock, even scandalize Irish audiences into questioning inherited political and religious beliefs and, indeed, reverential national attitudes on all levels of public life. . . . It is not the familiarity of the subject-matter . . . that affects native or non-native audiences so much as it is the author's deliberate and disturbing manipulation of such experience.[15]

If a play elicits stock responses, it resembles Szanto's model of integration propaganda, in that it perpetuates accepted channels of reaction. But if a play can elicit a stock response and proceed to show it in an effective alienated light, it will begin a change in the audience's consciousness by setting up contradictory reactions in them; standard reactions will be called into question and, ideally, the spectator will attain a new self-consciousness and moral autonomy. A point of sympathy must be established in the audience, and then negated by another viewpoint, if consciousness is to be changed. As David Hare has observed, 'A play is not actors, a play is not the text; a play is what happens between the stage and the audience. A play is a performance. So if a play is to be a weapon in the class struggle, then that weapon is not going to be the things you are saying; it is the interaction of what you are saying and what the audience is thinking'.[16] David Edgar has identified the 'upending of received forms' as one of the main sources of potency in recent British political plays, along with the power of a shocking on-stage revelation. In a fundamental break with the Brechtian tradition of distancing the audience from occurrences, many writers of the seventies 'involve the audience, provoking them into thought by the very shock and surprise of the images'.[17] But the final effect remains the same, namely a disruption of conventional response.

It is also useful to discriminate between the comparative aims and styles of political *drama* (or plays) and of political *theatre*, for which Sandy Craig has proposed a good working definition:

> the important feature which distinguishes political plays from political theatre is this: political plays seek to appeal to, and influence, the middle class, in particular that section of the middle class which is influential in moulding 'public opinion'. The implication of this is that society can be reformed and liberalized, where necessary, by the shock troops of the middle class – and, of course, such people are influential in campaigns for reform. But further, political plays in bourgeois theatre implicitly realize that the middle class remains the progressive class within society. Political theatre, on the other hand, as embodied in the various political theatre companies, aims – with varying degrees of success – to appeal to, and be an expression of, the working class. Its underlying belief is that the working class is the progressive class within society.[18]

A clear and realistic assessment of one's potential audience is particularly important for a playwright to write to maximum effect.

What can political drama do beyond exposing the contradictions within society via the individual consciousness? Theoretically, it can posit alternatives to the current situation. In the promotion of general moral imperatives, it can work to great effect, as in the mothers' prayer for peace that recurs in *Juno and the Paycock*, but drama does not lend itself easily to an exposition on any grand scale of definite social reforms; the ambitious imaginativeness of *Back to Methuselah* far outweighs its dramatic potential. Drama thrives on conflict expressed through action and dialogue, whereas Shaw's prescriptive vision frequently resembles a lecture or sermon, so superficial are its conflicts. As Robert Brustein suggests, drama without debate approaches mere fantasizing.[19] Hence, political drama will usually depict a clash of values within society with the intention of providing a negative critique of that society. There is considerably more scope and potential dramatic vitality in exposing the iniquities of capitalism than in attempting to present an engaging, practical image of a socialist society (David Hare's *Fanshen* being a recent notable exception, although this gains its dramatic impetus from conflicts that are engendered within a new community). The successful political dramatist will ensure that his drama retains an engaging vitality from the debate of conflicting viewpoints, taking care that his personal viewpoint is not mitigated to the point of ineffectuality, nor allowed unopposed victory at the expense of dramatic tension. By these means, effective political drama can manoeuvre its audience into a critical position towards the social status quo, provided the drama moves on premises that are sufficiently imaginatively convincing.

1   Socialist Supermen and Pilgrims' Progress

BERNARD SHAW

All who achieve real distinction in life begin as revolutionists. The most distinguished persons become more revolutionary as they grow older, though they are commonly supposed to become more conservative owing to their loss of faith in conventional methods of reform.

The Revolutionist's Handbook[1]

Ibsen's plays provided great inspiration and direction for Shaw, whose dedication to 'Ibsenism' was really a commitment to a specifically political reading of the Norwegian's works and to an attitude towards society that could be distilled from Ibsen's dramatic technique:

In the theatre of Ibsen we are not flattered spectators killing an idle hour with an ingenious and amusing entertainment: we are 'guilty creatures sitting at a play'; and the technique of pastime is no more applicable than at a murder trial.

The technical novelties of the Ibsen and post-Ibsen plays are, then: first, the introduction of the discussion and its development until it so overspreads and interpenetrates the action that it finally assimilates it, making play and discussion practically identical; and, second, as a consequence of making the spectators themselves the persons of the drama, and the incidents of their own lives its incidents, the disuse of the old stage tricks by which audiences had to be induced to take an interest in unreal people and improbable circumstances, and the substitution of a forensic technique of recrimination, disillusion and penetration through ideals to the truth, with a

9

free use of all the rhetorical and lyrical arts of the orator, the preacher, the pleader, and the rhapsodist.[2]

In his own plays, Shaw does *not* in fact reject 'the old stage tricks'. He never ceases to use such tricks to elicit conventional stock responses from the audience; but then Shaw brings the characters, circumstances and audience responses into contact with a realistic perspective (the 'forensic technique', often personified) which will indict their idealism as ridiculous and dangerous. Both of these stage tricks – old and new – have theatrical merit, and Shaw uses to the full the vitality *both* of the traditional devices (or parodies of them) to create larger-than-life characters *and* from new dramatic techniques that cut through conventions with wit and intelligence. This programme would seem a recipe for self-conscious metadrama but for a crucial identification which gives Shaw a dramatic technique brilliantly congruent with his moral intentions. This identification is born of his days as a theatre critic: 'When my moral sense revolted, as it often did to the very fibres, it was invariably at the nauseous compliances of the theatre with conventional virtue.'[3] Contemporary theatre's support of conventional values, and provision of characters who, as models of behaviour and thought, were likely to perpetuate these values, Shaw identified as a vicious spiral of romantic idealism which he attempted to break by falsifying simultaneously the social convention, the theatrical convention that supports the social convention, and the part of the audience's sympathies that is unthinkingly accorded to the social convention through the theatrical convention. *Plays Pleasant* (1894–97) and *Captain Brassbound's Conversion* (1899) are intended to debunk a romantic, theatricalized view of life which might otherwise flourish. Thus, the audience gains a critical detachment from (and often laughs at) its previously unquestioned preconceptions; Shaw says, 'I must . . . warn my readers that my attacks are directed against themselves, not against my stage figures.'[4] The moral failures of society are condemned, and our complacency implicates us in the continuance of this immoral society. *Widowers' Houses* (1892) presents a sharp anatomy of an unacceptable capitalist society which, nevertheless, we continue to accept. Like the young romantic hero Trench, the audience is taken on a pilgrimage to guilty self-knowledge; it is his (and the audience's) investments that give Cokane and Sartorius their power, much as Trench would like to dissociate himself from the crooks' dealings. The play satirizes social standards of propriety: when Sartorius threatens Lickcheese with unemployment (a scene that may be a comic echo of the Bernick-Aune dialogue in Ibsen's *Pillars of the Community*), Lickcheese protests, 'Which of us is the worse, I should like to know? Me that wrings the money out to keep a home over my children, or you that spend it and try to shove the blame on me?', only to receive the rejoinder, 'A most improper observation to address to a gentleman, Mr Lickcheese! A most revolutionary sentiment!'[5] Similarly, Sartorius refuses to improve his slums because, he says, 'if we made the houses any better, the rents would have to be raised so much that the poor people would be unable to pay, and would be thrown homeless on the streets'. Blanche suggests 'Well, turn them out and get in a respectable class of people.' Sartorius sympathizes with her heartlessness: 'It is the ladylike view of the matter.'[6] Such satirical grotesquerie urges dissociation from its implications, but it is precisely this dissociation that is shown as impossible for Trench and the audience. The play is a fine example of what Shaw termed the Ibsenist art of 'sharpshooting at the audience': 'Never mislead an audience, was an old rule. But the new school will trick the spectator into forming a meanly false judgment, and then convict him of it in the next act, often to his grievous mortification.'[7] *Mrs Warren's Profession* (1902) follows the same line. Mrs Warren rebukes the society that has driven her to prostitution, and the audience may, like Vivie, temporarily sympathize sentimentally with her. But then Mrs Warren is revealed as a self-interested perpetuator of the system, not its moral superior, and Vivie is shown to be tainted by the same crime. As Crofts tells her, 'If youre going to pick and choose your acquaintances on moral principles, youd better clear out of this country, unless you want to cut yourself out of all decent society.'[8] Shaw now uses Vivie to rebuke Mrs Warren for *her* faults, the most telling criticism being that she is 'a conventional woman at heart',[9] thereby aiding society to continue unchecked in its moral damage.

Shaw does not present easily identifiable, stylized villains (except, as in *The Devil's Disciple*, to question society's stock valuation of them); rather, as he points out about *Mrs Warren's Profession*, 'Society, and not any individual, is the villain of the piece.'[10] One might say the same for the works of Ibsen, Strindberg and Chekhov. The difference is that Shaw has a

definite remedial programme to which the apparently unanswer-
able dilemmas of *Widowers' House* and *Mrs Warren's Profession*
implicitly refer us, namely socialism. But Shaw stresses, 'I am,
like most Socialists, an extreme Individualist',[11] and accordingly
many of his critiques of society have their basis in the same
Nietzschean objections to the mediocrity of social life raised by the
naturalists, but more consciously so, as the title of *Man and
Superman* (1905) reveals. The play is a striking literalization of a
comment Shaw made years before he wrote the play: 'The
pleasures of the senses I can sympathize with and share; but the
substitution of sensuous ecstasy for intellectual activity and
honesty is the very devil.'[12]

Man and Superman steps back from the propagandist plays and
their bids to identify society's disorders and imply remedies; it
focusses rather on the *ability* to identify society's disorders and to
find fruitful methods of reacting to them. Don Juan is conceived as
a super-social moral spokesman, splendidly suitable for Shaw's
purposes because he represents the man who 'follows his own
instincts without regard to the common, statute or canon law; and
therefore, whilst gaining the ardent sympathy of our rebellious
instincts (which are flattered by the brilliances with which Don
Juan associates them), finds himself by fraud and force as
unscrupulously as a farmer defends his crops by the same means
against vermin'.[13] These rebellious instincts associate him with
his descendant John Tanner, who shares that 'sense of reality that
disables convention'.[14] When nineteenth- and twentieth-century
nations have embarked on such potentially ruinous courses
through these conventions, Shaw stresses that 'there is no future
for men, however brimming with crude vitality, who are neither
intelligent nor politically educated enough to be Socialists'.[15] Jack
is provided with a set of conventional foils to deflate, scoring off
the standard 'jeune premier' Tavy and the reactionary Ramsden
in the same sparkling comedy-of-manners way that Bluntschli
scores off the standard heroic model of Sergius in *Arms and the Man*,
but Ann Whitfield can (in dramatic if not intellectual terms) make
Jack 'collapse like a pricked bladder' at the moments when his
personal pride and excessive zeal threaten to eclipse all other
standards of conduct, and Enry Straker's bluff realism also
provides a comic perspective on the satirist. The complexity
increases in the central Hell debate which sets Don Juan's
social-existentialist commitment to the Life Force against the

romantic–tragic perspective of the Devil and the Statue, who exemplifies the way 'the moral sense remains dormant in people who are content with the customary formulas for respectable conduct'.[16] Ann, as Everywoman, has to make her choice between these worldviews, and elects to join Juan/Tanner in bringing about the Superman. The subtle balance of the debate is a long way from the stark moral–economic fables, *Widowers' Houses* and *Mrs Warren's Profession*, but this does not indicate a lapse in commitment. The Devil is persuasive and appealing, but anyone who prefers his arguments misunderstands Juan's criticisms of them; the Devil speaks eloquently to trick the audience into sympathizing with his views, only for Juan to dismiss these views as ignorant, short-sighted and defeatist. Tanner's earthly capitulation to Ann is no repudiation of his beliefs or conversion into conventionalism, despite his fears; rather, pride and austere rationality are deflated as he receives a corrective nudge from the Life Force in order that he may fulfil the work set by this presiding genius more (not less) efficiently. Ann mocks his pretentions ('it sounds like the Life Guards'), but aids his purpose in a super-rational way even Tanner cannot perceive. As Shaw explains in the Preface, the sexual initiative is 'politically the most important of all the initiatives, because our political experiment of democracy, the last refuge of cheap misgovernment, will ruin us if our citizens are ill bred'.[17] Thus, from a practical concern with socialist reform, we see Shaw extend his philosophy of social amelioration into metaphysics. Realizing the limitation of a democracy that 'cannot rise above the level of human material of which its voters are made', Tanner and Shaw posit 'a democracy of Supermen'.[18] The interim rises of fascism and Nazism make this objective sound unattractive to modern ears, but Shaw takes care to add the antidogmatic qualification: 'The proof of the Superman will be in the living; and we shall find out how to produce him by the old method of trial and error, and not by waiting for a completely convincing prescription of his ingredients.'[19] Shaw also defends himself by saying 'I have been accused of preaching a Final Ethical Superman: no other, in fact, than our old friend the Just Man Made Perfect!'[20] As Carl Levine has commented, Shaw inherits some of Nietzsche's distaste for the herd instinct of the common man,[21] but whereas the more literally individualistic Nietzsche proposes the creation of a new ethical class, Shaw seeks to raise the lot of all men (initially through

democratic socialism, then increasingly through creative evolution) in a more utilitarian manner. Also, Shaw opposes strict
ethical determinism as the mark of the stifling convention against
which his heroes are matched; for him, as for Brecht afterwards,
'The golden rule is that there are no golden rules.'[22]

Although a theme of *Man and Superman* is raising the lot of all
men, many of Shaw's other plays are more concerned with the
progress of Don Juan's Life Force ideal than with the progress of
John Tanner's revolutionary socialist principles within a capitalist social context. *The Man of Destiny* (1896), *The Devil's Disciple*
(1897), *Caesar and Cleopatra* (1898) and *Saint Joan* (1924) trace this
Life Force, as manifested through certain gifted individuals,
struggling against romantic convention, reactionary stagnation
and general symptoms of the 'herd morality' in an attempt to
shape history. As Don Juan says, 'The philosopher is Nature's
pilot. And there you have the difference: to be in Hell is to drift: to
be in Heaven is to steer.'[23] Unlike the social tragedies of Ibsen,
Strindberg and Chekhov, Shaw's plays are concerned to inspire
by depicting a superman triumphing over his stifling, conformist
environment, not to present a defeatist image of that superman's
thwarting. Only *Saint Joan* has a tragic flavour, and there the
tragedy concerns Joan's persecutors rather than the posthum-
ously victorious saint. Men of basic integrity are shown to be
warped by their service to an excessively rigid, short-sighted
convention: 'The tragedy of such murders is that they are not
committed by murderers. They are judicial murders, pious
murders; and this contradiction at once brings an element of
comedy into the tragedy: the angels may weep at the murder, but
the gods laugh at the murderers.'[24] *Saint Joan* makes us party to
this dual cosmic perspective. It is the same perspective from
which the god Ra speaks the Prologue to *Caesar and Cleopatra*, but
Ra brings a theatrical and political immediacy to cosmic contempt for the human:

> Peace! Be silent and hearken unto me, ye quaint little islanders
> . . . neither do any of ye regard it seemly to do aught until ye see
> all the rest do so too; wherefore it commonly happens that in
> great emergencies ye do nothing, though each telleth his fellow
> that something must be done.
> . . .
> look to it, lest some little people whom ye would enslave rise up

and become in the hands of God the scourge of your boastings
and your injustices and your lusts and stupidities.

. . .

ye are a dull folk, and instruction is wasted on you; and I had
not spoken so much but that it is in the nature of a god to
struggle forever with the dust and the darkness, and to drag
from them, by the force of his longing for the divine, more life
and more light. . . . Farewell: and do not presume to applaud
me.[25]

Back to Methuselah (1921) represents the full flowering of Shaw's
philosophical interest in, and dramatic exposition of, creative
evolution theory, which becomes an increasingly attractive ideal
for Shaw as he grows increasingly despairing of conventional
channels for social reform, particularly democracy. *Back to
Methuselah* extends Ra's divine perspective on the audience, who
are increasingly encouraged to view themselves as intolerably
imperfect in the process of evolution. As Shaw admits:

A doubt . . . had grown steadily in my mind during my forty
years public service as a Socialist: namely, whether the human
animal, as he exists at present, is capable of solving the social
problems raised by his own aggregation, or as he calls it, his
civilization.

. . .

The real Class War will be a war of intellectual classes; and its
conquest will be the souls of the children.[26]

Back to Methuselah presents us with scenes from this intellectual
class war as creative evolution struggles towards its millennium,
whilst forcing the audience to align their hostilities against their
own evolutionary stage. In 'The Gospel According to the Brothers
Barnabas', contemporary politicians Asquith and Lloyd George
are lampooned and merged, emphasizing triviality and ineffectuality amongst professional politicians and their inability to
countenance any progressive ideal, creative evolution or otherwise. 'Tragedy of an Elderly Gentleman' shows a short-liver like
the audience to be a childish anachronism from the point of view
of long-livers, but the play is so weighted in favour of the
long-livers as to weaken dramatic conflict and hinder the
audience's identification with the obstacle to progress. The

automata in 'As Far as Thought Can Reach' fulfil the same role as the Elderly Gentleman by representing modern mindless romanticism, but their extermination is accomplished more quickly and has more comic vitality, because they are made to express the more ridiculous aspects of twentieth-century attitudes whilst the Newly-Born acts as a focal agent for our education in the ways of the new world, and we consequently share her condescending, comic view of Ozymandias and Cleopatra. But generally, *Back to Methuselah* suffers from a deficiency in dramatic conflict, previously recognized by Shaw as so vital to his art: 'Now unity, however desirable in political agitations, is fatal to drama; for every drama must present a conflict. The end may be reconciliation or destruction; or, as in life itself, there may be no end; but the conflict is indispensable: no conflict, no drama.'[27] The intentions of *Back to Methuselah* are 'metabiological' rather than political, but the Pentateuch uses techniques found in more socially oriented plays, albeit to less effect. Shaw's doctrines of creative evolution and the Life Force extend the plays' concerns from the political to the metaphysical through a common basis in Nietzschean will-to-power, commitment to self-overcoming and to consequent social amelioration. However, while impatience for progress may infect the audience of *Back to Methuselah*, its injunction to become a higher form of life is less easily realised and less guilt-provoking than would be a diatribe against capitalism combined with proof of our own moral blame in capitalism's continuance. *Man and Superman* is more successful than *Back to Methuselah* in that it blends cosmic–evolutionary and socialist–political impulses in the figure of Juan/Tanner, demonstrating their connected and complementary qualities.

Major Barbara (1905) constituted a return to the theme and style of *Plays Unpleasant*, as suggested by its working title, *Andrew Undershaft's Profession*. *Major Barbara* combines *Plays Unpleasant*'s implication of an audience surrogate with *Man and Superman*'s conscious address to social reform and debate between alternative programmes. The sheer weight of convention makes identification with a Salvation Army leader over a gleeful arms manufacturer almost inevitable, but Barbara's financial and moral association with Undershaft is revealed first as unavoidable, then as a positive blessing. In *Widowers' Houses*, Trench's education as an Everyman figure indicted the audience for unacceptable immorality, to which Trench then submitted wholeheartedly with deliberately shocking ease. Barbara's education in the dishonesty of her creed brings her disillusionment, but her subsequent embrace of Undershaft's brutally realistic enterprises gives her and Cusins an opportunity of reforming the system the only way possible – from the basis of crude martial and intellectual realism, the preparedness to kill which is 'the final test of conviction, the only lever strong enough to overturn a social system, the only way of saying Must'.[28] Like Strindberg's Jean in *Miss Julie*, Undershaft is a determined elemental force breaking into the torpid world of ineffectual social aristocracy, a true Dionysus with a motto 'Unashamed'. Along with Cusins and Barbara, the audience has its liberal reformism debunked by Undershaft, who says '*I* am the government of your country',[29] but also proves that he is the means of changing governments by trading moral and spiritual principles for decisive practical action. Along with Cusins, the audience is brought to acknowledge that Undershaft's analysis of the basis of power is true. 'But it ought not to be true'[30] – at least according to conventional morality. Undershaft's rejoinder is that 'If your old religion broke down, get a new and better one for tomorrow.'[31] As for social reform, Undershaft says, 'Whatever can blow men up can blow society up. The history of the world is the history of those who had courage enough to embrace this truth'[32] This is an anticipation of Brecht's famous 'Sink in filth / Embrace the butcher, but / Change the world'[33]). Cusins's rejection of the Armorer's Faith promises to give the play's Dionysian energy a moral direction and ends the play optimistically, echoed by Barbara's acknowledgment that 'the way of life lies through the factory of death' and that instead of bringing religion to the masses, she must aid 'the raising of hell to heaven and of man to God'.[34] Few plays can move an audience so rapidly to such unconventional and radicalized conclusions as *Major Barbara*. Shaw forces the spectator into a 'meanly false judgement' and convicts him of it in the next act, and makes him embrace previously insupportable realities which were apparently diametrically opposed to the initial false ideals. If *Widowers' Houses* identified the audience as guilty capitalists, *Major Barbara* manoeuvres the audience into the position of something approaching ruthless revolutionaries.

The spinelessness and purposelessness of the English aristocracy, which is compared disparagingly to Undershaft, the Nietzschean aristocrat, in *Major Barbara*, becomes the theme of

Misalliance (1910) and *Heartbreak House* (1919). Both plays depict representative households and assemble a cast of representative characters to illustrate the aimless drifting of ostensible national leaders. These depictions of genteel sterility recall Chekhov's representative networks of failed characters, whilst the frankly fantastic turns of plot, schematic characterization and airs of busy (*Misalliance*) and languid (*Heartbreak House*) purposelessness anticipate absurdism. Both plays follow the Chekhovian model. They present intensified images of 'cultured, leisured Europe before the war'[35] turned 'helpless wasters of their inheritance'.[36] The title *Misalliance* refers partially to the breakdown of satisfactory continuity between generations: 'children and parents confront one another as two classes in which all the political power is on one side'.[37] Moreover, because 'liberty is the one thing that parents, schoolmasters, and rulers spend their lives in extirpating for the sake of an immediately quiet and finally disastrous life',[38] the children are forced into constricting moulds which leave them with all energies dissipated: 'We are a mass of people living in a submissive routine to which we have all been drilled from our childhood.'[39] The resultant misfits are represented in *Misalliance* by Johnny, 'all body and no brains'; Bentley, 'all brains and no more body than is absolutely necessary'; and the reckless, iconoclastic but finally ineffectual Hypatia, who at least manages to formulate her dissatisfaction with the role determined for her:

> Girls withering into ladies. Ladies withering into old maids. Nursing old women. Running errands for old men. Oh, you can't imagine the fiendish selfishness of the old people and the maudlin sacrifice of the young. It's more unbearable than any poverty: more horrible than any regular-right-down-wickedness. Oh, home! home! parents! family! duty! how I loathe them! How I'd like to see them all blown to bits![40]

(Hypatia's wish is almost granted in *Heartbreak House*; and her consciousness of her wealth as an imprisonment foreshadows the patient of *Too True to be Good*.)

Although *Misalliance* portrays Tarleton with affectionate humour, his capitalist attitudes have helped to create the existential pathos of surrounding characters. At one point he exclaims, 'I believe I ought to have made Johnny an author',[41] as if referring to a piece of plasticine. When the dangerously living Nietzschean aristocrat Lina arrives to shame the national aristocrats, Tarleton cannot but be attracted to her energy and feel repulsion at his own conventional, professional role ('I can't help that ridiculous old shopkeeper . . . I loathe him because he's a living lie. My soul's not like that; it's like yours'[42]). Julius Baker is a farcical caricature of a revolutionary, but his protests sound a real note of pain:

> Do you know what my life is? I spend my days from nine to six – nine hours of daylight and fresh air – in a stuffy little den counting another man's money. Ive an intellect: a mind and a brain and a soul. . . . How can a man tied to a desk from nine to six be anything – be even a man, let alone a soldier?[43]

The other fantastic entrant, Lina, can also pinpoint failings in the Heartbreak House when she finds herself being treated like a regular aristocrat:

> Old pal: this is a stuffy house. You seem to think of nothing but making love. All the conversation here is about love-making. . . . It is disgusting. It is not healthy. Your women are kept idle and dressed up for no other purpose than to be made love to. I have not been here an hour; and already everybody makes love to me as if because I am a woman it were my profession to be made love to.[44]

The other misalliance of the title is the lack of spiritual fertility in the concluding marriages. Lina's adventurousness will benefit Bentley, but it lures him away from the house he should take charge of; and Hypatia's union with Percival is summarized by her plea 'Papa: buy the brute for me'.[45] *Misalliance* is hilarious, but fulfils Shaw's criteria for comedy as 'a destructive, derisory, critical, negative art . . . shewing an uneasiness in the presence of error which is the surest symptom of intellectual vitality'.[46] *Heartbreak House* is more sombre than *Misalliance*, with the threat of disaster imminent. Its preface also indicts English aristocrats:

> They hated politics. They did not wish to realize Utopia for the common people: they wished to realize their favourite fictions

and poems in their lives; and, when they could, they lived
without scruple on incomes which they did nothing to earn.
. . .
power and culture were in separate compartments.[47]

Like Trench, Vivie and Barbara, Ellie Dunn serves as the
audience's focal point as she learns about the house and suffers
crushing disillusionment; and like Barbara she is brought to
perceive a truth and more realistic hope for the future beyond her
lost ideals and search for happiness. Assembled in this English
menagerie are the romantics Hector and Hesione, Ariadne ('Oh,
how I longed! – to be respectable, to be a lady, to live as others did,
not to have to think of anything for myself'[48]), the ineffectual
liberal Mazzini Dunn, the wastrel Randall, the philistine capitalist Mangan and Captain Shotover, the Shavian genius who is
permitted remarkably direct comments on the representative
figures around him:

> CAPTAIN SHOTOVER: What then is to be done? Are we to be kept
> forever in the mud by these hogs to whom the universe is
> nothing but a machine for greasing their bristles and filling
> their snouts?
> HECTOR: Are Mangan's bristles worse than Randall's love-
> locks?
> CAPTAIN SHOTOVER: We must win powers of life and death over
> them both. I refuse to die until I have invented the means.
> HECTOR: Who are we that we should judge them?
> CAPTAIN SHOTOVER: What are they that they should judge us?
> Yet they do, unhesitatingly. . . . They believe in themselves.
> When we believe in ourselves, we shall kill them. . . . We kill the
> better half of ourselves every day to propitiate them. The
> knowledge that these people are there to render all our
> aspirations barren prevents us from having the aspirations.
> And when we are tempted to seek their destruction they bring
> forth demons to delude us, disguised as pretty daughters, and
> singers and poets and the like, for whose sake we spare them.[49]

The parabolical style allows Shaw to identify the problematic
members and forces of society with a clarity and power beyond the
naturalistic playwright's constrictions. The Shavian voice of the
Captain grows in command for the redeemable erstwhile roman-

tics Ellie and Hector. Mazzini's complacency is undercut by these more authoritative voices and shown to be conventionality rather than culture. His opinion that the Heartbreakers are 'rather a favourable specimen of what is best in our English culture'[50] serves as an ironic indictment of that culture. He is convinced that 'Nothing ever does happen.' 'It's amazing', he says, 'how well we get along, all things considered.'[51] This is refuted decisively by the final bombing attack. Again, the despairing Hector serves to draw a forceful remedial prescription from the Captain:

> HECTOR: And this ship we are all in? This soul's prison we call England?
> CAPTAIN SHOTOVER: The captain is in his bunk, drinking bottled ditch-water; and the crew is gambling in the forecastle. She will strike and split and sink. Do you think the laws of God will be suspended in favour of England because you were born in it?
> HECTOR: Well, I don't mean to be drowned like a rat in a trap. I still have the will to live. What am I to do?
> CAPTAIN SHOTOVER: Do? Nothing simpler. Learn your business as an Englishman.
> HECTOR: And what may my business as an Englishman be, pray?
> CAPTAIN SHOTOVER: Navigation. Learn it and live; or leave it and be damned.[52]

Heartbreak House stops just short of fulfilling Hector's nihilistic impulse 'Fall. Fall and crush.'[53] The play offers a tellingly tenuous prescription for survival which is as schematic as an algebraic formula: Ellie's youthful vigour plus Shotover's Nietzschean will minus Mangan and the burglar ('the two burglars – the two practical men of business'[54]) equals hope for England. But then it is suitable that a comic conclusion should discourage complete despair as voiced by Hector, and that the play should be more concerned to hold up an intensifying mirror to national complacency and the misguided nature of trust in Mangans.

Shaw's late 'political extravaganzas' develop the fantastic qualities of *Back to Methuselah*, *Misalliance* and *Heartbreak House*, and often add a sense of the specific contemporary political background. *The Apple Cart* (1930) expresses Shaw's increasing dissatisfaction with parliamentary democracy and their channels of reform. King Magnus is the higher evolutionary man above party politics who wittily exposes its failings, as in his conversation with Boanerges (a caricature of John Burns, as is Proteus of Ramsay MacDonald) when he leads the social democrat into exposing the crude mechanisms of the power he represents:

> BOANERGES: I talk democracy to these men and women. I tell them that they have the vote, and that theirs is the kingdom and the power and the glory. I say to them 'You are supreme: exercise your power.' They say, 'Thats right: tell us what to do'; and I tell them. I say 'Exercise your vote intelligently by voting for me.' and they do. That's democracy; and a splendid thing it is too for putting the right man in the right place.
> MAGNUS: Magnificent. I never heard it better expressed.[55]

From this exposure of democracy's farcical distance from its ideals, Magnus uses his supposed weakness, his limitation of referentiality to 'great abstractions', against his parliamentary adversaries, knowing that these abstractions make him a more attractive figure in the eyes of the public, to who he is not required to pander for votes. He also considers the situation in which England, rather than be dominated by America, 'might raise the old warcry of Sinn Fein, might fight for [its] independence to the last drop of [its] blood',[56] a consideration of patriotism which forces the audience to consider Anglo-Irish relations in a new light. Hope would seem to reside in Lysistrata's suggestion for Magnus to lead a new party against the multi-corporations, but Magnus demurs as being 'too old fashioned'; 'This is a farce that younger men must finish'.[57] Similarly, Shaw can only expose the contradictions in politics; he must leave remedial action to the audience, who are once more encouraged to place their sympathies in an unexpected quarter, namely with monarch and against ostensible parliamentary democrats. In the Preface, Shaw meets criticism that says he has 'packed the cards by making the King a wise man and the minister a fool . . . that is not the relation between the two. Both play with equal skill; and the King wins, not by greater astuteness, but because he has the ace of trumps in his hand and knows when to play it. As the prettiest player of the two he has the sympathy of the audience'.[58] However, we know who determined that Magnus should be the prettiest player! *The Apple Cart* is another scene from Shaw's intellectual class war in which the more progressive spirit defeats the regressive fools, despite (and contrary to) the conventional standings of both.

The underrated *Too True to be Good* (1934) returns to the problems of wealth first suggested in *Misalliance*. Given that 'Our society is so constituted that most people remain all their lives in the condition in which they were born', Shaw suggests 'real opposition to Socialism comes from the fear (well founded) that it would cut off the possibilities of becoming rich beyond those dreams of avarice which our capitalist system encourages'.[59] Shaw attacks this fear of social change with the thesis that the capitalist system 'with its golden exceptions of idle richery and its leaden rule of anxious poverty, is as desperate a failure from the point of view of the rich as the poor'.[60] *Too True to be Good*'s moral anarchy, black humour and grotesque fantasy frequently anticipate the tone of Howard Brenton and Howard Barker's political comic nightmares; in fact, the play's particularly strange atmosphere is given a partial rationalization in that it might be the Patient's fevered dream, just as *Heartbreak House* could be Ellie's Shakespeare-influenced rapture. The dream also allows for the Patient's wish fulfilment, that liberates her from the constrictions of wealth, home, family, morality and social position. As she tells the criminals:

> Lucky for you that I'm asleep. If I wake up I shall never get loose from my people and my social position. It's all very well for you two criminals: you can do what you like. If you were ladies and gentlemen, youd know how hard it is not to do what everybody else does.[61]

Like Ellie, the Patient acts as a guide for the audience through her (and perhaps their) fantasy of amoral freedom and unfettered self-interest; and, like Ellie, Trench, Barbara, Vivie and others, she and the audience become disillusioned with an ideal before disillusionment allows a truth to be confronted. Shaw's casually disorientating attitude towards the audience is exemplified by the final lines of Act One, when a human-sized personified microbe addresses the audience to emphasize that the initial leap of fantasy has constituted the important move: 'The play is now virtually over; but the characters will discuss it at great length for two acts more. The exit doors are all in order. Goodnight.'[62]

The Patient, once freed from social and material encumbrances is actually frustrated by her purposelessness. The conventional ideal of happiness without responsibilities proves as hollow for her as did the conventional ideal of happiness through wealth. Consequently she entertains a neoromantic, nihilistic view of man and life that would not be out of place in a fragmented character from an early Brecht or Brenton play: 'We do nothing but convert good food into bad manure. We are walking factories of bad manure: thats what we are.'[63] The hollowness of social success is seen also in Tallboys, who would love to exchange his superior rank and pay for Private Meek's integrity – an integrity denied him by his professional duties. Even the immoral burglar Aubrey is revealed as a man of intelligence and principle, who has been made a cynic and criminal by the hypocrisy of postwar capitalist society:

> You cannot divide my conscience into a war department and a peace department. Do you suppose that a man who will commit murder for political ends will hesitate to commit theft for personal ends? Do you suppose you can make a man the mortal enemy of sixty million of his fellow creatures without making him a little less scrupulous about his next door neighbour?[64]

If World War I sounded the death knell for Heartbreak House, it also left the subsequent generation without any sense of moral purpose. *Too True to be Good* takes these young people and the audience on a journey of discovery that points up the falsities in the ideologies fed to them by society, until they feel themselves 'falling, falling, falling endlessly and hopelessly through a void in which they can find no footing'.[65] Even Mrs Mopply, representing the older generation, comes to realize the truth: 'Everybody told me lies. The world is not a bit like what they said it was. I wasnt a bit like what they said I ought to be. I thought I had to pretend. And I neednt have pretended at all.'[66] The conspiracy of silence that constitutes social convention is broken; and, appropriately, the characters launch into lengthy, ruthless analyses of society and selves. The Sergeant can identify the brutalities of world war as 'innocent men killing each other', for 'the devilment of the godless leaders of this world'.[67] The army chaplain turned burglar, Aubrey, recognizes 'we have outgrown our religion, outgrown our political system, outgrown our own strength of mind and character':

But what next? Is NO enough? for a boy, yes: for a man, never
... I must have affirmations to preach. Without them the
young will not listen to me; for even the young grow tired of
denials. The negative-monger falls before the soldiers, the men
of action, the fighters, strong in the old uncompromising
affirmations which give them status, duties, certainty of
consequences; so that the pugnacious spirit of man in them can
reach out and strike deathblows with steadfastly closed minds.
Their way is straight and sure; but it is the way of death; and the
preacher must preach the way of life.[68]

Aubrey seems to find consolation in the hope of divine inspiration,
but Shaw confesses his preference for the Patient, who moves from
shattered illusions and a life of dissipation to redemptive social
commitment:

THE PATIENT: ... I was devoured by parasites: by tourist
agencies, steamboat companies, railways, motor car people,
hotel keepers, dressmakers, servants, all trying to get my money
by selling me things I dont really want; shoving me all over the
globe to look at what they call new skies, though they know as
well as I do that it is only the same sky everywhere; and
disabling me by doing all the things for me that I ought to do for
myself to keep myself in health. They preyed on me to keep
themselves alive: they pretended they were making me happy
when it was only by drinking and drugging – cocktails and
cocaine – that I could endure my life.
AUBREY: I regret to say it, Mops; but you have not the instincts
of a lady.
THE PATIENT: You fool, there is no such thing as a lady. I have
the instincts of a good housekeeper; I want to clean up this filthy
world and keep it clean.
    ... I dont belong to the poor, and dont want to. I always
knew that there were thousands of poor people; and I was
taught to believe that they were poor because God arranged it
that way to punish them for being dirty and drunken and
dishonest, and not knowing how to read and write. But I didnt
know the rich were miserable. I didnt know that I was
miserable. I didnt know that our respectability was uppish
snobbery and our religion gluttonous selfishness, and that my

soul was starving on them. I know now. I have found myself out thoroughly – in my dream.[69]

Too True to be Good concludes Shaw's trilogy of fantastic explorations of the aimlessness of the English aristocracy with a savage directness absent from the earlier plays *Misalliance* and *Heartbreak House*. Perhaps the only reason for the neglect of *Too True to be Good* is that, as its title suggests, it has been judged too mercilessly accurate to be hailed as the remarkable play it is.

On the Rocks (1934) follows *The Apple Cart* in demonstrating the crippling failings of postwar parliamentary democracy, but has a more immediate setting, with discontented unemployed besieging Downing Street. However, the play suffers from the absence of a Magnus to bring intellectual vitality to the stage. We are given instead a simple demonstration of our politicians' incompetence and petty careerist self-interest:

LADY CHAVENDER: The country isn't governed: it just slum-mocks along anyhow.
SIR ARTHUR: I have to govern within democratic limits. I cannot go faster than my voters will let me.
LADY CHAVENDER: Oh, your voters! What do they know about government? Football, prizefighting, war: that is what they like. And they like war because it isn't real to them: it's only a cinema show. War is real to me; and I hate it, as every woman to whom it is real hates it. But to you it is only part of your game: one of the regular moves of the Foreign Office and the War Office.
SIR ARTHUR: My dear, I hate war as much as you do. It makes a Prime Minister's job easy because it brings every dog to heel; but it produces coalitions; and I believe in party government.[70]

The government of Sir Arthur is shown to be a 'game', and this frivolously selfish approach to its tasks has run the country onto The Rocks, of which Captain Shotover warned the ship of state. The values Sir Arthur has neglected are represented by the ghost of the future, who stresses that 'women and men who are ahead of their time . . . alone can lead the present into the future'; Sir Arthur and his fellow politicians are ghosts from the past who can 'only drag the present back'.[71] At least Sir Arthur, like the other Shavian pilgrims, comes to see the folly of his harmfully conventional attitudes and develops greater integrity: 'I am enjoying the enormous freedom of having found myself out and got myself off my mind. That looks like despair; but it is really the beginning of hope, the end of hypocrisy.'[72] However, he will not lead the revolt against the acknowledged parliamentary 'white-washing'. In fact, he says, 'I shall hate the man who will carry it through for the cruelty and the desolation he will bring on us and our like.'[73] He is left musing on the possibility 'Suppose England really did arise!',[74] despite the unpromising sound of police batons quelling the unemployed protesters outside. Whilst *On the Rocks* might have powerful effects in the unlikely effect of its being played to a theatre full of ministers, it fails to provide opportunities for a more probable audience to engage sympathetically with characters other than inadequate politicians, making the play one of Shaw's less complex and compelling works. *Geneva* (1939) extends Shaw's exposé of government as a game played by trivial-minded incompetents into the international arena and includes caricatures of Chamberlain, Hitler, Mussolini and Franco, but the play is flimsy. It shows the international leaders as childish cowards when the threat of natural world destruction promises to render their petty squabbling meaningless, although this threat later transpires to be a hoax. *Geneva* is essentially an unremarkable political cartoon given a farcical final twist.

Shaw's predominantly verbal address to his audiences provides us with some of the most perfect technical models and powerfully articulate examples of political drama. His work is based on the passionate use of the intellect. Because he believes that 'The roughly threefold division into average, superaverage and sub-average is a natural division, and will persist in spite of any development of factory legislation or Socialism',[75] Shaw makes bids to inspire the average with images of the superaverage victorious in their struggle for the long-term greater good, and he believes the most effective practical channel for this is socialism fired by the Nietzschean Will to Power. The weaknesses in Shaw's philosophy, his bombastic public tone and his ability to make audiences laugh should not obscure his artistic successes and fundamental seriousness and commitment, which make his contribution to the evolution of political drama's own Life Force so vital.

2 Kathleen ni Houlihan's Other Island

BERNARD SHAW, SEAN O'CASEY

> your Kaithleen ni Houlihan has th'bent back of an oul woman
> as well as th'walk of a queen. We love th'ideal Kaithleen ni
> Houlihan, not because she is false, but because she is beautiful;
> we hate th'real Kaithleen ni Houlihan, not because she is true,
> but because she is ugly.
>
> _Red Roses for Me_[1]

Shaw's most direct address to the specific problems of Irish
society was _John Bull's Other Island_ (1904), and he retrospectively
described its reception as follows:

> Writing the play for an Irish audience, I thought it would be
> good for them to be shewn very clearly that the loudest laugh
> they could raise at the expense of the absurdest Englishman
> was not really a laugh on their side; that he would succeed
> where they would fail; that he could inspire strong affection and
> loyalty in an Irishman who knew the world and was moved only
> to dislike, mistrust, impatience and even exasperation by his
> own countrymen; that his power of taking himself seriously,
> and his insensibility to anything funny in danger and destruc-
> tion, was the first condition of economy and concentration of
> force, sustained purpose, and rational conduct. But the need for
> this lesson in Ireland is the measure of its demoralizing
> superfluousness in England. English audiences very naturally
> swallowed it eagerly and smacked their lips over it, laughing all
> the more heartily because they felt they were taking a caricature
> of themselves with the most tolerant and large-minded
> goodhumour.[2]

John Bull's Other Island dramatizes the rivalry of the confident, materialistic Englishman, Broadbent, and the realistic but comparatively ineffectual Irishman, Doyle, which culminates in Broadbent's inevitable victory. However, Shaw presents a complex model of mutual commentary along the lines of the Mrs Warren–Vivie relationship, in that Broadbent turns the complacent superiority of the local Irish *lumpenproletariat* to his own advantage, whilst Doyle and Keegan provide an abstract and spiritual sphere of superiority. As Doyle observes (but cannot alter), 'the Englishman does what the caterpillar does. He instinctively makes himself look a fool, and eats up all the real fools at his ease while his enemies let him alone and laugh at him for being a fool like the rest'.[3] But Shaw states directly in his Preface that 'I am persuaded that a modern nation that is satisfied with Broadbent is in a dream. Much as I like him, I object to being governed by him, or entangled in his political destiny.'[4] Correspondingly, the audience should identify with the source of superior awareness, which seems to be Keegan, and his observations:

> Mr Broadbent spends his life inefficiently admiring the thoughts of great men, and efficiently serving the cupidity of base money hunters. We spend our lives efficiently sneering at him and doing nothing. Which of us has any right to reproach the other? . . . Standing here between you the Englishman, so clever in your foolishness, and this Irishman, so foolish in his cleverness, I cannot in my ignorance be sure which of you is the more deeply damned . . .[5]

In fact, both Irishman and Englishman have the right to reproach the other, but not the grounds to bolster their own complacency at the other's expense. Even Keegan's dream of an ideal future is perhaps the thought of a great man, but so out of place in the prevailing circumstances that he concludes 'I am better alone, at the Round Tower, dreaming of heaven'[6] rather than attempting to translate it into reality. Doyle probably provides the most stable ground for audience sympathy in his awareness of his own shortcomings amongst this pattern of partially attractive, mutually critical viewpoints. Doyle can meet Broadbent's practical self-defence ('I shall collar this place, not because I'm an Englishman and Haffigan and Co are Irishmen, but because

theyre duffers, and I know my way about'[7]) by placing the
practicality upon which it relies within the broader political
context of society's cause-and-effect chain:

> The real tragedy of Haffigan is the tragedy of his wasted youth,
> his stunted mind, his drudging over his clods and his pigs until
> he becomes a clod and a pig himself – until the soul within him
> has smouldered into nothing but a dull temper that hurts
> himself and all around him. I say let him die, and let us have no
> more of his like. And let young Ireland take care that it doesnt
> share his fate, instead of making another empty grievance of it.[8]

Doyle moves towards an awareness of Ireland's continued
obeisance to materialism and capitalism as the root of its own
social tragedies and necessary fealty to English capital, but finally
he resolves to throw in his personal lot with the most efficient
businessman. However, the play links Ireland's perpetuation of
its heritage of dreams to its perpetuation of capitalism, in that
Broadbent falls in love with an unreal romance-Ireland *below*
reality which the locals keep up for the sake of his money (and lose
their own rights in the process), whilst Keegan's unreal dream
flies too far *above* reality to do anything but keep him on the hill in
isolation. Both dreams, whatever their intents, prevent social
change. Only the most blindly nationalistic Irish or English
audiences could avoid concluding with Doyle 'I wish I could find
a country to live in where the facts were not brutal and the dreams
not unreal.'[9]

The dichotomy of brutal facts and unreal dreams is a crucial
factor in the work of Sean O'Casey, who was greatly inspired by
Shaw. O'Casey's early career as a political activist with the Irish
Citizen Army and Transport and General Workers' Union
predates his playwriting career, and the disillusionment produced
by these ill-fated experiences informs his work with a rueful
realism. *Kathleen Listens In* (1923) is an allegorical fantasy showing
Kathleen ni Houlihan, symbol of Ireland's traditional and
mystical beauty, driven to distraction and illness by the Babel of
her persistent suitors; thus, O'Casey presents a cartoon-like
image of Ireland's clamouring internal self-divisions driving it
towards disaster. The Dublin Trilogy traces the effects of, and
responses to, larger political events in naturalistic domestic
microcosms, beginning with *The Shadow of a Gunman* (1922) and its

tenement viewpoint on the 1920 hostilities between the Black and
Tan British auxiliaries and the Republicans. Comedy arises from
pathetic windbags of both ideological sides, Owen and Grigson,·
offering their mistaken support to the least appropriate of
recipients, the narcissistic poet Davoren with his artist's elitist
contempt for the common people (which does not prevent him
courting this support for his own selfish ends). Shields and
Davoren constitute a mutually critical partnership like Broadbent
and Doyle, but without the redemptive features of Shaw's duo;
Shields inhabits a world of brutal facts, his earthy vitality mingled
with irrationality, superstition and complaints about the country
when his own petty designs are thwarted; Davoren inhabits a
world of unreal dreams, being a poetic dilettante who curses the
people and causes disaster through his condescension. This is not
to deny their considerable dramatic attractiveness, especially
when provided with a set of comic foils who are revealed as even
greater fools by their lionization of Davoren. The ridiculous
tenement dwellers who debate on the presence of two k's in
'shockin' are equally pretentious in their aspirations to martial
spirit when seen from the only partially superior awarenesses of
Shields and Davoren. The ideals of Kathleen ni Houlihan and
martial support for the vision she embodies have faded:

SHIELDS: The country is gone mad. Instead of counting their
beads now they're counting bullets; their Hail Marys and
paternosters are burstin' bombs – burstin' bombs, an' the rattle
of machine-guns; petrol is their holy water; their Mass is a
burnin' buildin'; their De Profundis is 'The Soldier's Song', an'
their creed is, I believe in the gun almighty, maker of heaven an'
earth – an' it's all done for 'the glory of God an' the honour o'
Ireland'.
DAVOREN: I remember the time when you yourself believed in
nothing but the gun.
SHIELDS: Ay, when there wasn't a gun in the country; I've a
different opinion now when there's nothin' but guns in the
country. . . . An' you daren't open your mouth, for Kathleen ni
Houlihan is very different now to the woman who used to play
the harp an' sing 'Weep on, weep on, your hour is past', for
she's a ragin' divil now, an' if you only look crooked at her
you're sure of a punch in th'eye . . . it's the civilians that suffer;
when there's an ambush they don't know where to run. Shot in

the back to save the British Empire, an' shot in the breast to
save the soul of Ireland . . . I believe in the freedom of Ireland,
an' that England has no right to be here, but I draw the line
when I hear the gunmen blowin' about dyin' for the people
when it's the people that are dyin' for the gunmen! With all due
respect to the gunmen, I don't want them to die for me.[10]

Shields's analysis of ideals invoked in crazed contradiction of the
values they ostensibly represent is perceptive and authoritative
within the context of the play's events. However, it suits the
dissolute natures of Shields and the egoist Davoren to externalize
the blame for their personal misfortunes. They are subjected to
the indignity of denying principles, even identities, and then
having to reinvent events for personal grandeur, when the
Auxiliaries raid the tenement. This accentuates their sad contrast
to the integrity of the naïve, mistaken, but nonetheless courageous
self-sacrifice of Minnie Powell. Mrs Grigson's disparaging comments about Minnie are the last in a long line of bitterly ironic
comedies of errors, in which the fleeting glimpses of redemptive
qualities – Seumas's realism, Donal's literary sensibilities, Minnie's courage – remain dissipated, even mutually destructive, in
the face of their social oppressions. Kathleen ni Houlihan and the
modern Tower of Babel become increasingly, comically, tragically, polarized.

This theme continues in *Juno and the Paycock* (1924), as a family
disintegrates under the political pressures of civil war. Johnny
Boyle is the focus for the theme of political activism, having lost an
arm fighting in the Anglo-Irish war of 1916 but found guilty of
informing by IRA men in 1922. His haunted idealism is
contrasted to Juno's practical domestic perspective:

JOHNNY (*boastfully*): I'd do it agen, ma, I'd do it agen; for a
principle's a principle.
MRS BOYLE: Ah, you lost your best principle, me boy, when you
lost your arm; them's the only sort o' principles that's any good
to a workin' man.
JOHNNY: Ireland only half free'll never be at peace while she still
has a son left to pull a trigger.
MRS BOYLE: To be sure, to be sure – no bread's better than half a
loaf.[11]

Bernard Benstock writes of Juno:

> O'Casey's handling of Juno Boyle is an odd instance of playing
> both for and against the dramaturgical convention. The traits
> that she at first exhibits [dislike of trades unions, of abstract
> idealism and of irreligious behaviour] are there to ingratiate her
> with the narrowly middle-class mentality of much of the
> audience, making acceptable her emergence as a truly heroic
> figure at the play's resolution, while those who see through her
> early narrowness and conventionality are witness to the
> transformation that produces the final Juno rising above her
> situation and her limitations.[12]

This may be an overly subtle model of her characterization, but
her dogged concrete values (anticipating those of Brecht's
resilient mother figures) act as powerful criticism of the sentimental patriotic attitudes struck by wastrels like Boyle and Joxer, who
continue Grigson's hollow boastfulness and Shield's blaming of
the modern 'chassis' for every grievance;[13] in contrast, Juno alone
attains the status of ideal courage, as prefigured by her mythological name, but by showing resilience and endurance in her front
room rather than on the front lines. The funeral of Mrs Tancred's
son also provides illustration of the misdirection of courage into
military channels and its realistic consequences:

> FIRST NEIGHBOUR: It's a sad journey we're goin' on, but God's
> good, an' the Republicans won't always be down.
> MRS TANCRED: Ah, what good is that to me now? Whether
> they're up or down – it won't bring me darlin' boy back from the
> grave.
> . . .
> FIRST NEIGHBOUR: Still an' all, he died a noble death, an' we'll
> bury him like a king.
> MRS TANCRED: An' I'll go on livin' like a pauper.[14]

But scarcely has the funeral procession departed than Boyle, with
his scant experience as a Liverpool collier, is proclaiming 'When I
was a sailor, I was always resigned to meet with a wathery grave;
an' if they want to be soldiers, well, there's no use o' them
squealin' when they meet a soldier's fate', whilst Joxer chimes in
'Let me like a soldier fall – me breast expandin' to th' ball.'[15] The

folklore and glorification of war remains inextricably rooted in the unrealistic male worldview, and this theme is given a more sinister reprise at the end of the act with the IRA man's conviction that 'no man can do enough for Ireland'.[16] Juno's repetition of Mrs Tancred's lament for her dead son has the deliberate stylization of Shakespeare's Father that hath Killed his Son and Son that hath Killed his Father in *3 Henry VI*, in that it is a representative echo designed to illustrate the fratricidal nature of civil war by exposing the fracture of familial ties beneath the preservation of political alignments. The play ends with Boyle's ironic comment that 'Irelan' sober . . . is Irelan' . . . free'[17] as he stumbles drunkenly into the ransacked wreckage of his home. O'Casey is not as yet attempting to examine the rights and wrongs of basic political disputes or injustices, but is concerned to present an intensified image of the anomalies of attempted political resistance that sacrifices the human values which it ostensibly wishes to preserve, particularly highlighting the discrepancy between traditional elevated Irish ideals of heroism and the base self-destruction perpetrated in their name. *The Plough and the Stars* (1926) dramatizes the same theme against a different martial backdrop, the Easter Rising of 1916. Although the Orator inspires the men with the glory of resistance against the English, the play focusses on the divisions and conflicts amongst the Irish and the various responses elicited by events. The plot of Jack and Nora Clitheroe firmly identifies the considerable part played by intoxicated male vanity in civil strife and the female domestic despair which necessarily follows. Brennan's belief that 'Mrs Clitheroe's grief will be a joy when she realizes that she has had a hero for a husband' is a bitter irony when Bessie and the audience know 'If only [he'd] seen her, [he'd] know to th'differ.'[18] More complex models of the breakdown in conventional partisan feeling and ideals of heroism complement this central theme; the cantankerous Bessie is reviled as a crotchety supporter of the British Empire but provides the play's most heroic action in attempting to save Nora, but Bessie is rewarded with a misdirected British bullet. There is also a telling exchange between Corporal Stoddart and the Covey, who share a belief in socialism but confront each other on opposite sides in the Rising:

CORPORAL STODDART: I'm a Sowcialist moiself, but I 'as to do my dooty.

THE COVEY (*ironically*): Dooty! Th'only dooty of a Socialist is th'emancipation of th'workers.

CORPORAL STODDART: Ow, a man's a man, an' 'e 'as to foight for 'is country, 'asn't 'e?

FLUTHER (*aggressively*): You're not fightin' for your country here, are you?[19]

Other effective moments of the debunking of conventional military heroics are the English Sergeant's protest that an Irish sniper is not fighting fair, much to Fluther's outrage ('D'ye want us to come out in our skins an' throw stones?'[20]), and the final tableau of the English soldiers' repose, drinking tea amongst the ruins of houses and lives – the agonizing implications of which we have seen from a crucially separate point of view – whilst the distant English soldiers sing an impossibly cheerful heroic song. This matches the vainglorious propaganda firing Irish rebels and affords us a privileged glimpse of both sets of men as duped tools in the hands of political leaders. O'Casey's satire of national totems struck home to the extent of provoking riots at the opening performances of the play.

In *Inishfallen Fare Thee Well*, O'Casey describes his own reaction to the uproar and his revulsion from this idealistic-sentimental aspect of the Irish public:

> For the first time in his life, Sean felt a surge of hatred for Kathleen ni Houlihan sweeping over him. He saw now that the one who had the walk of a queen could be a bitch at times. She galled the hearts of her children who dared to be above the ordinary, and she often slew her best ones. She had hounded Parnell to death; she had yelled and torn at Yeats, at Synge, and now she was doing the same to him. What an old snarly gob she could be at times; an ignorant one, too.[21]

O'Casey then moved to England, and one might justifiably expect that his anger at his country's hypocrisy would goad him to creating increasingly savage portraits of a sordid reality beneath the veneer of national complacency. But the plays written after the Dublin Trilogy tend to attempt something other than the Shavian goal of destroying ideals, and O'Casey's dramatic style also changes from the slightly heightened naturalism of his chronicles of grim tenement life outside the principle focus of political events but subject to their shockwaves. Instead he tends to favour expressionistic visions with a damaging tendency to self-insulation, a fault which may stem from his deliberate self-severance from his native Irish audience, and consequent sacrifice of his piquant understanding of their basic political realities and attitudes (and how to react against these attitudes to the maximum dramatic effect). *The Silver Tassie* (1929) is a partial extension of the Dublin Trilogy's scathing anatomies of martial idealism, but set against the Europe of World War One. Act Two's expressionistic nightmare vision of trench warfare continues the protest begun in *The Plough and the Stars* against the common soldier's pawn-like status for his superiors, who mystify the men with an amalgam of spurious idealism to preserve their co-operation whilst themselves remaining detached from this idealism's awful results. The padre informs the men that 'Your king, your country an' your muvver 'as you 'ere',[22] whilst superior officers link current activity with the heroic image of 'The Yellow Plumes that pull'd a bow at Crecy, / And gave fame a leg up on the path to glory.'[23] The weary shell-shocked soldiers are contrasted to the inhumanly cheerful, jargon-spouting Visitor, whose 'cautious nibbling / In a safe, safe shelter at danger' enables him to pretend 'he's up to the neck in / The whirl and the sweep of the front-line fighting'[24] and thus perpetuate the mistaken ideal. But the main focus of blame falls on the church through the setting of the ruined monastery and the climactic Mass chanted to the cannon. O'Casey's identification of the church as the crucial support of a hypocritical social system permeates many of his later plays and also tends to limit their effect beyond this highly personal, slightly hysterical analysis. Harry Heegan's bitterness at his sacrifice strikes a vivid note of vengeful outrage, but it can find no practical outlet, dooming him to a life of frustrated impotence whilst the surrounding dancers choose to edit him out of their world-view, and the play's final scene, so as not to disturb the merriment. *Within the Gates* (1934) continues the expressionistic style in its depiction of the economic and spiritual slump of the 1930's, but the treatment works against the material's contemporary immediacy. The ghost-drum of the chanting down-and-outs provides a striking cautionary corrective to the glorified image of Drake's drum, but O'Casey's critical response to the prevailing tissue of conciliatory ideals remains as vague as the ideals themselves, an uncertain fusion of economics and religious hypocrisy ('Your Christ wears a bowler hat, carries a cane, twiddles his lavender gloves, an' sends out gilt-edged cards of thanks to callers'[25]). The seasonal cycle against which the action is set seems inappropriate and pretentious, distancing rather than harmonizing the events. The figures of the Everywoman prostitute (!) Jannice and the visionary Dreamer suffer from insufficient authorial distance, resulting too often in a sentimental tone; and whilst Jannice can act as a touchstone to the beliefs of the other one-dimensional park inhabitants (greeting the song 'Gold and silver's grown a god' with 'Let it fall to pieces then'[26]), she is, by virtue of her pivotal role, incapable of further insight. It is characteristic of O'Casey at this period that the two figures struggling for her soul are the Bishop, a stereotypical hypocrite, and the Dreamer, whose detachment from life (as his title suggests) and vague Yeatsian espousal of art as creed sounds alarmingly close to Shaw's Eugene Marchbanks. Restricted to such abstractions, the play cannot but fail in practical political terms.

The Star Turns Red (1940), in contrast, addresses itself to political conflict with directness unprecedented for O'Casey, no doubt attributable to his movement towards communism under the aegis of Shaw and others, and the consequent vehemence of his reaction to the Spanish Civil War. However, this very vehemence hinders O'Casey's self-distancing from his material, resulting in the same sentimentality and melodrama that crippled *Within the Gates*. Criticism of schematic characterization is almost laughably tautological in a play whose cast list divides into the Red Guards, the Saffron Shirts, the Brown Priest and the Purple Priest, and O'Casey's firm espousal of communism is, in the conventional theatre of the day, almost uniquely bold. But while the play might provide heroic inspiration for existing communists on a very elementary level, there is little or no intellectual analysis to complement the play's emotional thrust, so that the action has few links with, or comments on, the world beyond O'Casey's intense personal vision of 'To-morrow, or the next day'. The fascists are shown to be bad by their actions in the play, which are not overtly and necessarily connected with their fundamental ideological brutalities, whereas the communists appear good and heroic in their opposition to the fascists, rather than through receiving any exposition of their amelioratory plans for the extant social system. O'Casey's infatuation with religion also gives the

clash an awkward dimension in the opposition of Brown and
Purple Priests, as active Christian Socialism and reactionary
repression respectively. Red Jim's invective against the heritage
of 'shame and rags and the dead puzzle of poverty' [27] continues to
identify religion with the brainwashing force that convinces the
crowd that 'Youth and all its thoughts are lies!' [28] O'Casey's
personal associations of comunism threaten to remain private in
such intense, unmediated form; more skilful is the debunking of
the 'dignity and loveliness that priests say poverty gives the poor'. [29]
However, *The Star Turns Red* is unlikely to fill any audience
members with enthusiasm for communism who are not already so
inclined. [30] *Oak Leaves and Lavender*, published in 1948, strives to
express solidarity with the Allies in World War Two – an
objective fraught with potential danger for the author of *The Silver
Tassie* – and negotiates the inherent problems by making the
sacrificial hero an Irish communist choosing to fight for 'the
people' rather than England, and inspired by the prospect of a
collective effort with the Russian Red Army. Indeed, the war has a
cathartic effect on the decadent, ghost-ridden mansion of England
– a dusty Heartbreak House which is converted into a tank-
producing factory. *The Star* and *Oak Leaves* set themselves the
difficult tasks of rejecting the same false idealisms as *The Plough
and the Stars* and *The Silver Tassie*, that is the idealisms which
produce exploitation and irresponsible loss of life, whilst also
affirming a positive idealism to present heroic images of self-
sacrifice for a worthy cause. The alteration in impulse is natural,
not its degree of success, as the later plays proceed by intellectually and dramatically tenuous means. *Red Roses for Me* (1946) is
the most successful of the heroic communist sacrifice plays
because of O'Casey's surer control of expression of his beliefs,
through Ayamonn Breydon, and the way the definite social
context for the political dispute emerges. Rather than dogma,
Ayamonn preaches enquiry, and the humour and affection of his
social milieu make him, by association, a more sympathetic
character than the austere Red Jim, or Drishogue of *Oak Leaves*.
Ayamonn's political debates with his comrades afford more
naturalistic and articulate formulations of convictions. Like all of
O'Casey's more convincing characters, Ayamonn hates what he
sees as a sham, but he is also gifted with the ability to see through
false ideals to worthy ones and inspire his fellows. He articulates
the interconnections of O'Casey's two categories of idealism and

two faces of Ireland when he says at one point: 'We love th'ideal Kaithleen ni Houlihan, not because she is false, but because she is beautiful; we hate th'real Kaithleen ni Houlihan, not because she is true, but because she is ugly'. The issues of the strike are also dangerous ground for the creator of union-wary Juno Boyle, but O'Casey anticipates 'practical' objections of her kind to industrial action by placing Ayamonn's beliefs in a firm idealistic context:

> BRENNAN: . . . money's the root of all evil.
>
> AYAMONN (*to the Inspector*): A shilling's little to you, and less to many; to us it is our Shechinah, showing us God's light is near; showing us the way in which our feet must go; a sun-ray on our face; the first step taken in the march of a thousand miles.[31]
> . . .
> 3RD MAN: It was a noble an' a mighty death.
>
> INSPECTOR (*from where he is near the tree*): It wasn't a very noble thing to die for a single shilling.
>
> SHEILA: Maybe he saw the shilling in th'shape of a new world.[32]

Red Roses for Me does not entirely escape the sentimentality which flaws the other plays of O'Casey's middle period, but it at least accommodates it the most comfortably, and stands as his most successful heroic drama.

The opposition of vital youth and repressive age which emotionally informs *The Star* and *Red Roses* finds its fullest expression in O'Casey's third major period, that of allegorical farce. These plays are Jonsonian routs of representative follies, gleeful satirical reductions of authority to Dionysian chaos. *Purple Dust* (1945) shows two Broadbentian Englishmen (who lack the saving graces of Shaw's character) creating their own Heartbreak House in Ireland, treating the inhabitants as mere 'newly painted toys' to people their regressive fantasy of the past. Stoke and Poges wish to forget 'the vile world and all its ways',[33] finding the present day and present men 'Paltry, mean, tight and tedious',[34] apparently oblivious both to their own materialism (exploiting Ireland and speculating in concrete in the wake of the bombing of England) and to the jibes of the more realistic Doyle-like locals, led by O'Killigain. Characteristically, O'Casey adds a reactionary Canon opposed to dances and courting couples, joining religious puritanism with English materialism as the cancers identified in Ireland. The resultant broad comedy includes a delight in the cheeky vandalism of a workman who scrapes his hobnailed boots across Poges's beloved quattrocento and culminates in the fall of the English capitalists' 'house of pride' [35] which is deemed to have had its day, but, unlike the symbolic prescription ending *Heartbreak House*, the expulsion of Stoke and Poges provides no model of progress for Ireland other than O'Killigain's realism and a trust in the efficacy of time and Celtic myth, which meet in the dark Figure's apocalyptic judgement on the ancient house and its subsequent flooding. The mythological scourge of joyless, pretentious authority continues in *Cock-a-doodle Dandy* (1949), with its account of the outraged hysteria which greets the mischief of the Cock, an animated fertility symbol. The united front of capitalists and priests 'embalming themselves in money' effects the Cock's exile, and that of the bright young generation, and even causes the rather melodramatic death of an inoffensive worker. The allegory ends with a satirical edge, when the Messenger leaves Ireland for 'a place where life resembles life more than it does here', recommending the sterile, tyrannical old order to 'Die. There is little else left useful for the likes of you to do.' [36] But, as C. Desmond Greaves points out, 'O'Casey has no *policy* for social transformation and it is always symbolised by a magical effect'.[37] Despite their surface vitality, *Purple Dust* and *Cock-a-doodle Dandy* have little substance beyond fantastic wish-fulfilment, a tendency that can also be detected in the heroic dramas of O'Casey's middle period. Satire of the present and affirmation of myth are uneasy bedfellows in the work of a progressive political playwright. The intervention of Irish legend incarnate may provide an inspiring ideal against which to measure contemporary depravity but bears scant relation to viable channels of political reform; therefore it runs the risk of being self-insulated fantasy or, worse, perverted faith and energy of the type displayed by the characters in the Dublin Trilogy and their imaginative divorce from cold, hard facts. *The Bishop's Bonfire* (1955) bewails the fraudulence of the materialistic organized clergy who control Ireland, and *The Drums of Father Ned* (1959) repeats the theme in more optimistic terms, but the guiding force of the counter-revolution is, again, a supernatural figure. The play also returns to the theme of *Kathleen Listens In*, namely the internal divisions which prevent Ireland's progress. The 'Prerumble' gives a harsh realistic image of this in the continued hatred of two Irishmen even in the face of a common enemy, the Black and Tans, whilst the more light-hearted body of the play shows their children united under the Keegan-ideal of Father Ned to fight the 'old and stale and vicious: the hate, the meanness their policies preach; and to make a way for the young and thrusting'[38] (a harmonious ending which echoes Larry Doyle's only hope for the future and is subsequently echoed by the ending of Howard Brenton's *The Romans in Britain* in 1980).

O'Casey's problematic relationships with Kathleen ni Houlihan and the native values of Ireland are instructive for political drama in general even when the products of the tension are less than satisfying artistically, for they show a playwright struggling to demolish regressive ideals by showing Kathleen ni Houlihan's unpalatable realistic face, and then to substitute a new progressive ideal. But whilst the first activity is worthy of a tough-minded, sceptical Larry Doyle and produces pungent, disciplined fusions of form and content, O'Casey's attempts at the second goal too often become reminiscent of Keegan, alone at the Round Tower, dreaming of a pure ideal – with all the necessary and damaging detachment from the basic fabric of contemporary society this involves. O'Casey's separation from his native audience and the tensions of their day-to-day realities may have taken their toll in creative terms.

3 Learn How To See and Not To Gape

ERWIN PISCATOR, BERTOLT BRECHT

> Consider even the most insignificant, seemingly simple
> Action with distrust. Ask yourself whether it is necessary
> Especially if it is usual.
> We ask you expressly to discover
> That what happens all the time is not natural.
> For to say that something is natural
> In such times of bloody confusion
> Of ordained disorder, of systematic arbitrariness
> Of inhuman inhumanity is to
> Regard it as unchangeable.
>
> *The Exception and the Rule*[1]

The theatrical experiments of the German director Erwin Piscator articulated the impulse 'to give artistic form to our revolutionary view of the world, the *epic* or political style' (as Piscator described it in his 1963 foreword to his 1929 book *The Political Theatre*[2]). Piscator also explained the relationship of epic theatre to its formal predecessors and influences:

Political theater as it developed in the course of each of my undertakings is neither a personal "invention" nor the result of the social grouping of 1918. Its roots reach back deep into the last century. It was then that the intellectual situation of bourgeois society was penetrated by forces which, either by design or by their mere existence, decisively altered that situation, in part even destroying it. These forces came from two directions: from literature[3] and from the proletariat. And at the point where they met a new concept arose, Naturalism.

. . .

42

But Naturalism is far from expressing the demands of the masses. It describes their condition, and restores a proper relationship between literature and the state of society.

Of course, Naturalism is not revolutionary, nor Marxist in the modern sense. Like its great predecessor Ibsen, it never got past stating the problem. Cries of exasperation stand where we should hear answers.[4]

In contrast to naturalism, epic theatre *was* designed to be revolutionary and Marxist, fusing corrective injunctions with cries of exasperation, and it required a new, sharper style of theatrical experience to accomplish this. Epic theatre was 'about the extension of the action and the clarification of the background to the action, that is to say it involved a continuation of the play beyond the dramatic framework. A didactic play was developed from the spectacle-play'.[5] The task of this style was 'to make the people who stream into the theater aware of what is slumbering in their unconscious, vague and incoherent',[6] forcing them to see things in a different light and react to them afresh. Piscator's prescriptions were mainly in the technical area of stage presentation, advocating the use of new stage effects made possible by mechanization, projected film backdrops and auditoria designed to break down the proscenium arch's conventional separation of actors and audience so as, literally as well as metaphorically, 'to draw the spectator into the middle of the scenic events'.[7] But Piscator outlined goals for the new epic theatre extending far beyond the technical. It soon became evident that even Piscator's large-scale theatre failed to attract proletarian audiences, leaving his company in the ideologically contradictory position of playing to bourgeois audiences, to which he replied:

it proves to be impossible to build up a proletarian theater within the framework of our current social structure. A proletarian theater in fact presupposes that the proletariat has the financial means to support such a theater, and this presupposes that the proletariat has managed to make itself into a dominant social and economic power. Until this happens our theater can be no more than a revolutionary theater which uses the means at its disposal for the ideological liberation of the proletariat and its theater from these contradictions.[8]

A new area of subject matter was also an intrinsic part of the new theatre, and was reflected in Piscator's orchestrations of large casts, crowds and dummies:

> The War finally buried bourgeois individualism under a hail of steel and a holocaust of fire.
> . . .
> It is no longer the private, personal fate of the individual, but the times and fate of the masses that are the heroic factors in the new drama.
> . . .
> It is not his relationship to himself, nor his relationship to God, but his relationship to society which is central. Whenever he appears, his class or social stratum appears with him. His moral, spiritual or sexual conflicts are conflicts with society.[9]

Recognizing the 'deep gulf between the life we live and the life we would wish to live',[10] Piscator claimed 'We, as revolutionary Marxists, cannot consider our task complete if we produce an uncritical copy of reality . . . nor can we present man as a creature of sublime greatness in times which in fact socially distort him'; instead, 'The business of revolutionary theater is to take reality as its point of departure and to magnify the social discrepancy, making it an element of our indictment, our revolt, our new order.'[11] Piscator's directorial methods have been dismissed by at least one hostile critic as 'empty formalism',[12] but his practical experiments and articulate theorizing both nurtured and focussed the epic theatre movement. His fellow German Bertolt Brecht acknowledged that Piscator was making political theatre before him, indeed that 'the theatre's conversion to politics was Piscator's achievement, without which the Augsburger's [i.e. Brecht's] theatre would hardly be conceivable'.[13] From the foundations of Piscator's theories of new theatre design and technical effects, the new role he posited for the audience and the new goals he posited for the author, director and actor, Brecht evolved his additional epic theatre theorizations, and wrote the first major works of dramatic literature specifically conceived with new effects in mind. For Shaw, the audience existed to be educated; for Brecht, to be re-educated.

Brecht's early plays are not informed by the same articulated Marxism as his later works, despite his rather strenuous and

uncharacteristically over-serious efforts to suggest so in late
theoretical writings, but all of his plays proceed from the
observation that 'The bourgeois theatre's performance always
aim at smoothing over contradictions, at creating false harmony,
at idealization', leading Brecht to write a consciously tougher,
more attacking drama. *Drums in the Night* (1922) traces events
which cause one character to protest 'Oh, don't make a drama out
of this. It's too squalid', and he earns the reply 'It isn't a drama.
It's political realism. Something we Germans are short of.'[14] This
self-conscious, Shavian attack on theatrical conventions for their
congruence with social conventions and false idealism appears
most directly in Kragler's last lengthy speech:

> I'm fed up to here. *He laughs irritably*. It's just play-acting.
> Boards and a paper moon and the butchery offstage, which is
> the only real part of it. . . . Stop that romantic staring! You
> racketeers! *Drum*. You bloodsuckers! *Laughing full-throatedly,
> almost choking*. You cowardly cannibals, you! *His laughter sticks in
> his throat, he cannot continue, he staggers around, throws the drum at the
> moon, which was a lantern, and drum and moon together fall into the river,
> which is without water*. Very drunken and infantile.[15]

The hollowness of theatrical props, cardboard red moons of
revolution and imaginary rivers, is debunked as the trappings of
misdirected idealism and romanticism, whilst Kragler's insults
to his off-stage adversaries for their 'romantic staring' can easily
apply to the audience and force them to question their own
motives for sharing vicariously in his feverish disillusionment.
The later Brecht, as a committed Marxist, felt unease that his first
play to be staged should satirize the revolution: 'Here was a case
where revolting against a contemptible literary convention almost
amounted to contempt for a great social revolt.'[16] In fact,
Kragler's nightmarish discovery of his personal dislocation from
both bourgeois and proletarian roles in the revolution is too
fiercely realised to be qualified, even by Brecht's subsequent
larger considerations. David Bathrick equates Kragler with true
revolution,[17] but it is probably more accurate to view him as
potential revolution whose identification with the larger movement
is stifled and alienated at the existing revolution's expense, thus
contributing indirectly to its failure. *Baal* (1923) also treads
uncharacteristic ground for the older Brecht by following the
revolt of an individual on grounds which Piscator would probably

have dismissed as fundamentally 'bourgeois individualism'. Nevertheless, there is no doubting Baal's elementary theatrical vitality as a cynical hedonist, part malcontent, part coney-catching trickster, who devalues the valuations of his socially conventional foils with amoral relish, 'anti-social, but in an anti-social society'.[18] His volatile anarchism is illustrated by the scene in the night club, where even the self-expressive potential of a stage is insufficient for Baal as he lurches into uncensored songs which provoke uproar, to the horror of the management.[19]

In the Jungle of Cities (1923) is a strange and haunting menagerie of self-destructive Jonsonian humours, proceeding from the 'vague realization' that 'under advanced capitalism fighting for fighting's sake is only a wild distortion of competition for competition's sake'[20] and seeking to provoke moral revulsion at (and perhaps a simultaneous amoral engagement in) the predatory psychological vandalism indulged in by Shlink and Garga, described in the Prologue as 'inexplicable' and carrying the advice: 'Don't worry your heads about the motives for the fight, concentrate on the stakes. Judge impartially the technique of the contenders, and keep your eyes fixed on the finish.'[21] It is, of course, impossible to take this injunction literally, especially when tantalising half-reasons for the fight are scattered amidst the savage wit. Shlink proceeds from the presumed self-evident truth that 'Money is everything. Right?'[22] and subverts Garga's sense of his own identity by upending the master-slave relationship between them and, as Garga puts it, 'withdrawing into my corner'.[23] Power and debt alike are shown to carry guilt as both Shlink and Garga strive simultaneously to cut themselves free of any obligation to another person and also deflect the sadism of their environment onto the closest available victim:

> GARGA: We're none of us free. It starts in the morning with our coffee, and we're beaten if we play the fool. A mother salts her children's food with her tears and washes their shirts with her sweat. And their future is secure until the Iron Age, and the root sits in their heart. And when you grow up and want to do something, body and soul, they pay you, brainwash you, label you, and sell you at a high price, and you're not even free to fail.[24]
> . . .
> MARY: How long have you had this disease?

SHLINK: Since I was a boy on the rowboats on the Yangtze Kiang. The Yangtze tortured the junks and the junks tortured us. There was a man who trampled our faces every time he stepped into the boat. At night we were too lazy to move our faces away. Somehow the man was never too lazy. We in turn had a cat to torture. She was drowned while learning to swim, though she'd eaten the rats that were all over us. All those people had the disease.[25]

Finally it transpires that Shlink's aggression was a perverse symptom of 'the black plague of this planet, the lust for human contact'.[26] But, like Volpone and the Jew of Malta, Shlink is defeated when his adversary takes his own cynical assumptions one step further and turns them against him; Garga refuses to fight, preferring to survive, leaving Shlink in utter isolation:

SHLINK: You never understood what it was all about. You wanted me dead. But I wanted a fight. Not of the flesh but of the spirit.
GARGA: And the spirit, you see, is nothing. The important thing is not to be stronger, but to come off alive.[27]

Even the contacts afforded by the conflicts of a heightened capitalism are seen as self-defeating, as Shlink and Garga lose not only all their possessions but also their human contacts in the struggle, and still fall short of the mutual understanding and respect of the most brutal prizefighters.

Man equals Man (1926) continues the style of magnifying social discrepancy from the ideal without overtly moralizing, and presents another acidly comic image of man distorted by social forces. Three British Army privates indulge in the dubious technological experiment of reassembling a personality for their own ends. Like Shlink, they start from a reductive, 'modern' assertion (here 'Man is nothing. Modern science has proved that everything is relative'[28]) and similarly find that their own assumptions, in extreme form, rebound upon them, as Galy Gay becomes a Frankenstein monster who appals even them with his blank malleability. His characteristic willingness to 'close an eye to what concerns myself/ And shed what is not likeable about me and thereby/ Be pleasant'[29] leads him to become the perfect tool of imperialism. Galy Gay's determination to be 'pleasant' leads

him to surrender to basic tribal aggression, to 'feel within
me / The desire to sink my teeth / In the enemy's throat / Ancient
urge to kill / Every family's breadwinner / To carry out the
conquerors' / Mission'.[30] In a sense, Galy Gay 'wins. And a man
who adopts such an attitude is bound to win',[31] but this provides
latent indictments of the system which encourages man to 'win'
by such inhumanity, and of the man so inhuman as to submit to its
'rules'.

From these challengingly bleak, intensified images of society in
which morality is conspicuous by its absence, Brecht moved on to
plays in which the themes and style reflected his full conversion to
Marxism and his development of the theory of epic theatre,
which, in contrast to the prevalent dramatic theatre, would force
the audience into a radical reassessment of responses normally
encouraged and confirmed by the hegemony of social and political
convention:

> The spectator was no longer in any way allowed to submit to an
> experience uncritically (and without practical consequences)
> by means of simple empathy with the characters in a play. The
> production took the subject-matter and the incidents shown
> and put them through a process of alienation: the alienation
> which is necessary to all understanding. When something
> seems 'the most obvious thing in the world' it means that any
> attempt to understand the world has been given up.
>
> What is 'natural' must have the force of what is startling.
> This is the only way to expose the laws of cause and effect . . .
>
> The dramatic theatre's spectator says: Yes, I have felt like
> that too – Just like me – It's only natural – It'll never change –
> The sufferings of this man appal me, because they are
> inescapable – That's great art, it all seems the most obvious
> thing in the world – I weep when they weep, I laugh when they
> laugh.
>
> The epic theatre's spectator says: I'd never have thought it –
> That's not the way – That's extraordinary, hardly believable –
> It's got to stop – The sufferings of this man appal me, because
> they are unnecessary – That's great art, there's nothing obvious
> in it – I laugh when they weep, I weep when they laugh.[32]

The intended effect was that outlined by Piscator, that the
audience would be forced to come to terms with the latent

contradictions within their own consciousnesses so as to provide a
theatrical experience which would continue beyond the walls of
the playhouse into a re-examination and ideally a re-adjustment
of behaviour in everyday social life: 'Human behaviour is shown
as alterable; man himself as dependent on certain political and
economic factors and at the same time as capable of altering
them.'[33]

A fine example of this is provided by *The Exception and the Rule*
(1938), in which an inhumane action, a merchant killing a coolie,
is pardoned because it works on the assumption of a hostility
which is part of the fabric of existent society. The coolie is blamed
for his own death because he acted on a generous impulse to a
fellow man rather than how society would expect. The judges
have to go by 'the rule, not the exception', despite the demonstration that 'In the system they've put together / Humanity is the
exception',[34] provoking the players to urge the audience:

What is not strange, find it disquieting!
What is usual, find it inexplicable!
What is customary, let it astound you!
What is the rule, recognise it to be an abuse
And where you have recognised abuse
Do something about it![35]

There is a firmer sense of a morality in opposition to society
here than in the earlier plays, and a more direct bearing on
audiences and their immediate lives is stressed as forcibly as
possible. Revolutionary outrage replaces blasé reductivity which
mirrored social conduct in *In the Jungle of Cities*. But Piscator also
outlined the need for the fate of the masses to be the heroic factor
in the new drama, and it is Brecht's dramatic explorations of this
theme which produced the most controversial plays of his canon.
The Measures Taken (1930), *He Who Says Yes* (1930), *He Who Says No*
and *The Didactic Play of Baden-Baden on Consent* (1929) are almost
unique even amongst political plays in their address to this theme
(a notable exception being Hare's *Fanshen*), reversing the
immeasurably commoner and far easier foregrounding of individual as critic of society, by making society the critic of the
individual who chooses to foreground himself. *The Measures Taken*
explores the dilemma of those who realize (like the characters in
Shaw's *Major Barbara*) that 'violence is the only means whereby

this deadly / World may be changed, as / Every living being knows. / And yet, we said / We are not permitted to kill'.[36] The conclusion, that 'Taught only by reality can / Reality be changed',[37] echoes and supports their resolve to 'Sink in filth / Embrace the butcher, but / Change the world: it needs it!',[38] which has received its most interesting gloss from Jan Needle and Peter Thomson: 'Brecht's failure in this play becomes blindingly clear: it is one of naïvety. He really should have realized that people who "embrace the butcher" in political and power terms can never under any circumstances acknowledge that this is what they are doing.'[39]

Mother Courage and her Children (1941) works by a double alienation of the concept of courage. There is the anti-heroic self-interested courage of the mercenary old trader which serves as a wry gloss on the conventional ideal of martial heroism; in fact she parries the title with bluff self-effacement and appeal to necessity: 'They call me Mother Courage 'cause I was afraid I'd be ruined. So I drove through the bombardment of Riga like a madwoman, with fifty loaves of bread in my cart. They were going mouldy, I couldn't please myself.'[40] But whilst her small-scale courage of survival is an apt reminder of less central, smaller dramas which war carries in its wake – as is that of Juno Boyle – she is in moral terms no better than Shaw's Mrs Warren, in that her courage is misdirected into perpetuating the very system which damaged, and continues to damage, her life. Mother Courage has no illusions about her own dignity ('We're prisoners. But so are lice in fur'[41]), but by this stage Brecht demands something more than jaded, worldly-wise submission to and identification with society's most basic machinations (which characterized the 'heroes' of *Drums in the Night* and *In the Jungle of Cities*); true courage is now the determination to take arms against a sea of reductive cynicism and by opposing disprove it. Katrin's selflessnes carries the apparently inevitable penalty but stands as a powerful corrective image to her mother's louse-like survival, and the ironic demonstration of the contradictory aspects of Courage's existence and the transfer of audience sympathies from Courage to Katrin are the crucial movements of the play. This model of historical parable, with its engaging central figure who nevertheless requires constant reassesment, is continued in *The Life of Galileo* (1943, 1947, 1955 in its various revised forms), which also has affinities with a Shavian antecedant, namely *Saint*

Joan; both plays show a vital, progressive figure hampered and effectively crushed by the petty-minded and short-sighted forces of deadly conventional society which forces its heroes to recant their aspirations. However, Brecht's departures from Shaw's play are as interesting as the common features. Unlike the momentarily wavering but finally defiant Joan, Galileo *does* recant and set back the progress of his theories through his own human weakness; but more importantly he comes to express misgivings about the potential progress (and potential disaster) of his theories when committed to the existent irresponsible channels of power, giving the play a final twist in its repeated attacks upon complacency. The figure of Galileo has a multifaceted richness in providing organic parallels with numerous Brechtian objectives. At the most basic level, he begins as an immensely engaging figure, a witty, enthusiastic, irreverent 'higher evolutionary man' gleefully exposing and discrediting the reactionary folly of those around him. His searching scepticism and restless enquiry charges the developments of his theory with infectious excitement; the demonstration of his beliefs to the boy Andrea communicates the thrill of 'a new way of seeing' to the audience in an example of epic theatre at its most successful, moving outside the conventional flow of perception to gain a fresh new radical insight. Galileo's theories also indicate new possibilities of progression and imply challenges to hitherto unquestioned hierarchies of cosmic and social power. Howard Brenton rightly draws attention to the fact that 'The new science of Galileo's time is, in a mighty double meaning at the heart of the play, marxism now'[42] (or in Galileo's words: 'That's what it's really about. You're right – it's not about the planets, it's about the peasants of the Campagna'[43]). The most powerful exposition of the social implications of his theories comes in Galileo's dialogue with the Little Monk, who is given a lengthy and engaging speech in which to build up an impression of the day-to-day courage to survive exhibited by his family, and their reliance on the continuity and sense of necessity provided by the old traditional religious (and thereby social) order; and Galileo's refutation of this worldview gains in power and compulsion on the shoulders, as it were, of the Little Monk's speech, as the astrologer points out that this courage, whilst not as scabrous as that of Mother Courage, is also misdirected, a cosmetic on the outrage of their conditions:

LITTLE MONK, *in great irritation*: The highest principles compel us to silence – for the peace of mind of suffering humanity!
GALILEO: . . . If I were prepared to be silent, it would be from really base motives – good living, no persecution, etc.
LITTLE MONK: But won't the truth, if it is the truth, prevail – with us or without us?
GALILEO: No. No no. As much of the truth will prevail that we make prevail . . . I see the divine patience of your people, but where is their divine anger?[44]

But Galileo himself becomes an object of criticism rather than unqualified identification (a transfer of sympathies led by the reactions of his pupils), not least because of his contradiction of earlier principles; indeed he does consent to be silent from what he previously identified as 'base motives', and his iconoclastic faith that 'It is not for scientists to ask where the truth will lead'[45] becomes subject to crucial modification as Galileo himself extends the criticism levelled against him by his followers and subsequently placated by the transfer of the Discorsi manuscript:

If scientists are scared off by dictators and content themselves with piling up knowledge for knowledge's sake, science will be crippled and your new machines will only mean new hardships. . . . The gulf between you and the people will become so great that one fine day you will cry out in jubilation over a new achievement – and be greeted by a cry of universal horror. . . . If only scientists had a hippocratic oath, like the doctors, vowing to use their knowledge only for the welfare of mankind! But now all we have is a race of inventive dwarfs who can be hired for anyting.[46]

The extension of the action's consequences into the future (for the audience, the present day and beyond) gives the play a provocative open-endedness which transcends its historical setting with a power rare amongst historical plays. *The Life of Galileo* is probably Brecht's masterpiece.

The Good Person of Szechwan (1943) provides an instructive view of Brecht's concept of society at this time by demonstrating how its values are in direct opposition to those of humanity, and how even success is self-defeating under such terms because of the sacrifices and moral degradation involved (thus continuing the themes of *In the Jungle of Cities* and *Mother Courage*). *The Good Person* achieves this with particular force and clarity, working from the premise that morality is natural and spontaneous whereas the ruthlessness demanded by capitalist society requires a constant effort, inducing schizophrenic divisions of the self, if not utter capitulation to brutal self-interest. The play operates through a continued questioning of the term 'good', especially as equated with 'respectable'; when the Gods arrive in search of a remaining good person in their world, the prostitute Shen Te protests that 'I am by no means sure that I am good. I should certainly like to be, but how am I to pay the rent?.'[47] Shen Te is not 'good' in the sense of respectable and honoured by society, because of her profession, although she is the most humane person in the play; but the Gods' gift of money gives her this respectability, which she is forced to defend as the eminently respectable but ruthlessly exploiting Shui Ta. Unfortunately the Gods fail to recognize the contradictory aspects of the two 'goods' and fail to recognize that Shen Te's reliance upon Shui Ta is ultimately self-defeating in everything but survival and appearances (similarly, Shui Ta transforms Sun into a 'useful citizen', that is, merciless overseer). The oppressive nature of the claims on Shen Te's goodness form a pungent dilemma in the early scenes of the play; only with the mask of Shui Ta over her natural features can she decide that 'the poverty in this city is too much for any individual to correct'[48] and thus absolve herself from any responsibility to amend it. Even the supposed fulfilments of sexual and maternal love only exacerbate her problems. Whereas Baal, Shlink and Mother Courage *chose* to identify themselves with the most savage, predatory aspects of their amoral environments, Shen Te *is forced* to descend to the law of the jungle to prevent it from consuming her and those she holds dear; progress, even survival, is seen as otherwise impossible in society as it stands. Yet, rather than change their traditional commandments, the inflexibly impractical Gods prefer to conclude that 'everything is as it should be',[49] a moral which the audience is led to react away from forcibly. The play's epilogue extends the central dilemma to the audience as directly as possible (and neatly continues the imagery of knife-edge economic disaster and vicious monetary circles into the very actor-audience relationship):

Ladies and gentlemen, don't feel let down:

We know this ending makes some people frown . . .
Indeed it is a curious way of coping:
To close a play, leaving the issue open.
Especially since we live by your enjoyment.
Frustrated audiences mean unemployment.
Whatever optimists may have pretended
Our play will fail if you can't recommend it.
    . . . But what would you suggest?
What is your answer? Nothing's been arranged.
Should men be better? Should the world be changed?
Or just the gods? Or ought there be none?
For our part we feel well and truly done.
There's only one solution that we know:
That you should consider as you go
What sort of measures you would recommend
To help good people to a happy end.
Ladies and gentlemen, in you we trust:
There must be happy endings, must, must, must![50]

Brecht cunningly makes the lack of artistic harmony experienced
by the audience appropriate to the lack of social harmony around
them, and gives them the responsibility for providing alternatives
to both, thus creating perhaps the most direct thematic fulfilment
of Piscator's objective of epic theatre's extension of a play's action
beyond the conventional dramatic framework. *Mr Puntila and his
Man Matti* (1948) shares the theme of dual personality, in this case
embodied in an oppressive landowner human and benevolent
when drunk. Whereas Shui Ta was the social perversion of Shen
Te's essential good nature, Puntila remains Matti's ultimate
enemy despite drunken attempts at contact which are cursory and
comic; in fact it is more tempting to see Puntila as a bumbling,
self-deluded Shlink, in that he seeks contact with the very person
he oppresses but only succeeds in alienating him altogether.
Puntila's camaraderie and self-accusatory guilt ('Let me have it,
Matti, I'm no good'[51]) fail to prevent Matti's final unsentimental
declaration of defiant independence:

You're halfway human when you're drunk enough.
But comradeship dissolves in boozer's gloom . . .
Sad as I am to find out in the end
That oil and water cannot ever blend

It's not much help, there's nothing I can do:
So – time your servants turned their backs on you.
They'll find a decent master pretty fast
Once they've become the masters here at last.[52]

Puntila should have the obvious ludicrousness of Stoke and Poges
in O'Casey's *Purple Dust* (not least to gain mileage from Matti's
smashing of Puntila's furniture to build Mount Hatelma just as
the mischievous workers damage Poges's treasured quattrocento),
although his drunken scenes tend to give him a more pathetic
quality. As in *The Good Person*, harmonious co-existence is shown
to be impossible under present conditions, except that in *Puntila*
aggression is turned against the landowner rather than against
the system which creates landowner-servant relationships; it is as
if the protagonists of *The Good Person* turned on the vaguely
well-intentioned but destructively impractical gods. To take the
epilogue at face value, *Puntila*'s essential function is that of highly
entertaining agitprop, which ostensibly requires Puntila to
remain within his stereotyped role, not threaten to transcend it
through pathos – unless Brecht intends the audience to move with
Matti away *from* amused indulgence towards the almost redeeming humour and ridiculousness of Puntila *to* an unsentimental
recognition of his basic irredeemability, leaving the only open
path that of enlightened self-interest, in which case fellow-feeling,
as for Shen Te, becomes a hazard. In any case, *The Good Person*
remains a more skilfully managed, as well as more ambitious,
work.

  The Resistible Rise of Arturo Ui (1958) follows a very different
track. A comic-strip version of Hitler's rise to power relocated in
the Chicago vegetable trade and fuelled by farcical humour rather
than by moral outrage, all sounds profoundly inappropriate if not
self-defeating. In fact, *Ui* is fantastic and ludicrous to a highly
serious end, namely to the point of encouraging disbelief that such
events could occur and then reminding us, even as we laugh, that
they *did* occur under cover of a less exaggerated disbelief. As the
Announcer reminds us, 'everything you'll see tonight is true. / Nothing's invented, nothing's new / Or made to order just for you'.[53]
Only the insanity of events has been heightened to brisk comic
effect so that we see the gulf (and also the proximity) between Ui's
public aphorisms and avowals such as 'Bitter experience /
Teaches me not to stress the human angle'[54] and the bloody deeds

they justify. But most of the comedy is directed against the complacency of those who enabled Ui/Hitler to rise to power and is concerned to anticipate and devalue the superiority an audience usually feels whilst watching comedy. Ui says 'If anyone's/Not for me he's against me and has only/Himself to blame for anything that happens.'[55] By the same token, the play suggests that anyone who is not against Ui is for him and has only himself to blame for anything that happens. The cautionary Epilogue brings these threads together with clarity and force:

> Therefore learn how to see and not to gape.
> To act instead of talking all day long.
> The world was almost won by such an ape!
> The nations put him where his kind belong.
> But don't rejoice too soon at your escape –
> The womb he crawled from is still going strong.[56]

If we neglect this advice in our own future conduct, the Epilogue suggests, the laugh will be on us.

No dramatist *up to* Brecht has such a well-focussed political intention and method in his address to creating a theatre where 'our representations must take second place to what is presented, men's life together in society; and the pleasure felt in their perfection must be converted into the higher pleasure felt when the rules emerging from this life in society are treated as imperfect and provisional. In this way the theatre leaves its spectators productively disposed even after the spectacle is over'.[57] This extension of dramatic effect into the lives of the audience was given a new level of successful directness by the production experiments of Piscator and the dramatic literature of Brecht, working in the conviction that political theatre had the power to alter briefly, with a view to transforming permanently, the patterns of perception sanctioned by an imperfect society; in short, that 'art can create a certain unity in its audience, which in our period is divided into classes'.[58]

4 The Hidden Situation

JOHN GALSWORTHY, C. K. MUNRO,
W. SOMERSET MAUGHAM, C. DAY LEWIS,
STEPHEN SPENDER, W. H. AUDEN &
CHRISTOPHER ISHERWOOD, J. B. PRIESTLEY

> Look at me, don't be a lot of damned fools; it's all bunk what
> they're saying to you about honour and patriotism and glory.
> Bunk, bunk, bunk.
>
> *For Services Rendered*[1]

Whilst Brecht developed and sharpened what he termed Shaw's
'terrorist' tendencies, British playwrights initially continued in
the tracks of the Irish dramatist's more traditional, naturalistic
points of departure. As Katharine J. Worth writes, 'Ibsen and
Shaw had made prolonged discussion of events seem the natural
theatrical mode', and subsequent British playwrights often used
this to express a Chekhovian mood of nostalgic decay, particularly 'the pathos of ordinary people's humdrum lives wasting
away in the relentless hand of time',[2] although handled in a more
self-consciously expository form. Such plays are often static,
verbal and express the self-critical doubts of a society whose
zeitgeist is lassitude – Heartbreak House seen from the inside – but
their focus remains largely within the domestic microcosm rather
than make any connection with larger social processes or
ideologies beyond a general humanism. In contrast to Shaw's
Heartbreak House, the cause of the illness escapes diagnosis.
However, individual dramatic moments can occur within the
works of certain writers which threaten to break through the
self-consciously stale decorum to create a more active and
passionate appeal to their audiences.

An interesting strength in the writings of John Galsworthy is his
concern and ability to present and criticize the self-critical, even
guilty, liberal bourgeois intellectual. *The Silver Box* (1906) shows

the plight of an actual Liberal Member of Parliament, John Barthwick, when his son acts irresponsibly but remains relatively unpunished by the law. The viewpoint of his wife Mrs Barthwick ('These Socialists and Labour men are an absolutely selfish set of people. They have no sense of patriotism, like the upper classes, *they simply want what we've got*'[3]) is discredited by an almost documentary concern to make the audience aware of the economic and ethical pressures upon the less privileged Jones family, the servants who suffer through young Jack Barthwick's spoilt-childishness. The repercussions prey upon John's mind, but fail to pierce his family's complacency, until a skilful modulation occurs at the end of the Second Act. A child is heard crying outside the dining room:

MRS BARTHWICK (*Sharply*): I can't stand that crying. I must send Marlow to stop it. My nerves are all on edge. (*She rings the bell.*)
BARTHWICK: I'll shut the window. You'll hear nothing. (*He shuts the window. There is silence.*)
MRS BARTHWICK (*Sharply*): That's no good! It's on my nerves. Nothing upsets me like a child's crying. (MARLOW *comes in.*) What's that noise of crying, Marlow? It sounds like a child.
BARTHWICK: It is a child. I can see it against the railings.
MARLOW (*Opening the window and looking out – quietly*): It's Mrs Jones's little boy, ma'am; he came here after his mother.
MRS BARTHWICK (*Moving quickly to the window*): Poor little chap! John, we oughtn't to go on with this!
BARTHWICK (*Sitting heavily in a chair*): Ah! but it's out of our hands!
(MRS BARTHWICK *turns her back to the window. There is an expression of distress on her face. She stands motionless, compressing her lips. The crying begins again.* BARTHWICK *covers his ears with his hands, and* MARLOW *shuts the window. The crying ceases.*
The curtain falls.[4]

The play's conclusion is similarly challengingly inharmonious. When the head of the Jones household is prosecuted, justice favours the rich 'nuisance to the community' Jack over his less economically powerful counterpart, but when Mrs Jones humbly seeks Barthwick's intervention:

(BARTHWICK *hesitates, then yielding to his nerves, he makes a shamefaced gesture of refusal, and hurries out of court.*
MRS JONES *stands looking after him.*
The curtain falls.[5]

Barthwick is clearly a sympathetic character when compared to his wife or son, in that he vaguely realizes an injustice and pays lip service to its correction. The final curtains suggest that liberal discomfort is not enough, but by showing the protagonist unable to articulate a coherent alternative of action may also fail to inspire the audience to any definite channel of reform beyond a broad, rather guilty sympathy with numerous viewpoints. Similarly, *Strife* (1909) seeks to give sympathetic private backgrounds to the leaders of both sides of an industrial dispute, who are finally both denounced by the bodies they represent on account of their intransigence. Roberts, the workers' leader, is given a powerful diatribe against capital, but Galsworthy gives the final word of the scene to an old man who exclaims 'Shame on your strife!'[6] when violence erupts; whilst Anthony, the company chairman, views the workers' uprising with a rhetorically potent but ideologically muddled speech which admits 'If I were in *their* place I should be the same. But I am not in their place.'[7] The final mutual respect of both broken leaders aims at producing a tragedy of irreconcileability, for all their common integrity. But this locates the dramatic interest in the respective wills to power of both men, rather than the rival claims of their politics, making the final tragedy human although against a volatile social background. It is also intriguing that both camps have their liberal, sympathetic representatives like Barthwick in *The Silver Box* (in this case, Anthony's children and the Trades Unionist Harness) but whose troubled, compromising souls cut poor dramatic figures next to the drive and energy of the aggressive hardliners they seek to mollify. Galsworthy extends sympathy so equivocally that the play remains intellectually paralyzed in a practical paradox. The conflict is both unavoidable and denounced for its human cost, and no means of practical resolution is indicated beyond the wry mutual respect of its burned-out former contenders – a sympathy which remains impossible when still in the heat of battle.

Galsworthy's *Justice* (1910) paves the way for Behan's *The Quare Fellow* (1956) in demonstrating to the audience the harshness of the social sanctions they tacitly support, and the cell mime in Act

Three scene three strives towards an enforced experience of oppressive conditions in a way developed by Edgar's *The Jail Diary of Albie Sachs* (1978) and Wesker's *Caritas* (1981): the imprisoned John Falder is shown in his cell wordlessly listening, sewing, pacing and finally hammering on the metal door with his bare fists. *The Foundations* (1917) returns to the theme of political protest with the adventurous choice of a revolutionary urban terrorist as central figure, and conducts a sharper analysis of political philanthropy than *The Silver Box*. There is little doubt that the complacently well-meaning gentry who gather together for a charity dinner, to 'eat ourselves silly to improve the condition of the sweated',[8] appear in a ludicrously ironic and condescending position under sustained dramatic analysis, and the discovery of a bomb on the premises intensifies the tensions in their professed sympathy:

> PRESS: . . . But would you allow yourself to be blown up with impunity?
> LORD W: Well, that's a bit extreme. But I quite sympathize with this chap. Imagine yourself in his shoes. He sees a huge house, all these bottles, us swilling them down; perhaps he's got a starving wife, or consumptive kids.
> PRESS (*Writing and murmuring*): Um-m! "Kids."
> LORD W: He thinks: "But for the grace of God, there swill I. Why should that blighter have everything and I nothing?" and all that.
> PRESS (*Writing*): "And all that." (*Eagerly*) Yes?
> LORD W: And gradually – you see – this contrast – becomes an obsession with him. "There's got to be an example made," he thinks; and – er – he makes it, don't you know?
> PRESS (*Writing*): Ye-es? And – when you're the example?
> LORD W: Well, you feel a bit blue, of course. But my point is that you quite see it.
> PRESS: From the other world.[9]

This aspect of the play forms an implicit critique of *Strife*'s multilateral sympathy in its cold scrutiny of the liberal conscience which effectively asks even the most compassionate upper or middle class audience members whether they are compassionate *enough* and from what motives – then queries the values of a compassion which permits its holder to be blown up with benevolent understanding. The ruthless discomfort to which the play subjects liberal smugness is witty and stimulating. Unfortunately, the figure of Lemmy the revolutionary is inconsistently realised; at times he is a bloodthirsty anarchist ('I don't care 'oose blood it is. I want to see it flow!'[10]), at others a lucid post-war malcontent whose objections to his mother, who 'believes in things', contain a justifiable bitterness:

> Wot oh! – they said, time o' the war – ye're fighting for yer children's 'eritage. Well, wot's the 'eritage like, now we've got it? Empty as a shell before yer put the 'igh explosive in . . . I did the gas to-dy in the cellars of an 'ouse where the wine was mountains 'igh. . . . When the guns was roarin' the talk was for no more o' them glorious weeds – style an' luxury was orf. See wot it is naow. You've got a bare crust in the cupboard 'ere, I works from 'and to mouth in a glutted market – an' they stand abaht in their britches in the 'ouses o' the gryte. I was reg'lar overcome by it. I left a thing in that cellar –[11]

In contrast to Lemmy, Lord William is dramatically and literally put out of countenance as his reassuring clichés break down:

> Ladies and gentlemen, the great natural, but – er – artificial expansion which trade experienced the first years after the war has – er – collapsed. These are hard times. We who are fortunate feel more than ever – er – responsible – (*He stammers, loses the thread of his thought – Applause*) – er – responsible – (*The thread still eludes him*) – er –[12]

There is another skilful dramatic moment when the aristocratic child, Little Anne, confronts the working class child, Little Aida:

L. ANNE: Do you hate the rich?
L. AIDA (*Ineffably*): Nao. I hates the poor.
L. ANNE: Why?
L. AIDA: 'Cos they 'yn't got nuffin'.
L. ANNE: I love the poor. They're such dears.
L. AIDA (*Shaking her head with a broad smile*): Nao.
L. ANNE: Why not?
L. AIDA: I'd tyke and lose the lot, I would.
L. ANNE: Where?

L. AIDA: In the water.
L. ANNE: Like puppies?
L. AIDA: Yus.
L. ANNE: Why?
L. AIDA: Then I'd be shut of 'em.
L. ANNE (*Puzzled*): Oh.[13]

This splendid dialogue prefaces the encounter of Lord Williams and Lemmy in person, which also contains some attitude-spoiling worthy of Shaw:

LEMMY: If I was a bit more noble, I might be tempted to come the kind-'earted on twenty thou' a year. Some prefers yachts, or ryce 'orses. But philanthropy on the 'ole is safer, in these dyes.
LORD W: So you think one takes to it as a sort of insurance, Mr Lemmy? Is that quite fair?
LEMMY: Well, we've all got a weakness towards bein' kind, somewhere abaht us. But the moment wealf comes in, we 'yn't wot I call single-'earted. If yer went into the foundytions of yer wealf – would yer feel like 'avin' any? It all comes from uvver people's 'ard, unpleasant lybour – it's all built on Muvver as yer might sy. An' if yer daon't get rid o' some of it bein' kind – yer daon't feel safe nor comfy.
LORD W (*Rather desperately*): I know – hunger and all the rest of it! And here I am, a rich man, and I don't know what the deuce to do.
LEMMY: Well, I'll tell yer. Throw yer cellars open, an' while the populyce is gettin' drunk sell all yer 'ave an' go an' live in Ireland; they've got the milennium chronic over there. . . . That's speakin' as a practical man. Speakin' as a synt – 'Bruvvers, all I 'ave is yours. To-morrer I'm goin' dahn to the Lybour Exchynge to git put on the wytin' list, syme as you!'
LORD W: But d--- it, man, there we should be, all together! Would that help?
LEMMY: Nao; but it'd syve a lot of blood. (LORD WILLIAM *stops abruptly* . . .) Yer thought the Englishman could be taught to shed blood wive syfety. Not 'im! Once yer get 'im into an 'abit, yer cawn't git 'im out of it agyne. 'E'll go on sheddin' blood mechanical – Conservative by nyture. . . . If all you wealfy nobs wiv kepital 'ad come it kind from the start after the war yer'd never 'a been 'earin' the Marseillaisy now. . . . Naow, *you've*

been in the war an' it's given yer a feelin' 'eart; but most of the nobs wiv kepitel was too old or important to fight. *They* weren't borne agyne. So naow that bad times is come, we're 'owlin' for their blood.[14]

Lemmy's metamorphosis into a comic character becomes complete in the final moments, although he retains the ability to score an unsettling point off his conventional upper class foils. In fact, he mitigates his own prophecy by defusing the threat of bloodshed in particularly comic terms, defending Lord William from the incensed crowd with a rather unflattering description:

> Wot I sy is: Dahn wiv the country, dahn wiv everyfing. Begin agyne from the foundytions. (*Nodding his head back at the room.*) But we've got to keep one or two o' these 'ere under glawss, to show our future generytions. An' this one is 'armless. His pypes is sahnd, 'is 'eart is good; 'is 'ead is *not* strong.[15]

He also has the wit to ensure that Lord William carries out his theoretical beliefs to the practical letter by distributing money: 'Nobody arst 'im – quite on 'is own. That's the sort 'e is. (*Sinking his voice confidentially*) Sorft'.[16] Urban terrorism fades into witticisms, and Lemmy becomes more closely related to Enry Straker than Jed of Brenton's *Magnificence*. Galsworthy's conclusion of *The Foundations* is regrettably as damp a squib as Lemmy's bomb, although he leaves the injunction 'Next time yer build an 'ouse, doan't forget – it's the foundytions as bears the wyte'[17] to haunt the final curtain. But its black jokes at the expense of the benign liberal conscience contain an uncomfortably stimulating edge which makes the play worthy of wider attention than has been accorded. If Galsworthy's use of comedy has been less cosmetic and distancing on its raw emotional edges, it would stand as an even more provocative examination of class war and political sympathy.

The plays of C. K. Munro stand as brave if inelegant bids to dramatize the sweep of large political developments in international and human terms. Munro's plays have a principally documentary aim, attempting to show the effect of greedy economic pressures on matters of international politics and what occurs 'behind the scenes' of everyday life as it is experienced by the mere citizens of the countries involved. The functional characterization gives the plays a stripped-down quality of enactment occasionally reminiscent of a training film in the attempt to present an x-ray anatomy of international dealings, but in consequence few of the characters have the necessary depth to engage audience sympathies. *The Rumour* (written in 1922) shows the self-interested speculation that sparks an international crisis and war, and accuses the self-defined 'men of business': 'To you a human being is nothing but an object to be destroyed by your minions. . . . You possess information which might save the lives of thousands, of tens of thousands of human beings, the happiness of a thousand homes. And you will not reveal it, because your *business* interests lie in another direction.'[18] Like Shaw's *Geneva*, it boasts an array of vacuous politicians and strives to bring the audience to the awareness that 'it's not the fighters that are to blame for [wartime bloodshed], but those who send them to fight; those through whom the fighting has come about'.[19] An interesting aspect of the play is the periodic choric comments of the Englishmen Smith and Jones who, ignorant of the secret self-interested machinations, respond with conventional heroic interest to the conflict between Przimia and Loria, until Jones learns of his son's consequent death; meanwhile, even war is settled by trade, as the comfortable materialist Ned adds the final revelation that Loria's defeat was caused by their lack of armament provisions on account of his advice. *Progress* (written in 1923) traces the process of imperial colonization and consequent warfare, again demonstrating that 'One of the main weapons used by all the combatants, not only on each other, but by each government on its own people, is lying'[20] and features a good dramatic debate between the expedient Prime Minister (who is about as worthy of power as his counterpart in Shaw's *On the Rocks*) and Lord Mang, who objects that the statesman's doctrine of justification by results 'has been responsible for every political evil, every social oppression and injustice, since the beginning of the world'.[21] Whereas the Prime Minister claims 'the right to do what I think is best for the people to whom I am responsible', Mang suggests 'You rate your foresight too high'[22] and that the Prime Minister also acts with too much of an eye to future election results. Like those of Smith and Jones in *The Rumour*, the reactions of Bert, Bole and The Count punctuate the developments of *Progress* and provide an ironic counterpoint to the backroom political dealing with their laymens' perspectives. Bert begins the play out of work, loses an arm fighting for his country and is acclaimed as a hero, then ends the play once more out of work; and all three remain utterly oblivious to the real nature of the power shaping their lives, even to the point of directing their blame and aggression at Mang and the Germans, exactly as the Prime Minister would want. This demonstration of the discrepancy between idealistically conditioned public opinion and the true base nature of the dispensation of political power is the most skilful effect in Munro's otherwise rather wooden and long-winded plays.

W. Somerset Maugham's *For Services Rendered* (1932) is a more sharp and bitter development of the predominant neo-Chekhovian domestic dramas of the time such as Priestley's *Time and the Conways* (1937) or *The Linden Tree* (1948). *For Services Rendered* explores the decaying and distorted nature of England in the aftermath of war through the microcosm of the Ardsley family and presents painful and ironic evidence of the continuing survival of the *Heartbreak House* malaise. The decorated wartime officer Colley finds himself unsuited to peacetime and frustrated by its economic harshness, so commits suicide rather than compromise his pride. Colley's decision is compared to the bitterness of the blinded Sydney, the unthinking sensuality of Howard and the blind complacency of Ardsley himself:

SYDNEY: When it was all over, we did think that those of us who'd died hadn't died in vain, and those of us who were broken and shattered and knew they wouldn't be any good in the world were buoyed up by the thought that if they'd given anything they'd given it in a good cause.
ARDSLEY: And they had.
SYDNEY: Do you still think that? I don't. I know we were the dupes of the incompetent fools who ruled the nations. I know that we were sacrificed to their vanity, their greed and their stupidity. And the worst thing of it is that as far as I can tell they haven't learnt a thing. They're just as vain, they're just as greedy, they're just as stupid as they ever were. They muddle on, muddle on, and one of these days they'll muddle us into another war. When that happens I'll tell you what I'm going to do. I'm going out into the streets and cry: 'Look at me, don't be a lot of damned fools; it's all bunk what they're saying to you, about honour and patriotism and glory. Bunk, bunk, bunk!'[23]

Although Sydney is blind, he has the vision to make connections far beyond the ability of Munro's Jones or Bert, and his speech carries a powerfully direct resonance far beyond the naturalistic framework of the play or the proscenium arch. But misguidedly conventional reactions to his appeal are also anticipated and incorporated by Maugham:

> HOWARD: Who cares if it is bunk? I had the time of my life in the war. No responsibility and plenty of money . . . I tell you it was a bitter day for me when they signed the armistice. What have I got now? Just the same old thing day after day, working my guts out to keep body and soul together. The very day war is declared I join up and the sooner the better if you ask me . . .
>
> ARDSLEY: . . . No one wants another was less than I do, but if it comes I'm convinced that you'll do your duty, so far as in you lies, as you did it before. It was a great grief to me that when the call came I was too old to answer. But I did what I could. I was enrolled as a special constable. And if I'm wanted, I shall be ready again.
>
> SYDNEY (*between his teeth*): God give me patience.
>
> HOWARD: You have a whisky and soda, old boy, and you'll feel better.
>
> SYDNEY: Will a whisky and soda make me forget poor Evie half crazy, Collie doing away with himself rather than go to gaol, and my lost sight?
>
> ARDSLEY: But, my dear boy, that's just our immediate circle. Of course we suffered, perhaps we had more than our share, but we're not everyone.
>
> SYDNEY: Don't you know that all over England there are families like ours, all over Germany and all over France? . . .
>
> ARDSLEY: The fact is, Sydney, you think too much.
>
> SYDNEY (*smiling*): I dare say you're right father. You see, I have little else to do. I'm thinking of collecting stamps.
>
> ARDSLEY: That's a very good idea, my boy. If you go about it cleverly there's no reason why it shouldn't be a very sound investment.[24]

The aftermath of war has also taken its toll on the female characters: Eva's loss of Collie denies her the means of escape from the Ardsleys' sterile home and drives her insane, whilst Lois finds that considerations of pre-war morality have little bearing on her desperate need to be free from her apathetic, moribund mother and the provincial suffocation offered by the family. The demented Eva provides an effective check to Ardsley's complacency in the last moment of the play:

ARDSLEY: Well, I must say it's very nice to have a cup of tea by one's own fireside and surrounded by one's own family. If you come to think of it none of us have anything very much to worry about. Of course we none of us have more money than we know what to do with, but we have our health and we have our happiness. I don't think we've got very much to complain of. Things haven't been going too well lately, but I think the world is turning the corner and we can all look forward to better times in future. This old England isn't done yet, and I for one believe in it and all it stands for.

    EVA *begins to sing in a thin cracked voice.*

EVA   God save our gracious King!
                Long live our noble King!
                  God save our King!

(The others look at her, petrified, in horror-struck surprise. When she stops LOIS *gives a little cry and hurries from the room.)*
CURTAIN [25]

For Services Rendered is a fine example of the bitter, rather than witty, means towads the Shavian goal of destroying ideals (in this case the patriotic myths invoked by political leaders, and the dangers of their complacent acceptance).

It is interesting to compare Maugham's play to J. B. Priestley's *An Inspector Calls* (1946), a later play which continues to use the domestic image of the microcosmic bourgeois family presided over by a complacent patriarch and combines it with the plot development of the murder thriller towards an effect quite different from either of these established forms, namely that of a super-rational social parable. Despite its date of composition, the play's action is set in 1912 to discredit the self-absorbed optimism of Arthur Birling's rosy predictions from the hindsight of the post-war world. The intrusion of Inspector Goole into Birling's rather too pat expressions of his 'common-sense' capitalist philosophy serves to bring the knowledge of a more painful existence into their secure, comfortable home. To the Birlings' smug conviction that 'we're respectable citizens and not criminals' the Inspector replies that 'Sometimes there isn't as much difference as you think. Often, if it was left to me, I wouldn't know where to draw the line.'[26] Despite Birling's rejection of community responsibility, Goole proves the connections of each family member with the ill fortune and death of a representative Everywoman figure, Eva Smith, demonstrating that 'we have to share something. If there's nothing else, we'll have to share our guilt'.[27] In fact, Mrs Birling's refusal of aid to Eva Smith places the blame and sentence upon her own son, leading to the destruction of his illegitimate child by the girl and, thereby, her own grandchild (a twist reminiscent of Ibsen's *Pillars of the Community* in the inadvertant destruction of future generations by one's ostensible work on their behalf; and the irresponsible son Eric recalls the spoilt Jack in *The Silver Box* except that in this case the father is hardly much better). The Inspector's final summing-up has the impact of a direct address to the audience similar to Sydney's crucial speech in *For Services Rendered*, but here with even less regard for considerations of realistic speech:

> INSPECTOR: But just remember this. One Eva Smith has gone – but there are millions and millions and millions of John Smiths and Eva Smiths still left with us, with their lives, their hopes and fears, their suffering, and chance of happiness, all intertwined with what we think and say and do. We don't live alone. We are members of one body. We are responsible for each other. And I tell you that the time will come when, if men will not learn that lesson, then they will be taught it in fire and blood and anguish. Good night.[28]

However, the lack of realism is consistent with Priestley's final development of the plot when the older Birlings are cheered by the discovery that Goole is not a member of the local police; they dismiss him as 'a socialist or some sort of crank' and regress to their old complacency, until the telephone rings to herald the arrival of a real police inspector. Goole, in retrospect, becomes an inhuman bearer of a prophecy, akin to the Jungian Shadow, and a supernatural chastiser of evils reminiscent of O'Casey's mythic intervenors in human iniquity (except that the Birlings, with their varying degrees of illusion and selfishness, give much more scope for audience identification than O'Casey's unashamedly farcical caricatures, so that the admittedly very generalized message of

Priestley's play has a closer relevance to everyday conduct).
Priestley's *They Came to a City* (1943) also uses a self-acknowledged
'symbolic' mode in its bid to project a vaguely socialist Utopia,
apparently inspired by 'the very different attitudes of mind that
people had to any post-War changes.'[29] The visionary City has
more than a hint of the afterlife, but finally comes to stand as an
inspirational glimpse of the ideal which two figures return to the
outside world to describe:

> Some of 'em'll laugh and jeer just because they don't *want*
> anything different. They're frightened of losing some miserable
> little advantage they've schemed and worked for. . . . They
> don't want to lose the whip-hand they've got over somebody.
> They'd rather have their little privilege and prestige in an
> ashpit than take a chance and share alike in a new world. . . .
> they will tell us we can't change human nature. That's one of
> the oldest excuses in the world for doing nothing. And it isn't
> true. We've been changing human nature for thousands of
> years. But what you *can't* change in it, Alice – no, not with guns
> or whips or red hot bars – is man's eternal desire and vision and
> hope of making this world a better place to live in . . . our city.
> Where men and women don't work for machines and money,
> but machines and money work for men and women – where
> greed and envy and hate have no place – where want and
> disease and fear have vanished forever – where nobody carries a
> whip and nobody rattles a chain.[30]

Any depth or contemporary relevance in *They Came to a City* has to
be applied in reverse from this final expository speech by Joe.
Unfortunately, the positive symbolism of *The Came to a City* is less
effective than the negative symbolism of *An Inspector Calls* because
of the former's distance from anything recognizable in reality.

Whilst Maugham's *For Services Rendered* was fundamentally a
Chekhovian response to the aftermath of World War One, a
number of plays appeared in the 1930s anticipating the political
upheavals of World War Two and particularly warning of the
dangers of fascism, but adopting a poetic, non-realistic style
moving towards Brechtian effects if not directly influenced by the
German playwright, and far removed from the domestic naturalism which maintained its grip on much of the mainstream theatre.
C. Day Lewis, in the Preface to his *Noah and the Waters* (published

1936) describes the play as in the tradition of the medieval morality play; and its chorus ensembles struggling for the commitment of a central Everyman accords with the image. Like O'Casey's *Purple Dust*, the play adapts the story of the Flood to represent a rising tide of political impatience, but in a more directly allegorical way than O'Casey's knockabout comedy. Noah and the personified Flood are addressed by the ruling Burgesses, who attempt to placate them, but the Flood deconstructs their arguments and lays the blame for contemporary decline firmly on their materialistic heads. Noah hesitates, unsure of which to trust, but finally accords with the Flood, and the waters of the world unite to rout the old order. Lewis's epigraph, from *The Communist Manifesto*, makes the allegory explicit:

> Finally, when the class war is about to be fought to a finish, disintegration of the ruling class and the old order of society becomes so active, so acute, that a small part of the ruling class breaks away to make common cause with the revolutionary class, the class which holds the future in its hands . . .

At least *Noah and the Waters* has no illusions about its potential audience and the effect the play wishes to have upon them, but its heightened tone is rather monotonous and one-dimensional, unlike that of Stephen Spender's *Trial of a Judge* (1938) which uses similar heightened speech, choric interjections and vacillating central figure to subtler effect. Its opposition of Black Fascist and Red Communist figures initially recalls O'Casey's *The Star Turns Red* but surpasses O'Casey's play because of its greater skill in drawing out the opposition of ideologies; for example, the fascists are given deeper things to say than 'Hail the Circle and the Flash', in fact they give a detailed account of their reasons for killing a Polish Jew and emerge as more truly terrifying figures in consequence. The focal figure of the Judge is an articulate spokesman for the liberal dilemma, trusting the framework of law against the belief that 'might is right', and motivated by a vague ideal of 'peace-mantled sunset villages' but never becoming a wholly ludicrous or unsympathetic character. *Trial of a Judge* is an effective example of one of political drama's fundamental impulses, namely the exposure of the incongruity between standard social law and the ideals it professes to represent, thus forming a powerful indictment of the society in question; and the

Judge, torn between his professional orthodoxy and his conscience-stricken witness of injustice, embodies this crucial tension when he finds the law inadequate defence against fascist violence; indeed, the dead Jew's fiancée accuses him 'You are the mask they wear.'[31] The Judge's criticism of his own contradictory position brings him to similar conclusions when, in a dream, he is himself put on trial for treason:

HUMMELDORF: . . . What has the prisoner to say?
JUDGE: That I am guilty.
For, by your law, the jungle
Is established; and the tiger's safety is guaranteed
When he hunts his innocent victim,
By all the iron of the police.
I condemned to death gunmen
And gangsters, but they are
The highest functions of this society
. . .
I was a traitor. That is true. Because
I might have made all of this otherwise.[32]

The Judge's speech even moves the substitute judge Hummeldorf to a crisis of conscience and he protests, only to be beaten down by the fascists who form the prosecution, and the trial ends on a memorably direct note:

THIRD BLACK PRISONER: . . . Destroy all photographs taken and all reports of speeches in this court. The last ten minutes are wiped out. *They never happened*.
BLACK TROOP LEADER (*advancing to the front of the stage*):
If your imaginations
Invent and publish any picture of this scene,
Remember that the lines cut by memory
Into the brain may cut so deep
They kill life altogether.
Delete those lines. Make your brains blank. Or –
You have seen and heard nothing
Except the fate of those who are traitors.
(*Calling behind the stage*). Ring down the curtain.
CURTAIN[33]

The sharp urgency of this effect and the well realized poetic
sinister atmosphere surrounding the fascists are two of the reasons
why *Trial of a Judge* deserves a revival, as does W. H. Auden and
Christopher Isherwood's *The Dog Beneath the Skin* (1935), written
for the same Group Theatre as Spender's play. The stage
directions to *The Dog*'s first scene specify that 'The scene suggests
the setting of a pre-war musical comedy', and the comic
provincial vicarage is one of many standard forms which the play
fills with unsettling new material. It partakes in turn of the
flavours of a morality play, an episodic revue, a dream play, a
sleazy cabaret and, most ingeniously, a traditional pantomime,
especially when the naïve Idle Jack of a picaresque protagonist,
Alan, delivers his tearful farewells to home and family before
embarking on his expedition with his trusted 'doggy' in a
somewhat deranged parallel to *Dick Whittington* or *Puss in Boots*.
Alan's adventures with his dog in the monarchy of Ostnia and the
fascist dictatorship of Westland provide many opportunities for
comparisons with contemporary Europe, and his excursion
'backstage' of international politics is reminiscent of a fantastic
view of the scenes denied to C. K. Munro's 'common men'; as the
Second Journalist sings:

> The General Public has no notion
> of what's behind the scenes.
> They vote at times with some emotion
> But don't know what it means.
> Doctored Information
> is all they have to judge thing by;
> The hidden situation
> Develops secretly.[34]

The Dog Beneath the Skin also sports a Chorus to address the
audience directly, as when Alan's voyage of discovery provides
scathing images of European moral decline:

> Do not comfort yourself with the reflection: 'How very
>   unEnglish'
> If your follies are different, it is because you are richer
>   . . .
> But already, like an air-bubble under a microscope slide, the
>   film of poverty is expanding

And soon it will reach your treasure and your gentlemanly
behaviour.
Observe, therefore, and be more prepared than our hero.[35]

Act Two's scene in a lunatic asylum, where a portrait of 'Our
Leader' with a megaphone instead of a face inspires the lunatics
with a hysterical love of homeland, is a blackly comic caricature of
Nazi Germany. Otherwise, the play sags slightly in the middle,
with the authors' excursions into poetic grotesquerie becoming
indulgent, akin to Bond's *Early Morning* (1968) (the dialogue
between Alan's Left and Right Feet particularly foreshadowing
Arthur's separation from his head in the later play). But one bid to
engage the audience in a conflict of emotions is particularly
successful and deserves quoting at length. When the lunatics
surround and close in on Alan, exciting each other with taunts
and threats, they behave frighteningly close to the fascist pack
mentality of subsequent generations, and correspondingly inspire
revulsion. In contrast, the cabaret act performed by Destructive
Desmond at the Nineveh Hotel blends on – and offstage audiences
in what is likely to be an unsettling exposure of vandalistic glee,
particularly heightened by a hapless Art Expert, whose only
gradual perception of the threatening atmosphere in the audience's attitude, his obliviousness to Desmond's knife, and his
despair and personal pain at the nihilistic display are crucial to
the scene's emotional impact. Having established his love for a
Rembrandt – worth £60,000 but really priceless as it constitutes
an irreplaceable work of genius – the Art Expert is horrified when
Desmond produces his knife:

ART EXPERT: Stop! I protest against this disgraceful exhibition!
I appeal to the ladies and gentlemen of the audience. Surely you
won't allow this to go on?
DESMOND: Aha! So you appeal to the audience, do you? Very
well! (*To the audience*) Ladies and gentlemen, I leave it entirely in
your hands; which picture would you rather see cut to bits, this
landscape which Mr Expert so despises, or old mahogany
Rembrandt?
ALL THE DINERS: Rembrandt! Rembrandt!
DESMOND (*Brutally to* ART EXPERT): You hear what they say? And
now, get off my platform? If you don't like it, you can do the
other thing!

ART EXPERT (*putting his hands to his head*): Either these people are mad, or I am! (*He jumps down from the stage and runs out of the restaurant.*)

(DESMOND *waves an ironic goodbye after him. The drums begin to roll. The audience groan with delight.* DESMOND, *standing before Rembrandt, works himself up into a state of hysterical fury. He makes faces at the canvas, shows his teeth, shakes his fist, spits*)

DESMOND (*as the drums reach their climax*): Grrrr! Take that, you brute! (*Slashes canvas with his knife*) and that! and that! (*Finale of trumpets. The* ATTENDANTS *hold up the slashed picture and* DESMOND *puts his arm through it several times. Then he strikes it from their hands and tramples it on the floor. Terrific applause.* DESMOND *bows and exits*.)[36]

Few scenes in drama can demonstrate the appeal of malicious anarchy better than this, but it also lends resonance to the later statement 'I think the most important thing to remember about Man is that pictures mean more to him than people'.[37] The attack on Rembrandt would have little appeal without the grief of the Art Expert – which may make the audience feel less far from the tribal circle of malevolent lunatics than before, especially when the Chorus states:

We show you man caught in the trap of his terror, destroying
 himself . . .
You cannot avoid the issue by becoming simply a community
 digger,
O you who prattle about the wonderful Middle Ages: You who
 expect the millennium after a few trifling adjustments . . .

Beneath the communities and the coiffures: discover your
 image.
Man divided and restless always: afraid and unable to forgive.
Beware of yourself . . .

You have wonderful hospitals and a few good schools;
Repent.
The precision of your instruments and the skill of your
 designers is unparalleled;
Unite.
Your knowledge and your power are capable of infinite
 extension;
Act.[38]

The Dog Beneath the Skin moves from forcing the audience into recognition of the capacity for evil beneath everyone's civilized veneer, towards an urgent injunction not to let this capacity gain the upper hand, particularly in the potentially disastrous sphere of international politics. The return of Alan and Francis to their native village affords further examples of this, for example when Mildred Luce addresses the militaristic Lads of Pressan:

> Wave your dummy rifles about! It's only play now. But soon they'll give you real rifles. You'll learn to shoot. You'll learn to kill whoever they tell you to. And you'll be trained to let yourselves be killed, too. I thought I'd just tell you. It isn't that I care. I'm glad! What does it matter to me if you're all murdered? My sons were all murdered, and they were bigger and stronger and handsomer than you'll ever be, any of you! So what do I care![39]

Francis continues the theme of man's conformity in destruction when he proclaims to the village:

> I was fascinated and horrified by you all. I thought such obscene, cruel, hypocritical, mean, cruel, vulgar creatures had never existed before. . . . It's an awful shock to start seeing people from underneath . . . I don't hate you anymore. I see how you fit into the entire scheme. You are significant, but not in the way I used to imagine. You are units in an immense army: most of you will die without knowing what your leaders are really fighting for or that you are fighting at all.[40]

The closing moments reveal the bestial qualities of the village's tinpot tyrants, who appear with the faces of grotesque animals, and once more the Chorus brings the lesson home to the audience in the Epilogue:

> Mourn not for these; these are ghosts who choose their pain.
> Mourn rather for yourselves; and your inability to make up
>   your minds
> Whose hours of self-hatred and contempt were all your majesty
>   and crisis
> Choose therefore that you may recover.[41]

Many plays are an anti-climax after *The Dog Beneath the Skin*, but
Auden and Isherwood's own subsequent efforts are particularly
disappointingly so, as the political qualities of their plays become
settings or bases for relatively esoteric poetic goals, and the works
are less organic or vital. *The Ascent of F6* (1937) also has a hero
caught between Britain and Ostnia's manipulations and forced to
act as a pawn for his country, but moves from there into more
poetic and psychological analyses. Ransom's position is neatly
summarized by Mrs A's vision, 'I have dreamed of a threadbare
barnstorming actor, and he was a national symbol';[42] and the
government's handling of the expedition and its presentation by
the media are shown in their effect by the choric reactions of Mr
and Mrs A, whilst all of these are pointedly contrasted to the
truth, as in Munro's plays. However, Munro's handling of the
duped average citizen is more compassionate, as Ransom identifies the A's as parasitical and sub-human against his
Nietzschean aspirations ('Was it to me they turned their rodent
faces, those ragged denizens of the waterfronts, and squealed so
piteously: "Restore us! Restore us to our uniqueness and human
condition!" '[43]). *On the Frontier* (published in 1937) is another
image of Ostnia and Westland, and even more reminiscent of
Munro in its simultaneous demonstration of the escalation of
pre-war tension and the identification of the industrialist as the
controller of destinies besides whom the ostensible leader is
comparatively powerless. Like *The Ascent of F6*, *On the Frontier* lacks
the clear, hard choric impact which punctuates *The Dog Beneath the
Skin* and complements its urgent message. *On the Frontier* is best
when exposing the discrepancy between public announcements
and private motive amongst national leaders. As the Leftists tell
the waltzers:

> These voices commit treason
> Against all truth and reason,
> Using an unreal aggression
> To blind you to you real oppression;
> Truth is elsewhere.
> Understand the motive, penetrate the lie
> Or you will die.
> . . .
> The country is in danger
> But not from any stranger.

Your enemies are here
Whom you should fight, not fear
For till they cease
The earth will know no peace
Learn to know
Your friend from your foe.[44]

Similarly, the entr'acte scene before Act Three, scene three, is a sharp demonstration of the Babel of English newspapers and their respective editorial policies. Another fine moment which belies the official national images of the situation is the near-breakdown of the barrier in the Ostnia-Westland room, as common human sympathy almost cuts through national partitions:

> ANNA (*as if listening to sounds in the very far distance*): Mother . . . can't you hear them, over there? They're crying, they're suffering – just like us!
> MRS VRODNY (*Speaking with a kind of terrible obstinacy that belies her words*): I hear nothing![45]

The interlude showing the troops in the trenches also shows the lack of malice but effective powerlessness of the privates in the hierarchy of the officer-dominated army, in a striking parallel to the central sequence of O'Casey's *The Silver Tassie*. Otherwise, much of the play, particularly the romance of Eric and Anna, is melodramatic, obvious or hazy in effect. But Auden and Isherwood's plays – like those of Munro, Maugham and Spender – stand together as underrated bids to expose the illusory nature of distractions from the 'hidden situation' of reality that are propagated in both wartime and peacetime, as well as indicating the rich potential of non-naturalistic techniques for the ends of political theatre.

5   Anonymity and Anger

JOHN OSBORNE, ARNOLD WESKER, BRENDAN
BEHAN, TOM McGRATH & JIMMY BOYLE

> I attract hostility. I seem to be on heat for it. Whenever I step
> out onto those boards – immediately, from the very moment I
> show my face – I know I've got to fight almost every one of those
> people in the auditorium. Right from the stalls to the gallery, to
> the Vestal Virgins in the boxes! My God, it's a gladiatorial
> combat! Me against them! Me and mighty Them! Oh, I may
> win some of them over. Sometimes it's a half maybe, sometimes
> a third, sometimes it's not even a quarter. But I *do* beat them
> down. I beat them down! And even in the hatred of the
> majority, there's a kind of triumph because I know that,
> although they'd never admit it, they secretly respect me.
>
> *Epitaph for George Dillon*[1]

Whilst Brecht strove towards the objective of a 'rational theatre'
or at least one which pushed the audience towards the formulations of logical connections between social structure and individual misery, the dramatists of the Fifties, Osborne, Wesker and
Behan, also made considerable impact by turning their dramatic
focus onto society. However, the latter playwrights' outrage was
unashamedly informed by emotional objections to the loss of self,
identity and integrity enforced by society, rather than by
reference to political ideologies exposing economic and judicial
inequality inherent in the social status quo. Without wishing to
denigrate their startling effect upon the direction of theatre,
Wesker, Behan and particularly Osborne have more in common
with their dramatic predecessors than with their successors; their
effectiveness frequently lay in the rediscovery and sharpening of
techniques and themes familiar from Shaw, O'Casey and the
naturalists. Osborne's plays continue to be an internal guide
through a modern Heartbreak House, but its lethargy is chal-

78

lenged by the vociferously protesting but primarily intuitive voices of its more intelligent sufferers – who nevertheless fail to escape from their tragic solitude. Osborne's most distinctive development is his impulse away from polite paralysis to vehement antagonism towards society and the actual theatre audience insofar as it represents the massed concensus of society. Wesker and Behan excel at showing the effect of political developments on an engagingly human canvas and at manoeuvring audience sympathies towards identification with unlikely and unfamiliar figures.

Osborne's flair lies in his development of the moment in *For Services Rendered* when Sydney Ardsley breaks out of the social compact of silent suffering to explode in a bitter tirade which lifts him out of the confines of a naturalistic framework and into a sphere of defiant, urgent personal address to the audience. The tragic tone of many of Osborne's plays stems from the fact that many of his protagonists go as unheeded as Sydney; as Alan Carter has claimed, 'The response . . . is from the audience, or from the action of the play, but rarely from the minor characters. In this way the audience notice the void around the hero and they hasten to fill it in themselves.'[2] Despite Osborne's ill-informed contempt for Shaw and the seriousness of his intentions,[3] he shares the earlier playwright's technique and skill in assembling a series of foils around an unconventional but highly principled spokesman for them to fuel his criticisms. It may in fact be more accurate to link both dramatists as developers of the basic theatrical energy of the Jacobean malcontent who fluctuates between identifying with and standing against the corruption, purposelessness and frivolity of his disjointed society. But, to provide a final dramatic analogue, Osborne's plays probably have their strongest similarity to those of Ibsen in their fundamentally Nietzschean sympathy with the strong, solitary individual who refuses to submit to the Procrustean bed of society's standards and thus alienates himself further from both the mediocrity and the fellowship which are represented by the common herd. It is appropriate that Osborne has written an adaptation of *Hedda Gabler* in that many of his original creations share Hedda's sensitive and witty dissatisfaction with the stifling pettiness of everyday life but fail to formulate any articulation of their protest beyond the immediately personal and emotional and are thus denied the capacity for channelling their thwarted energy into any remedial gesture beyond an impulse towards oblivion.

In *Look Back in Anger* (1956), Jimmy Porter spends much of his time baiting those closest to him in order to goad them into some form of response. As he says of Alison, 'Don't think I could provoke her. Nothing I could do would provoke her. Not even if I were to drop dead.'[4] Nevertheless, he continues his almost hysterical spiral of rhetorical extremity and abuse, from the impassioned ('Nobody can be bothered. No one will raise themselves out of their delicious sloth. . . . Oh heavens, how I long for a little ordinary human enthusiasm. . . . Let's pretend that we're human beings and that we're actually alive'[5]) to the calculated shock of his cynicisms and personal attacks on Alison and Helena. A certain amount of this seems a coherent response to the apathy of his surroundings ('My heart is so full I feel ill – and she wants peace!'[6]), but his much-quoted lament for 'good, brave causes' is directed to be '*semi-serious*'[7] and is finally unsatisfactory as a decisive link between his futile bids for emotional reciprocity and his social climate. Jimmy has nothing but contempt for those who escape into a glib identification with a self-conscious modern mood and are content with this as an excuse to let things float, as they are the ones likely to 'want to escape from the pain of being alive'[8] or of effort or of love. Although he rails against the injustice of life, 'The wrong people going hungry, the wrong people being loved, the wrong people dying!', this has the air of personal slight particularly when followed by the self-romanticizing notion that 'The heaviest, strongest creatures in this world seem to be the loneliest. Like the old bear, following his own breath in the dark forest. There's no warm pack, no herd to comfort him.'[9] This mixture of complaint, appeal and self-assertion is probably closer to the core of Jimmy than his mourning of 'good, brave causes'. The frequently similar title figure of *Epitaph for George Dillon* (1958) also opposes 'Me' to 'mighty Them' in his 'hatred of the majority' and finds the supreme expression of this conflict in his ability to break through the indifference of a theatre audience, and there is no doubting the power of the unscrupulous, articulate, defiantly provincial Jimmy and George to upset the complacency or purge the frustrations of a contemporary London theatre audience (Alison is a particularly effective audience surrogate in her status as 'a sort of hostage from those sections of society [Jimmy] had declared war on'[10]); however, Osborne leaves his heroes stranded by their uncompromising aloofness until they opt for compromise, and either will not or cannot imagine the victory of their vague if vehement ideals. George, the seething challenger of audiences, ends up absorbed into the plot and cast of what he himself wryly describes as one of 'those really bad suitable-for-all-the-family comedies they do all the year round in weekly rep in Wigan',[11] and is finally described as becoming suitably 'mechanical', whilst Jimmy himself retreats from the pain of life by playing at 'little furry creatures with little furry brains'[12] with his erstwhile hostage-target. George's theatrical metaphors attain full fruition in *The Entertainer* (1957), in which Archie Rice enacts the professional confrontation with the audience, who are given a fictional role within the play. Archie's entropic personal life acts as a grim counterpoint to his forced comedian's cheer, and his songs form a mocking echo of the 'modern mood' of apathy and self-interest, but most importantly his act fails to connect with the presumably sparse music-hall audience. In the words of Robert Wilcher:

> By exploiting our double awareness of Archie as man and as entertainer and by making us, in our role as music-hall audience, mutually responsible for the failure to achieve that 'vital, electric moment of contact'. . . . Osborne brings the 'national decadence' of post-war Britain home to us in a uniqely powerful way. Archie's failure as a comedian is mirrored in our failure as an audience. The breakdown of the laughter contract becomes an intellectual metaphor and a theatrical experience of the flagging vitality of post-war Britain.[13]

The ideal, to which this breakdown is contrasted, seems to be provided by Archie's memory of the solitary negress singing in a bar so that 'you knew somehow in your heart that it didn't matter how much you kick people, the real people, how much you despise them, if they can stand up and make a pure, just natural noise like that, there's nothing wrong with them, only with everyone else'.[14] The self-expression, self-justification and final successful emotional reciprocity of the negress's song seems to be an ideal to which many Osborne heroes aspire with their own personal forms of 'blues shouting', and an end in itself. In contrast, Archie's act is doomed and he is defeated because, while still in England, 'I'm dead, just like the whole inert, shoddy lot out there. It doesn't matter because I don't feel a thing, and neither do they. We're just as dead as each other.'[15] The audience never receive the chance to answer this charge within the play; rather they are directed to their public lives when Archie has the parting-shot, 'Let me know where you're working tomorrow night – and I'll come and see *YOU* !',[16] and thus salvages some self-respect by breaking out of the safe, cosy confines of his act and his relationship with the audience, referring them to a conventionally inappropriate consideration of his integrity as a similar working human being. *The Entertainer* acts as a metaphor for national decline, but offers few reasons for this decline other than emotional frustration and misplaced nostalgia. It is mainly notable for its provocative involvement of the audience in a negative role, as is the 1960 television play, *A Subject of Scandal and Concern*. One of Osborne's less engaging 'blues shouters', George Holyoake, opposes the religious hypocrisy of nineteenth century society, and a condescending narrator provides a modern epilogue:

> This is a time when people demand from entertainments what they call a 'solution'. They expect to have their little solution rattling away down there in the centre of the play like a motto in a Christmas cracker. . . . For those who seek information, it has been put before you. If it is meaning you are looking for, then you must start collecting for yourself. And what would you say is the moral then? . . . If you are waiting for the commercial, it is probably this: you cannot live by bread alone. You must have jam – even if it is mixed with another man's blood. . . . That's all. You may retire now. And if a mini-car is your particular mini-dream, then dream it. When your turn comes, you will be called. Good night.[17]

This can act as an inbuilt guard against the trivializing, pre-packaging, integrationist air with which the medium of television can infect many of its presentations, but hardly gives any more weight or relevance to the curiously self-insulated historical episode of Holyoake. Similarly, *Luther* (1961) seems chiefly concerned with an individual's rebellion against orthodoxy rather than with the fundamental clash of Luther's values with those of a corrupt, materialistic church.

1968's *Time Present* needs and gives little excuse for letting its heroine rail wittily against the phoniness of modern society, and makes for an interesting comparison with *Look Back in Anger*;

Jimmy's diatribes against the apathy and mediocrity of society had the compelling note of an irreverent, lower-class outsider, whereas Pamela is a successful actress with sufficient access to society to satirize its superficial follies and fashions, and declares herself a Tory because 'I don't see why you should get on at my expense.'[18] Pamela pushes the play further towards the cool mockery of society's hypocrisy and self-absorbed 'stylishness' which characterizes comedy of manners and reaches its purest form in Osborne's work with *The End of Me Old Cigar* (1975). *West of Suez* (1971) is Chekhovian in its meandering dialogue and description of a sterile old social order passing on, but also in its view of the decadent old in collision with the brutally destructive new. Osborne's verbal powers support the sardonic old writer Wyatt rather than the insensitive young revolutionary Jed, whose obscene anti-verbal tirade of hate significantly lacks the poetic venom of his namesake in Howard Brenton's *Magnificence* (1969).

A Sense of Detachment (1972) seems to return to the emotions which informed the epilogue to *A Subject of Scandal and Concern* and make them the basis of a full-length stage play; but whereas *A Subject*'s Narrator expressed a pessimistic scepticism about the indiscriminacy of effect and audience to which television broadcasting was likely to succumb, *A Sense of Detachment*'s rambling disgust is even less controlled and defined. The weary banter of aimless actors stuck in a 'bit of your old Pirandello, like', ostensibly textless confrontation with an audience (characterized by the prissy Interrupter and the groundling Box Man) flirts (with deliberate lack of conviction) with the occupation of Northern Ireland, female stereotyping, the British heritage of patriotism and the voyeuristic nature of pornography, but these only provide 'some safe bit for the audiences, so that they can delude themselves that there is some intention and continuity' (when 'Either way they won't know').[19] Osborne also provides directions for the immediate effects of his most extreme journey into this self-styled 'theatre of antagonism'[20] by suggesting insults to trade with genuine hecklers, whom he welcomes to the point of relish. Neither does *A Sense of Detachment* have any illusions about its possible effects; in the Second Act, the Chap is instructed to address the audience 'If there is still any left.'[21] But whilst there is an undeniable tactical effectiveness available to the political playwright through the insulting or threatening of an audience or audience surrogate (as *Serjeant Musgrave's Dance*, *Comedians* and

The Churchill Play can successfully demonstrate), this dramatic tone is usually adopted to sting the audience into an awareness of their own complicity in the perpetuation of an unjust society or of their privileged position within it, so that the immediate emotional sensation of guilt or even fear may trigger off renewed intellectual examination of their role in society. This would comprise a successful example of implicating the audience with reference to a definite political end. In contrast, *A Sense of Detachment* seems content with alienating the audience with no coherent, fruitful reason beyond their status as an audience in the Royal Court theatre or wherever it is performed. There may be circumstances under which Osborne's gut-level impulse to attack them for this very reason could be genuinely sympathetic, but the effort of communicating it is obviously deemed unworthwhile, so finally *A Sense of Detachment* communicates little beyond a personal disgust with its own medium of the theatre and with that medium's intrinsic relationships, and thus constitutes at best a wasted opportunity and at worst a counter-productive piece of irresponsibility. Osborne's next play, *A Place Calling Itself Rome* (published 1973), is a modernized rewriting of Shakespeare's *Coriolanus*. Whilst one can imagine the original play's appeal to Osborne's taste for opposing strong solitary individuals to a spineless herd (although an adaptation of *An Enemy of the People* may have been even more characteristic), Osborne adds little to what can be accomplished by a modern-dress production of Shakespeare's play and loses the subtleties of language and characterization. The slick satire of *The End of Me Old Cigar* seems less ambitious but more comfortable, and Osborne seems to confirm Sartre's suggestion that 'when the writer instead of remaining on the margin of the privileged class, is absorbed by it . . . literature identifies itself with the ideology of the directing class; reflection takes place within the class; the challenge deals with details and is carried on in the name of uncontested principles.'[22]

Many of Wesker's objections to modern society are, like Osborne's, concerned with its damaging effect upon human integrity and identity in the process Wesker terms 'fragmentation', which prevents its victims from understanding or transcending their assigned stereotypical social role through communication with their fellows; but Wesker's imaginative revolt is significantly less purely individualistic than Osborne's. Many of

Wesker's plays are concerned with the testing of socialist principles in everyday life, through opposition and compromise towards a final position of tragic defeat or battered resilience, and his main concern is with the depiction of characters inspired with ideals, rather than with the direct propulsion of an audience towards a specific channel of reform (although they may be moved by the exemplary courage and integrity of Wesker's protagonists, even if their battles are usually humbler than those of Shaw's higher evolutionary men or Osborne's vituperative rebels). Wesker's plays may indeed be more true to lived experience than many political plays, and certainly contain a uniquely blended tone of compassion and defiance, but thereby forfeit access to the political immediacy attained by other dramatists. Instead, Wesker's long-term humanist impulses impel him towards the sphere of Chekhovian social drama, presenting images of social–existential commitment besieged by a hostile, dehumanizing society, with tragic reflections on the loss of interpersonal communication. For example, the socialism of the Kahns in *Chicken Soup with Barley* (1958) mainly comes over as a generalized ideal of brotherhood which meets disillusioning obstacles and a debate as to the practical form by which it is to be lived. Sarah embodies many fundamental values:

> SARAH: What's the good of being a socialist if you're not warm. . . . Everything cold and calculated. People like that can't teach love and brotherhood.
> PRINCE: Love comes later, Sarah.
> SARAH: Love comes now. You have to start with love. How can you talk about socialism otherwise?[23]

Sarah is criticized by Monty and Ronnie for her lack of familiarity with formal political economics and her tendency to view life in black-and-white terms, but her conviction gives her a spiritual strength which they lack in their cynical capitulations and bruised vacillations. Contrastingly, Beatie in *Roots* (1959) has to combat a negative (against Sarah's positive) form of old-fashioned, unflinching conviction when she challenges her family's provincial prejudices and the habitual lack of distinction in their daily life which keeps them in a stunted existence. Dave and Ada Simmonds, in *I'm Talking About Jerusalem* (1960), discover that their personal form of socialism endows their retreat and enterprises with an impractical self-righteousness which also makes their vision self-insulated to the point of sterility. In each part of the Trilogy, the protagonists pass through encounters with persuasive cynics and themselves experience brief flashes of despair and misanthropy, but finally emerge with a wary resilience; and in each case, the audience is invited to sympathize with the characters on the basis of their treatment of their fellows rather than by a practical vindication of their social analysis. Whilst non-socialist audience members may be encouraged to support the socialist characters' endeavours (no mean feat in itself, particularly at the time of the plays' premières), the socialism *per se* is a long way from a Marxist analysis of social power structure and, more importantly, may become so general an ideal as to lose its dramatic impact in deference to the characters it motivates (although Wesker would probably claim that this is a false distinction because socialism is necessarily to be tested in an everyday human context; but then it is possible that the characters' actions could be similar under the ideological impetus of, say, christianity or existentialism rather than specifically socialism when considered in practical terms alone).

Their Very Own and Golden City (1956) is in many ways a flawed but compelling thematic extension of the Trilogy in its cross-patterning of conviction and compromise, revolutionary impulse and 'patchwork', which pervades Andy Cobham's architectural ambition. The main flaw is the vision of the City, which, like Priestley's in *They Came to a City*, is so vaguely realised and unrecognizable from the standpoint of contemporary reality as to draw damaging attention to its essentially poetic substance. Also, Andy's apparently inevitable compromise of his ideal in practice produces an apparently inevitable sense of defeat and bitterness which eclipses the protagonist's, and potentially the audience's, sense of his achievement ('I don't suppose there's such a thing as democracy, really, only a democratic way of manipulating power. And equality? None of that either, only a gracious way of accepting inequality' [24]), especially when counterpointed with the ironic scenes of his youthful enthusiasm. Kate's recognition that 'those of us who build the Golden City can never live in it' [25] and Andy's self-delivery to the opinion of future generations give them a tragic stature, but the play falls from the tightrope between optimism and pessimism which the Trilogy previously negotiated. Writing a successful social tragedy is, of course, a considerable achievement, and the unfolding events of *Their Very Own and Golden City* have a melancholy grandeur and may be true to much human experience; but it is itself a tragic distinction that fully-fledged political drama finds this form of truthfulness inadequate for the same reasons that Shaw and Brecht objected to tragedy itself – namely its demonstration of the futile if courageous littleness of human achievement from a long-term (if not eternal or cosmic) perspective. Andy's career is not so different from Galileo's, but Brecht adds Andrea to have the last word and sustain the inspiration of resistance against the status quo whilst not diminishing the power of his master's more guarded opinions. A less marked tragic tone also pervades subsequent Wesker plays, but the equally characteristic resilient aspiration never comes quite as close to being crushed as in *Their Very Own and Golden City*. *The Friends* (1970), *The Old Ones* (1972), *The Journalists* (1975) and *The Merchant* (1976) all demonstrate the problems of maintaining personal integrity and optimism and living through social contradictions which are particularly threatening to the protagonists' political sensibilities. *The Merchant* shows, in its opposition of Shylock Kolner and the young Venetian philistines, the difference between revolutionaries and mere rebels, as formulated by a character in *The Friends*: 'My brother is a rebel because he hates the past, I'm a revolutionary because I see the past is too rich with human suffering and achievement to be dismissed. . . . Do you know one of the reasons why I despise a capitalist society? Because it produces men who *enjoy* the violence of opposing it.'[26] The distinction is crucial both for Wesker's beliefs and for those of his characters.

The more light-hearted play *The Wedding Feast* (1974, 1977), based on a short story by Dostoevsky, is a comic examination of the effects of social fragmentation and echoes Brecht's *Mr Puntila and his Man Matti* in its basic situation of a drunken, cheerful employer attempting to fraternize with, and win the respect of, his unconvinced workers. However, Louis Litvanov is, although self-deluded and overly paternalistic, a more sympathetic figure than Puntila. Despite the lapsed Marxist Kate's instruction to the prone Louis ('don't be ashamed or apologetic for your money. You go around behaving like that, how shall we be able to hit you when the time comes, bor?'[27]), Wesker's attitude to the lost opportunity for human contact seems more regretful than that of his characters or Brecht's. Louis is more in love with the idea of being welcomed to the feast as Knocker's boss than as an ordinary man, but his painful failure at socializing and the hardening of antagonism on both sides constitute pathetic evidence of the failure of communication because of social compartmentalization, rather than a welcomed escalation of potential revolutionary tension. The role of Stephen Bullock, the journalist, is an odd one; his initial direct address to the audience and choric commentary might make him seem, traditionally, to be an authorial figure, but it soon becomes evident that Bullock's slick, reductive sarcasm constitutes an insensitive anti-humanistic response, with which the audience will feel uncomfortable to be associated. Unfortunately, Bullock's comments are not consistently maintained, as he becomes absorbed into the action of the play never to break through to the audience again – indeed, his authority and control of events are literally anticipated during the play's action. The idea of this unreliable narrator is intriguing, but his effect is strangely half-digested, and severely impaired by his peculiar Christopher Sly-like disappearance as a framing voice.

Wesker tends to attract sympathy for his socialist idealists on a humanistic rather than expressly ideological level by showing their resilient compassion and emotional integrity in a world mainly ruled by reductive cynics. But the human and emotional development of a character can also be used to expand their importance to the point of breaking an exclusively social mould of categorisation into which they have been forced, when the social mould in question becomes reductive, faceless and thereby another instance of Wesker's 'fragmentation' which acts as a block to basic human sympathy. O'Casey's *Juno and the Paycock* is such a case, with its dramatically powerful opposition of the mourning mothers Mrs Tancred and Juno, united by their laments for their sons if not by their families' political convictions. Too exclusively political a judgement of others is seen as a disintegrating effect, a crime against humanism. Brendan Behan's *The Hostage* (1958) is a splendidly unsentimental, blackly comic illustration of this thesis. Pat's close relationship with the audience and his cheerfully basic view of life acts as a telling contrast to the idealism of Monsewer, whose head is so full of ancient, abstract antagonisms as to be oblivious to much of reality, let alone the presence of the audience. Pat explains that the petty factionalism implied by the co-existence of the IRA, RAF, Red Army, US Marines, etc., is comically outdated by the existence of the H-bomb and its power to ensure that in death no one is divided. From this *carpe diem* position, Monsewer's fanaticism is even more ridiculous, especially when we learn that he is in fact half English, educated at Oxford and apparently spurred on by Oedipal rebellion. Similarly, the likeable humanity of the captive English soldier Leslie Williams mocks the diminution of men to faceless pawns, on which the hostage system depends in its ruthless 'eye for an eye' justice. The inaccuracy of the guiding sense of national stereotypes is also established to comic effect by the low-life characters' sympathy for Leslie and respect for the British Royal Family, despite his own contempt for such considerations; but Behan remains open-eyed about his hapless English representative by also making him prey to petty factionalist mentality in other terms ('I wish the Irish and the niggers and the wogs / Were kicked out and sent back home'[28]). Behan even anticipates and comically defuses the reductive nationalistic interpretations his play might attract:

> SOLDIER: Brendan Behan, he's too anti-British.
> OFFICER: Too anti-Irish, you mean. Bejasus, wait till we get him back home. We'll give him what-for for making fun of the Movement.
> SOLDIER (*to audience*): He doesn't mind coming over here and taking your money.
> PAT: He'd sell his country for a pint.[29]

Leslie transpires to be as much of a pawn to England as to the IRA; the distinction between Leslie and Monsewer is more marked by the separations of class than nation, as Leslie has unpretentiously perceived ('You're what I call a cricket person and I'm what I call a soccer person. That's where your race lark comes in'[30]), further debunking the narrow principle governing his capture:

> SOLDIER: You're as barmy as him if you think that what's happening to me is upsetting the British Government. I suppose you think they're all sitting around in the West End clubs with handkerchiefs over their eyes, dropping tears into their double whiskies. Yeah, I can just see the Secretary of State for War now waking up his missus in the night: 'Oh Isabel-

Cynthia love, I can hardly get a wink of sleep wondering what's happening to that poor bleeder Williams.'[31]

The irony of the situation is compounded by the fact that Leslie is shot by his own troops when they storm the building, although at least he dies in a wryly resigned state of mind about his predicament ('Perhaps I'll meet that Belfast geezer on the other side. We can have a good laugh about it'[32]); and the tone of gleeful irreverence is continued to the anti-illusionistic Curtain, at which the actor playing Leslie arises and the company remind the audience that the conflict has not really claimed his life, but continues in theirs ('The bells of hell, / Go ting-a-ling-a-ling, / For you but not for him'[33]). *The Hostage*'s successful blend of provocativeness and humorous zest is thus fittingly maintained.

On the other hand, some of Wesker and Behan's most successful plays work through the strategy of presenting a challengingly intensified image of man's enforced anonymity in modern compartmentalized society, and showing the steady rise in tension in this insupportable situation. Wesker's *The Kitchen* (1959, 1961) is an appropriately bustling and frantic anatomy of industrial society which also establishes the spiritual and emotional toll exacted from the men in their separate duties. The many characters only emerge gradually and partially, as befits the tautness of their working relationships, and it is significant that it is only in the brief lull between sittings that the cooks manage to talk in a friendly, unpressurized manner and reflect upon their situation. Paul seems the most perceptive in his description of his relationships with a neighbouring bus driver, which acts as illustration of social fragmentation and its costs in human integrity:

he says 'Did you go on that peace march yesterday?' So I say Yes, I did go on that peace march yesterday. So then he turns round to me and he says, 'You know what? A bomb should have been dropped on the lot of them! It's a pity,' he says, 'that they had children with them cos a bomb should've been dropped on the lot!' And you know what was upsetting him? The march was holding up the traffic, the buses couldn't move so fast! . . . but what terrifies me is that he didn't stop to think that this man helped me in my cause so maybe, only *maybe*, there's something in his cause. I'll talk about it. No! The buses were held up so drop a bomb he says, on the lot! And you should have seen the hate in his eyes, as if I'd murdered his child. Like an animal he looked. And the horror is this – that there's a wall, a big wall between me and millions of people like him. And I think – where will it end? What will you do about it? And I look around me, at the kitchen, at the factories, at the enormous bloody buildings going up with all those offices and all those people in them, and I think, Christ! . . . But then I think: I should stop making pastries? The factory worker should stop making trains and cars? The miner should leave the coal where it is? (*Pause*.) *You* give *me* an answer. You give me your dream.[34]

The Kitchen is also an effective play in its demonstration (not just description) to an audience of the pressurized situation it depicts, with its frantic dashing figures and roaring ovens; the two crucial modulations in mood, noise and activity are the afternoon break, when interpersonal relations become more tolerant, and the point where Peter's tolerance snaps after an argument with a waitress about territorial rights in the kitchen, leading to a national slur. Peter seems '*about to attack her, but she is not the enemy*'[35]; instead, he strikes at the kitchen's gas lead. The restaurant owner, Marango, is at a loss to understand his employee's destructive frustration, again because he inhabits a different compartment of society and works on the reductive premise 'He works, he eats, I give him money. This is life, isn't it. . . . What is there more?.'[36] Marango's own partial view of life denies him the chance to perceive a more holistic existence, and thereby denies his men the chance of attaining it. Wesker's later play *Chips with Everything* (1962) uses the hierarchy of an RAF training camp as a similar metaphor for society in general, with the gradations in rank afforded by the system of officers, NCO's and new conscripts. In Act Two scene four, the officers victimize the rebellious conscript Pip by striking at his squad; they deflect their anger onto Corporal Hill, who deflects his anger onto the squad using exactly the same words as the officers, a fine example of the normally unseen pattern of resentment escalated by social fragmentation. Pip, in contrast, can perceive the dehumanizing whole, in the camp and beyond, as shown when he picks Hill up on his hopelessly innocuous, partial form of social criticism:

HILL: I hate royalty more than anything else in the world.

Parasites! What do they do, eh? I'm not in this outfit for them,
no bloody fear, it's the people back 'ome I'm here for, like you
lot. Royalty –
PIP: Good old Corporal Hill, they've made you chase red
herrings, haven't they?[37]

Like the kitchen and many other institutions, the RAF needs to
dehumanize its workforce to ensure maximum efficiency, the
main emphasis in training falling upon 'obedience and discipline'
– in the words of the Wing Commander, 'God give us automation
soon.'[38] Pip's attempts to resist the inhumanity encountered by
the conscripts again involves him in conflict with Hill's fragmented perceptions, when Pip's coke-stealing plan has produced
an effective act of defiance against the authoritarian élite and he
finds himself being elevated into an élite class of heroic authority:

HILL: You always need leaders.
. . .
PIP: Always, always, always! Your great-great-grandfather said
there'll always be horses, your great-grandfather said there'll
always be slaves, your grandfather said there'll always be
poverty and your father said there'll always be wars. Each time
you say 'always' the world takes two steps backwards and stops
bothering.[39]

Nevertheless, Pip's resistance to their dehumanization proves
problematic. In Act One scene seven, the conscripts' substitution
of a menacing folk song for the innocuous pop song, that the
officers patronisingly request them to sing, stands as a personal
and collective triumph; but Pip bows to pressure and permits
himself to be absorbed into officer training, then he himself
absorbs into respectability the conscripts' final defiant gesture of
refusing to stand in an officer's presence. Pip claims that their act
of solidarity with the persecuted Smiler displays valuable loyalty,
thus neatly fragmenting the action from its cause and principle.
Wesker gives the audience the opportunity to deviate from or
mimic this capitulation with the final ironic playing of the
National Anthem, a device which has unfortunately lost much of
its edge since the play's first date of production. *Chips with
Everything* remains flawed and unsatisfactory because of the
obscurity of Pip's motivation which, like Andy's bitterness in
Their Very Own and Golden City, can almost support an integra-

tionist or defeatist reading of the conclusion. It is damagingly reductive for a piece of left-wing drama to suggest that any resistance to established authority is impelled by opportunistic self-interest or personal pique, as Pip's victorious superiors suggest. Unfortunately the generalized social metaphor of the RAF camp pulls the play in a different direction to the particular (if vague) case of Pip Thompson's personal compromise, which would have been better dealt with separately and more clearly. The play's non-realistic, representational, generalized aspects and the private psychological development of Pip soften each other's full impact when taken in harness. Nevertheless, *Chips with Everything* ends with a provocative image of the RAF's success which recalls the fate of Galy Gay in *Man equals Man*; it is the 'one solid gliding ship' of anonymous ruthlessness to which our society appeals for its protection.

Caritas (1981) is another parable of compartmentalization and obedience, taken to a moving, almost Beckettian extreme of concentration and intensity. Set in the fourteenth century, the play traces the impulse of Christine Carpenter to become an anchoress and isolate herself in extreme, exemplary fashion in order to come closer to the realisation of religious principles, whilst her erstwhile fiancé Robert participates and dies in Wat Tyler's peasant uprising. The link between the religious and political themes remains vague and undeveloped – the relationships seems imposed rather than organic – but Wesker dramatizes Christine's situation to great effect by minimizing any distraction from the meanness of her repetitious, lonely existence in what amounts to a form of sensory (or for the audience, dramatic) concentration through deprivation. Thus it provides a sympathetic but highly critical image of self-dedication to an ideal's literalist dogma, showing how austerity can build up the walls which the ideal ultimately hopes to dissolve, with the end result of madness and waste. *Caritas* is, in this respect, a powerful testament to Wesker's fundamentally humanist attitude to the over-zealous dogmatic practise of religious or political theory which may subvert its original ends. Christine's avowed vocation, which is intended to transcend worldly complications, instead distorts the holisticity of her personality into a spiralling tension of self-destruction, even more fearsome than the mechanical inhumanity which men are forced to assume in *The Kitchen* and *Chips with Everything*.

The dehumanizing 'dirty work' seen in the latter two plays, on which society depends but which it prefers not to acknowledge, also forms the basis of Behan's *The Quare Fellow* (1954), which uses a prison to demonstrate institutional callousness and develops Galsworthy's *Justice* in its depiction of the human consequences of the penal system the audience tacitly supports – a factor played upon by the sign on which the curtain rises, facing the audience and ordering 'SILENCE'. Warder Regan is distinguished from the Chief Warden, Holy Healey and the other 'screws' by his inability to lose sight of the human dimension of capital punishment. With the exception of Regan, the wry humour of the prisoners makes them more theatrically engaging than the prison officials, who attempt to maintain a tense, efficient, mechanical atmosphere about the execution (even to the point of assigning the victim a number for his gravestone, which the Chief cannot even be bothered to dictate correctly to the stone carver). If the prisoners' jokes constitute one form of relief from this tension, Regan's outbursts provide a more harrowing response by confronting, rather than escaping from, the full horror of the event. As he says of the Hangman in a bid to share the blame (and thus extending it into the theatre auditorium), 'Himself has no more to do with it than you or I or the people that pay us, that's every man or woman that pays taxes or votes in elections. If they don't like it, they needn't have it.'[40] When the Chief protests at Regan's need to dull his sensibilities with a drink before facing the witness of the ordeal, his response is a swift and articulate outburst:

WARDER REGAN: You think the law makes this man's death someway different, not like anyone else's. Your own, for instance.
CHIEF: I wasn't found guilty of murder.
WARDER REGAN: No, nor no one is going to jump on you in the morning and throttle the life out of you, but it's not him I'm thinking of. It's myself. And you're not going to give me that stuff about just shoving over the lever and bob's your uncle. You forget the times the fellow gets caught and has to be kicked off the edge of the trap hole. You never hear about the warders down below swinging on his legs the better to break his neck, or jumping on his back when the drop was too short.
. . .

CHIEF: Regan, I hope you'll forget those things you mentioned just now. If talk the like of that got outside the prison. . .
WARDER REGAN (*almost shouts*): I think the whole show should be put on in Croke Park; after all, it's at the public expense and they let it go on. They should have something more for their money than a bit of paper stuck upon on a gate.[41]

Several more recent authors have continued the tradition of prison drama in which the emotional resilience of the imprisoned is celebrated over the dehumanizing oppressiveness of the institution and its servants: Dale Wasserman's adaptation of Ken Kesey's novel *One Flew Over the Cuckoo's Nest* (1963), Peter Weiss's *Marat/Sade* (1964), Howard Brenton's *The Churchill Play* (1974), David Edgar's *The Jail Diary of Albie Sachs* (1978), and Howard Barker's *The Hang of the Gaol* (1978), whilst Wesker's *Caritas* depicts the perils of this secular image in its self-imposed religiously sanctioned form. But the most intense and unflinching look at the current British penal system is probably Tom McGrath and Jimmy Boyle's *The Hard Man* (1977), which can present a much harsher image of the relationship between prisoner, warder and society than *The Quare Fellow*, just as *The Quare Fellow* could record grim details in a way denied to *Justice*. *The Hard Man* is also a more complex dramatic experience than *The Quare Fellow*'s protest against capital punishment, in so far as it brings the 'quare fellow' as threateningly close to the audience's world as possible. Johnnie Byrne's life of violent crime is by turns amorally exciting and terrifying, in that his percussion-laced rampages have the dramatic thrill of self-affirmation in a hostile world until Byrne prevents any sentimentalization of his activities by keeping in close focus just whom he regards as this hostile world. He introduces himself to the audience: 'I'm speaking to you tonight from a Scottish prison where I am serving life-sentence for murder. What you are going to see is my life as I remember it. What you are going to hear is my version of the story'.[42] Byrne learns a particularly violent contempt for the twin gods of 'authority and private property' which he exercises with his two partners Slugger and Bandit:

BANDIT *Slightly derisive. Looks around him, taking in the audience.* Thair they go, Slugger, the honest workin people. Whit a bunch o mugs! They get up in a mornin and goo out tae wurk and get their miserable wages ut the end o the week tae help them pay fur their miserable wee hooses an' their miserable wee lives. Wance a year they're released fur two weeks. The Glesca fair! An' thae aw go daft! Eejits! Two weeks later it's back tae the grindstone again fur another year.

SLUGGER: Either that or they cannae get a job an' they go aboot in fuckin poverty.

BANDIT: Well thank Christ that's no fur us. When we want something – we take it. And it doesnae matter who it belongs tae.

SLUGGER: When we take it, it belongs tae us.

BANDIT: Aye an aw the toffs and intellectuals hate oor guts. Because we're the wans that kick in thir doors an climb in thir windaes and run oaf wae aw their nice new presies an their family hierlooms. An they know we don't give a fuck. Efter we've done a place an left it in a mess, ah'll bet they can still feel us in the air roon aboot thaim an they wonder who we are. What we're like. Because it's obvious we don't give a fuck . . .[43]

Byrne himself prefaces the aiming of a gun at the audience with the following:

BYRNE: *To audience*. There is so much none of you can understand about me and the world I come from and there doesn't seem to be any way of telling it that will finally get you to see the bitterness and indifference I inherited from whatever the system was the series of historical priorities that created the world into which I was born . . .

There were the have-nots that worked and the have-nots that thieved, then there were the rest of you – living away out there somewhere in your posh districts in aw your ease and refinement – what a situation!

It made me laugh to see you teaching your religions and holding your democratic elections – and it made me sick with disgust. That was why I enjoyed the sight of blood because, without knowing it, it was your blood I was after.[44]

A sufficiently intense small-scale production of *The Hard Man* defies the most radical of sympathies not to feel an almost personal note of hatred in Byrne's vehemence and a consequent revulsion, to the good effect of not minimizing the ethical conflict posed by the second half. Slugger and Bandit become prison guards – a specific dual role recalling the doubling of Hepple and Macleish in Brenton's *Revenge* (1969) – and the relatively sympathetic screw Johnston (who recalls Regan in *The Quare Fellow* and Thompson in *The Churchill Play*) is replaced by Paisley, who introduces himself with a directness echoing Byrne's:

> I'm Paisley. I'm the one. The bad screw. The one who brings disrepute on all his hard-working colleagues who are making the best of a very tough job. I'm the sadist. The one that's got too much of a taste for the sight of blood. That's what they say. I know it only too well. The prisoners don't like me because they know I don't mess about. I believe in discipline and I believe in using hard methods to tame hard men. And the other *Pause* screws don't like me because they know I'm the one that does the dirty work for them.
>
> . . . I'm *their* hard man. And they feel a wee bit guilty about me because I'm an aspect of themselves they don't like to admit to. Just like you should be feeling guilty about us because we're the garbage disposal squad for the social sewage system. You people out there, that's the way it works for you – you've got a crime problem so you just flush it away one thug after another in behind bars and safely locked away. The cistern's clanked and you think you can leave it floating away from you to the depths of the sea. Well, I've goat news fur you – its pollution. Yir gonnae huv tae look ut it. because if yae doan't, wun day it's gonnae destroy yae. But in the meantime, dirties like me, well, let's just say we're a necessary evil. Very necessary.[45]

Paisley's brutal campaign to break Byrne physically and spiritually contains the same sadistic glee as Byrne's First Act exploits; but then, as Paisley reminds the audience to prevent any easy moralizing, 'Listen, if you excuse him *indicates* BYRNE on the grounds that he's a product of this shit-heap system, then you'd better excuse me on the same grounds.'[46] However, Byrne refuses to be broken and takes his savage feud with Paisley into increasingly bestial depths until, surrounded by a baton-wielding team of screws:

> *He cakes his body in shit from the chamberpot.*
> So come on. Come on and get me.

Smears over his face.
How much of it can you accept?[47]

Byrne's cry is as much to the audience as to the screws, as he literalizes Paisley's earlier sewage system speech and strips the conflict down to who is prepared to sink the lowest in their uncompromising, descending spiral of hatred, secure in the knowledge and challenge that he is less defiled than anyone who touches him. *The Hard Man* takes to their logical extreme the intensified images of dehumanization with which Wesker and Behan agitate society's collective conscience, and also boasts a threatening, challenging central figure who can express an even more scathing antagonism (and with its own haunting coherence) than Osborne's betrayed, belligerent spokesmen.

6 Beyond 'Good' and 'Evil'

JOHN ARDEN & MARGARETTA D'ARCY, EDWARD BOND

> On the road to hell there is no half-way house run by a liberal landlord.
>
> *The Activists Papers*[1]

The first appearance of a genuinely Brechtian impulse and influence in British and Irish political drama takes place in the plays of John Arden and Margaretta D'Arcy and Edward Bond. Both Arden and Bond were always concerned with dramatizing social problems, undercutting the self-proclaimed forces of 'law and order' and demonstrating the human tragedies which are the direct result of their power; but both writers also proceeded to develop increasingly articulated and radical political philosophies supporting active socialism and the overthrow of capitalist society and imperialistic regimes. The increasing involvement of Margaretta D'Arcy in the life and work of Arden appears to have contributed considerably to this development, whereas Bond's insistent questioning of social power structures on the grounds of their threats to human integrity has led him to evolve his concept of 'rational theatre' (the expression of moral self-consciousness as characteristically – and perhaps too auto-matically and 'self-evidently' – identified by Bond with socialist consciousness) which he seeks to exemplify in his plays and identify in his essays. Arden and D'Arcy and Bond also share a fundamental interest in the individual's attempted self-definition in the face of a predatory society which would mould him in its own functional, destructive image.

Perhaps John Russell Taylor's best comment on Arden's work is his highlighting of the way that Armstrong and Lindsay in *Armstrong's Last Goodnight* and the Sawneys and the Jacksons in *Live Like Pigs* live 'in two different worlds according to two different codes . . . separate and incompatible. And neither wins in the end'.[2] Certainly Arden has always excelled at mobilising contradictory, exclusive patterns of perception as incarnated in different characters (or character groups) when the audience is likely to occupy the pivotal position in which the dramatic tension is also located. *The Waters of Babylon* (1957) details the attempts of the arch-survivor Krank to elude 'time, place, society and accident'[3] even in his capacity as pimp and slum landlord. But Krank is finally unable to escape implication in political wrangles or even human mortality when the play's broad, extrovert comedy climaxes in his shooting. For once, the charming if morally repugnant, Volpone-like figure cannot slither out of responsibility: 'Place, time and purposes, / Are now chosen for me',[4] although we can scarcely feel complacent at the manner of his downfall. Krank's death ends a public meeting at which various local despots jockey for the attention and sympathy of the audience, played by the actual theatre audience, which the Falstaffian rogue Butterthwaite tries to rouse in his own manner:

> BUTTERTHWAITE (*rudely*): O shut your cake-hole, Alfred. This meeting wants livening up. Let's hear from the true Working People, let's see if they can't make a bit more noise. (*He addresses the audience, dividing them into groups.*) Now then, all you lot to the left of my hand, you're Austria. You lot to the right, you're Prussia. And you lot up top, are you listening? You're Russia. Now what I want you to do is tell me who you are, and tell me all at once, when I give you the one–two–three. It's a grand way to get a gathering going this. They say old Wilf Pickles used it to warm up his legless pensioners before his broadcasts. All right now, on the one–two–three: Austria, Prussia and Russia. Shout them names out and shout 'em loud.
>
> (*He picks up the cymbals and prepares to clash them.*)
> KRANK (*violently checking him*): No. Not now.[5]

Krank actually rescues the audience from a public self-display, but Arden lets them go to the verge of choosing to comply with the trivializing distraction of the 'true Working People' from the (admittedly hazy) serious issues or respond to the pantomime vitality of Butterthwaite's appeal and participate in a popular ritual rarely associated with 'serious drama'; in the words of

Robert Wilcher, 'The techniques of the popular comedian are here used to disturb the equilibrium of the spectators and make them uneasily aware of their cultural and social prejudices.'[6] *Live Like Pigs* (1958) presents the collision of the Sawney family's lively anarchy with the Jacksons' scrupulous order when they are housed next door to each other by blind council officialdom, ridiculous in its attempt to fit two temperamentally opposed families into neighbouring slots of land without catering for the impingement and conflict of values. This comic but unsentimental view of the official regimentation of resistant humanity continues in Arden's first collaboration with D'Arcy, *The Happy Haven* (1960), an anti-illusionistic account of an insurrection in an old people's home, and *Ars Longa, Vita Brevis* (1963) with its obsessed art-teacher's bid to impose his authority in the classroom.

Arden's *Serjeant Musgrave's Dance* (1959) explores the problem of regimentation in darker, more overt fashion. Four refugees from a colonial war adapt their military tactics and sense of 'duty' to act out their own political drama before the inhabitants of a strike-bound town, determined to demonstrate the dehumanization of man in war (whether as killer or victim), to atone for the blood on their own hands and 'to work that guilt back to where it began',[7] that is, bring a display of violent pacifism back to the doorstep of the people in whose name they are supposedly fighting. But, although Musgrave believes that 'their riots and our war are the same one corruption',[8] he fails to engage his struggle with that of Walsh and his striking collier community against the common enemy of the complacent Mayor, Constable and Parson. The final scene constitutes Musgrave's last chance, when he succeeds the cosy platitudes of the town rulers at a public meeting (with the theatre audience playing the town audience, as in *The Waters of Babylon*). Fresh and wild from 'a little country without much importance except from the point of view that there's a Union Jack flies over it and the people of that country can write British Subject after their names',[9] Musgrave reveals 'the one flag' he fought for, the skeleton of his own colleague, in a bid to emphasise 'there's one man is dead, but there's *everyone's* responsible'.[10] He tries to win the colliers' active support, but Hurst is eager for more direct tactics, namely armed force, and his threat is instructed to be delivered to the audience over the barrel of a Gatling gun:

So you've just got five minutes to make up your mind. . . .
We've earned our living by beating and killing folk like
yourselves in the streets of their own city. Well, it's drove us
mad – and so we come back here to tell you how and to show
you what it's like. The ones we want to deal with aren't, for a
change, you and your mates, but a bit higher up. The ones as
never get hurt. (*He points at the* MAYOR, PARSON *and* CONSTABLE)
Him. Him. Him. You hurt them hard, and they'll not hurt you
again. And they'll not send *us* to hurt you neither. But if you let
'em be, then us three'll be killed – aye and worse, we'll be
forgotten – and the whole bloody lot'll start all over again.[11]

Again, the audience is 'saved', but only when Hurst is on the very
brink of opening fire. Attercliffe's completely pacifistic revolt
conflicts with Hurst's armed belligerence, whilst Musgrave's
religious idealism is betrayed by the unprincipled, opportunistic
Bargee. Arden's own standpoint on militant pacifism and anti-
idealism seems to have altered since he wrote the play, but there
remains no doubt as to which climactic image in the play is the
most dramatically powerful; and Arden would now probably seek
to qualify Hurst and Musgrave's addresses to the audience even
less.[12] The character of the Bargee is interesting for his resemb-
lances in character and function to those of the traditional fool,
particularly in his leading of the audience's responses and his
grotesque deflationary postures;[13] but his irresponsible eagerness
for 'Rapine and riot' and 'breaking open the boozers' finally
identifies him as a dangerously reductive, repulsive figure, a
low-life counterpart to the opportunistic Krank. Like many other
Arden characters, his mixture of attractive energy and moral
bankruptcy provides a challenge to hasty or conventional audience responses.

Arden's *The Workhouse Donkey* (1963) is a return to *The Waters of
Babylon* in its citizen comedy style, thematic address to corruption
in local government and use of the northern Labour MP
Butterthwaite. *Armstrong's Last Goodnight* (1964) returns to the
historical parable form and animated ballad tone of *Musgrave*.
This time, the conflicting worlds are those of King James V of
Scotland and the Highland chieftain Armstrong, whose hot
fierceness the king would channel to his own cool, official
purposes. Lindsay, the go-between, makes an attractive figure for
audience identification in his pivotal role and direct addresses, as

well as, perhaps, his initial faith in the power of 'craft and humanity' to prevail against the troublesome ruffian Armstrong. However, Lindsay's 'craft and humanity' come to assume the derogatory connotations of the word 'politics' when compared to Armstrong's bluff integrity; Lindsay's smug dealings lead to the double-crossing of Armstrong on a technicality, and then the laird's execution. We may be unsettled by the assurance that the King went on to be 'weel instructit in the necessities of state' by Lindsay, 'that poet that was his tutor',[14] when we have seen the 'necessities of state' to which a supposedly, self-congratulatory humane and sensitive man can address himself.

The subsequent sequence of Arden–D'Arcy collaborations reinterpret familiar tales or historical episodes by developing the principal character in a highly unconventional way so as to force a re-examination of the audience's standard response, and often restoring a political dimension to their existence which their frequent socially ratified invocations blur or omit; also, these plays have been for the most part written with a non-legitimate theatre setting and production style in mind. *The Business of Good Government* (1960), a nativity play written for production by a church hall amateur group, shows Herod in an untypically sympathetic light, as an all-too-human politician akin to Lindsay, forced to perform a conscious evil for the sake of earthly political expediency.[15] Arden's *Left-Handed Liberty* (1965), written to commemorate the anniversary of the Magna Carta, gives a characteristic twist to the document's history by the opposition of politic politician Pandulph to the whimsical authority of King John. *The Hero Rises Up* (1968) shows the heroic figure of Lord Nelson given an unromantic treatment with particular regard to the tension between his private life and his socially-manufactured public image, and also between the actions of a national warrior and the ideals which native society claims he represents, even in such politically embarrassing hard realities as the treatment of prisoners. As in *Armstrong*, the official forces come to recognize an unsettling contradiction between their ends and their means: 'We turn the world into a wilderness and have the nerve to call it peace.'[16] The final tableau is deliberately and tellingly forced, as, on their mount to heaven, Nelson and his followers become *'suddenly conscious of their own artificiality'* when he falters over a speech. Nelson, like Musgrave and Armstrong, has been made a tool of by his rulers.

The Island of the Mighty (1972) contains unglamorous departures from our standard received images of King Arthur's reign. There are modern relevances to the myth of a divided land, in the Dedication's assertion that 'Green Fields of Britain were always someone else's land' and Arden's expression of consciousness that 'British Imperialism in decline had much in common with its Roman precursor',[17] a parallel made even more overt in Brenton's *The Romans in Britain* (1980). If the presentation of Arthur is deflationary, like that of Nelson, then the relationships and language of the other characters are permitted some effective haunting, mythical-poetic qualities by Arden and D'Arcy, despite the Brechtian staging of the whole. Traditional plots and motifs are used to support modern morals: for example, the fratricidal conflict of Balin and Balan is used to demonstrate the inability to make political connections which leads to the misdirection of aggression, despite the Bondswoman's appeal to Balin to fight at least in her defence, not to 'help a little King grow into a bigger one'.[18] Arthur's address to the audience at the end of Part One, designed to win their sympathy, is balanced by the similar appeal of Gwenhwyvar and Medraut in Part Two, with both opposing forces playing on a patriotic commitment to the 'Island of the Mighty', although it is likely that both sides will be viewed with equal detachment after their unofficial private deviousness has been made manifest. The role of the artist and wordsmith is also a developing theme, as Merlin's Lindsay-like 'craft' breaks down and drives him aggressively insane, with the effect that he fails in his traditional function of reconciliation. In contrast, the emergent poet Aneurin's greater sense of realism and integrity makes him an increasingly authoritative figure as he comes to realize his profession's duty to the people rather than to kings and courtiers: 'All we can do is to make loud and make clear their own proper voice. They have so much to say . . .'.[19]

Arden's own progression to what he would probably see as a similar resolution is charted obliquely by two fine radio plays, *The Bagman* (1970) and *Pearl* (1978). *The Bagman* is a fantastic version of Arden's trip to India, in which the Narrator is armed with his bag of little men, dramatic creations about whose use he is vague, beyond acknowledging their capacity to reflect the audience. But in a genuinely revolutionary climate, the over-nice little men mutiny:

Men of war do not require
To see themselves in a truthful mirror.
All that they need to spur them to action
Is their own most bloody reflection
In the white eyeballs of their foe.
We are neat and well-considered little people –
If you bring us into battle
You bring us only into grief and woe
Fracture and breakage that we cannot repair
They will snap our wooden joints
And pull out our cotton hair.
Please let us please let us get back into the sack
When the battle has been won
We can peep out again and creep back.[20]

The narrator of *The Bagman* refuses to 'choose' and concludes that he can only continue to 'look at what I see' (a position condemned by Arden in the Preface as 'reprehensible, cowardly and not to be imitated'). *Pearl* is set in the seventeenth century, a historical distancing of political tensions well justified in the author's prefatory note:

> maybe there is still good reason for re-examining an earlier period of history when disastrous decisions were taken for the most plausible motives, when everyone was aware that the times were highly critical, and yet so few could divest themselves of their erroneous received ideas.

The messenger Pearl brings news to the mainland of the Lord Deputy's regime in Ireland, intended for Grimscar (who fears that 'the army he raises in Dublin is intended not only to coerce the rebellious Scots, but to be used within England for the oppression of the entire kingdom'[21]), but Pearl later joins with the dramatist Backhouse in designing 'a story cuts forward and back both ways'[22] with which to impregnate a scheduled conventional dramatic performance. Their enemies object that they 'do most apprehensively misdoubt the suitability of this play at such a critical time in the fortunes of the kingdom',[23] and their vengeance on Pearl and Backhouse (like the irresponsible neutrality of the Narrator in *The Bagman*) poses a challenging image to the listeners. These dramatic 'implications of the author' and explorations of the potentialities of his art describe Arden's own development but also demonstrate its possibility and necessity for others.

His change of heart is reflected by the more directly Marxist line and less conventional theatrical settings of his subsequent collaborations with D'Arcy. The twenty-six hour long cycle on the life and political development of Irish socialist James Connolly, *The Non-Stop Connolly Show* (1975), traces Connolly's various conflicts with the ubiquitous capitalist Vice, Grabitall, and ends with Connolly's personal defeat but idealistic defiance as he reminds the audience in the closing lines: 'This was not history. It has not passed' – unfortunately the cycle has received scant subsequent performance. *The Ballygombeen Bequest* (1972), a dark farce on British exploitation in Ireland, was supplemented at its Edinburgh Festival production (by 7:84 Theatre Company) by the distribution to the audience of the address and telephone number of an absentee English landlord currently engaged in an eviction case with a family of tenants in Ireland; and a later piece for 7:84, *Vandaleur's Folly* (1978), charts an ill-fated attempt to establish a socialist co-operative estate in 1831 and the economic pressures that impel several characters to participate in the formative organization of the Republican Movement. Perhaps the best of these recent plays is *The Little Gray Home in the West* (published 1982), which returns to many of *The Ballygombeen Bequest*'s themes and devices, and describes how an Irish family is persecuted by the forces of English capitalism, with the crucial estate forming a self-conscious analogy to the Irish Free State (at one point, the disputants even flash back into the characters of Michael Collins and Lloyd George). The English legatee and entrepreneur Baker-Fortescue applies every pressure in his considerable power against the O'Leary family, secure in advice from his solicitor that one is mistaken to confuse 'morality with legality', and his legal and economic attacks escalate into the full-scale internationally martial, when he arranges for contacts in the British Army to dispose of the Republican son of the family. *The Little Gray Home* is D'Arcy and Arden's most successful attempt to link nationalist and economic forces, and its bleak themes are handled with a deft, blackly farcical zest which would have been usefully deployed in leavening some of their Seventies plays. The stormy history of Arden and D'Arcy's involvements with more legitimate theatre venues (and therefore more conventional methods of production) suggests that these plays may well set the pattern for any future dramatic ventures.

Most of Edward Bond's plays have continued to appear in conventional theatre settings, but his work, like that of Arden and D'Arcy, has reflected the increasing radicalization and articulation of his political beliefs. *The Pope's Wedding* (1962) and *Saved* (1965) are modern social tragedies with characters struggling, mainly unsuccessfully, for self-articulation. Scopey in *The Pope's Wedding* envies the hermit Alen's apparent transcendence of a claustrophobic society and takes his place, but Alen has no secret to be learnt beyond that of impotent withdrawal; whilst *Saved* shows the deadening of any humanity amongst its futureless city-dwellers, with the central challenging shock-image of the killing of a baby – which has ceased to exist except as an object for its mother and attackers alike. *Early Morning* (1968) uses a dream-like surrealistic shorthand to handle similar themes: without access to knowledge of their rulers' sordid intrigues and self-interest, people (literally as well as metaphorically) cheerfully consent to consume each other in order to live. Only the more sympathetic Arthur comes to reject conventional sheep-like obedience (and with it, his erstwhile Siamese twin, George), passing through a stage of reductive cynicism (like the Patient in Shaw's *Too True to be Good*) as well as a gallery of black, gruesome authority caricatures before being delivered from the communal blindness and passing on elsewhere. Like Scopey, Arthur escapes from society; but his direction of escape is vague and may prove no more satisfactory than that of the earlier character. Still, he has at least acquired the knowledge and experience to define himself in terms other than those imposed by the dominant society, so *Early Morning* represents the abstract hope that is crucially denied to the brutally material and realistic problems of the characters in *Saved*.

The sparse dramatic style and Chinese peasant setting of *Narrow Road to the Deep North* (1968) makes overt the beginning of a profound Brechtian influence in Bond's work. Like Arden and D'Arcy, Bond is highly concerned with the function of the artist in society, and the initial self-introduction of the poet Basho appears to earmark him as a sympathetic figure. In fact, Basho has more in common with Merlin than Aneurin from *The Island of the Mighty* – in *The Bundle* he shares Merlin's fate of mental breakdown – and behaves in an irresponsible, basely politic manner as the play progresses, forcing the audience to modify their judgements and suspend their conventionally immediate allocations of sympathy or disapproval. Shogo's sphere of ruthless action is an extreme counterbalance to Basho's contemplative withdrawal, and Kiro is a child-like innocent who struggles to find his own place in or between the two systems of valuation. Shogo's socially successful cruelty is also opposed to Georgina's christianity, a textbook example of Nietzsche's identification of religion as a power to inhibit, even cripple, social action through moral guilt. All the characters are allowed a measure of self-justification and accorded an equally unsettling measure of condemnation. Basho's pompous self-absolution is the greatest fundamental evil, but the proliferation of negative examples drives Kiro to despair and suicide. Bond's qualification of his viewpoint, by giving the audience the added awareness of the emergent man from the river, is thematically crucial but theatrically demanding. Like Basho, Kiro has abnegated his responsibility to aid his fellow men, preferring the ultimate gesture of withdrawal, but Bond's uncompromising insistence on the cool epic stylization of his scenes hinders the immediacy of this impression by underestimating the audience's probable desire for emotional directive and overestimating the clarity and appeal of his avowedly rational or intellectual presentation-analysis.

Lear (1971) brings a new maturity to Bond's work. As well as creating its own harsh poetic atmosphere, the play is a cunning and effective reinterpretation of Shakespeare's *King Lear* which gains the same startling emphasis for its departures from the familiar original as Arden and D'Arcy's use of Arthurian legend and, more recently, Howard Brenton's use of *Macbeth*'s plot outline for his own *Thirteenth Night* (1981). *Lear*, with its hauntingly nightmarish scrambling of recognizable historical settings, demonstrates with great force Bond's sense of violent social restriction as an uncontrollable self-generating cycle of aggression through the dramatic metaphor of the wall, simultaneous symbol of defence and entrapment. Bond's most effective departure from his pattern may well be, as Malcolm Hay and Philip Roberts suggest, the lack of any conventional good character (Edgar, Kent, Albany) and the status of Lear's spiritual daughter Cordelia as a Stalinist figure who both differs from and resembles the other daughters she supplants; 'It is not only deliberately done, but the withholding of Cordelia's name until the end of Act One at the very moment when the Gravedigger's boy is about to

be shot and his wife raped, is specifically aimed to destroy any
lingering notions on the part of the audience that someone in the
play will represent conventional goodness.'[24] *Lear* demonstrates
how fear and belief in natural evil lead to their own confirmation
and perpetuate repressive social institutions; Lear's suspicion
alienates him and his daughters from any chance of harmony, but
they replace him only to continue as slaves to power, 'trapped' in
its 'straitjacket'; and Cordelia's counter-revolution, despite her
initial belief that 'When we have power these things won't be
necessary',[25] continues to destroy men in the name of duty and
perpetuate the wall. Lear's emergence as a critical social prophet
brings about an urgent, compelling debate with Cordelia's forces
on the validity of means to ends. Lear points out that the meekest
'law-abiding citizen' may be helping to maintain a rule of terror
by his complaisance ('you decent, honest men devour the earth!';
'your morality is a form of violence'[26]), then manages to engage
Cordelia herself:

CORDELIA: But if you listened to everything your conscience told
you you'd go mad. You'd never get anything done – and there's
a lot to do, some of it very hard.

. . .

LEAR: Don't build the wall.
CORDELIA: We must.
LEAR: Then nothing's changed! A revolution must at least
reform!
CORDELIA: Everything *else* is changed!
LEAR: Not if you keep the wall! Pull it down!
CORDELIA: We'd be attacked by our enemies!
LEAR: The wall will destroy you. It's already doing it. How can
I make you see? . . . You have two enemies, lies *and* the truth.
You sacrifice truth to destroy lies, and you sacrifice life to
destroy death. It isn't sane.[27]

Lear and his play end on an affirmatory existential note as he
'makes his mark' towards the wall's destruction, rejecting the
Basho-like withdrawal urged by the Ghost for a triumphant
moment of exemplary action in the name of 'pity', without which
man is 'mad', an uncompromising conclusion to a harrowingly
powerful play.

Bond's lighter social comedy *The Sea* (1973) demonstrates the
absurdity, xenophobia and insanity generated by class structure

and personal hubris in an oppressively small provincial community, from which the hero escapes with the inspiration to 'change the world' rather than simply join or replace Evens – a more thoughtful version of *The Pope's Wedding*'s Alen – in his beach hermitage. The next two plays, *Bingo* (1973) and *The Fool* (1975), give central importance to the role of the artist in society, and the tensions and contradictions he encounters. The protagonists, Shakespeare and Clare, both act for the audience as guides and touchstones in the currents of their societies. *Bingo* works on the simple but effective device of having Shakespeare confronted at every turn by the ultimate practical consequences of his (and his society's) inaction or compromise: the Old Man's ravings, the Young Woman's corpse, Combe's ruthless, reductive philosophy and wielding of power, the peasant's revolt and finally open aggression on the heath. Shakespeare's resistance to acknowledging his own role in this is gradually eroded. Whilst not embodying the active predator in the same way as Combe, Shakespeare's trance-like distance and 'protecting' of his 'own interests',[28] even his writing at the expense of participation, becomes identified as the eventual, combined exacerbation of hardship:

> even when I sat at my table, when I put on my clothes, I was a hangman's assistant, a gaoler's errand boy. If children go in rags we make the wind. If the table's empty we blight the harvest. If the roof leaks we send the storm. God made the elements but we inflict them on each other.[29]

Other effective touches include the dependence of every scene's action upon considerations of money and property, from the central Welcombe enclosure debate to the prostitute's trade, the reported dog-fights and bear-baiting, Judith's embarrassment at the Young Woman's soliciting 'On one's own property'[30] and her final frantic search for her father's will. Also the choice of Shakespeare as protagonist has the effect of subverting a popular literary stereotype with its associations of serene humanism, which Bond demonstrates as teetering on the edge of bland inhumanity in certain social conditions. The scene with the tougher, earthier Jonson makes for a lively conflict of values and attitudes, and the general fallible humanity of Bond's Shakespeare gains added effect from its contradiction of the isolation and deification conferred upon our major dramatist by some of his least realistic 'enthusiasts'. The figures of John Clare in *The Fool* lacks the same instant associations, though Bond vividly portrays the contradictions experienced by a rural peasant writer forced to seek patronage and sales amongst aristocratic townsfolk. Otherwise *The Fool* is considerably less successful than *Bingo*, with Clare's appeal and structural relevance being blurred by the way in which he is not the central character of the first half; Hay and Roberts claim of the earlier play that 'The audience is left to determine the relevance of the statement to their own lives',[31] which is a stylistic tendency of Bond less problematic in *Bingo* than in *Narrow Road* or *The Fool*. Scene Five's juxtaposition of prizefight and genteel conversation is a sharp dramatic image to contradict the Admiral's assurance 'Who controls the beast in man? Polite society',[32] but the earlier, rather simplistic handling of the workers' uprising offers an oddly skimped impression of a familiar opposition, which may be further endangered by the group attack on the naked Parson. The initial complacency of Milton and the Parson makes them unattractive, but an audience may find difficulties in endorsing completely the workers' disturbing debasement of the Parson on these grounds alone, unless they are already disposed to flow with the traditonal romantic landlords–and–peasants opposition (an insufficient response, as Bond himself has recognized: 'I don't believe in reducing characters to caricatures of their class role or function. That can only confirm in audiences what they already know'[33]). Hay and Roberts point out that the scene is balanced by the agony of the wounded man,[34] but the general effect remains potentially dangerously ambivalent when offered to an audience's primarily emotional sympathies in performance (unless vaguely intended as an assault on these very criteria of judgement). Bond's use of what he terms 'aggro-effects' seems, as yet, uncertain, a concept to which I will return when considering *The Bundle*.

A-A-America! (1976) is also rather too simple and easy in its gaudy cartoon perspective on American racism, especially its first half, *Grandma Faust*, in which there is no attempt to look beneath the stereotypically monstrous.[35] *The Swing* is more interesting and unsettling, primarily for its climactic scene in which the audience is forced into the collective role of a theatre full of bloodthirsty rednecks who empty their revolvers into a racial transgressor, urged on by a leering, sadistic clown.

The Woman (1978) is a historical demythologisation in the

tradition of *The Island of the Mighty*, in which the Trojan wars are fought over a supposedly lucky statue rather than a living Helen, an amendment by which Bond emphasises the futility, superstition and self-generating brutality of Heros's vainglorious brand of military imperialism. The recipe for checking such destructive idiocy is identified as an alliance of the more rational, discontented female characters, Hecuba and Ismene, with the new, self-conscious activity of the Dark Man, who rejects his previous status as a human instrument for his belligerent leaders.[36] *The Bundle* (1978) is a partial revision of *Narrow Road to the Deep North*, but a more compelling play than its previous incarnation. Basho continues to be a counter-productive figure, irresponsible in his withdrawal, but this time 'Shogo' grows up to be Wang, a character whose capacity for unflinchingly direct social action Bond is determined to show in a more positive light than before. The other complementary ghost hovering in the background of *The Bundle* is Brecht's *The Caucasian Chalk Circle* (1947), with its motif of the difficulty of evil, as crystallized by Grusha's inability to desert the child of her class enemy. In *The Bundle*, reactions to a deserted baby characterize the major characters (as in *Saved*): Basho is too self-interested to extend aid, the Ferryman too generously human to do anything else (in defiance of hard economic necessities), and Wang is uncompromisingly determined not to admit the distraction it constitutes from his mission (a direct attack on the selfsame economic 'necessities' that he views as being unjustly imposed). The fate of the Ferryman is also a critique of Brecht's Shen Te, the Good Person who is a 'tiger' to all else in defence of her own, blocking any social change by her impulsive humanity; and we might also recall Wesker's Andy Cobham of *Their Very Own and Golden City*, who found a grim embittered consolation in the 'patchwork' he created rather than the revolutonary changes he envisioned. *The Bundle* is Bond's attack on the temptations of 'patchwork' and its tendency to distract from major revolutionary change. In contrast to Basho who turns away from the world and condemns the poor to ignorance, and the Ferryman who is slow to make political connections and then shrinks away from their implications, Wang grows to have a capacity for clear, simple socialist analysis (demonstrated by his exposition before Tiger's gang) and the resolution to act on his austere conclusions. Wang's dialogue with the Ferryman is as compelling as Lear's with Cordelia, but Bond

comes to importantly different conclusions on this occasion. The
Ferryman shrinks from Wang's equation of 'food and clothes and
knowledge' with 'rifles',[37] as may the audience, but Wang pursues
his point relentlessly:

WANG: Then you're an enemy.
FERRYMAN: No.
WANG: Yes! If you don't help now, you'll make other mistakes!
Listen to their arguments too long. Hesitate. Be patient at the
wrong time. One day people like you will take us to be shot!
. . .
You pick up one child. What about the tenth child? Or the
hundredth child? You leave them to rot! Drown them with your
holy hands . . .
    You saints who crucify the world so that you can be good!
You keep us in dirt and ignorance! Force us into the mud with
your dirty morality![38]

Like Shaw's Andrew Undershaft, Wang proposes a new realistic
morality which takes full account of the potential of rifles; and his
point of view ('We have not yet earned the right to be kind. . . .
Here only the evil can afford to do good'[39]) is supported by later
developments. There is a splended moment when two formerly
competitive water-sellers give water to a suffering woman in
defiance of their usual capitalist procedure, although here they
follow the dictates of emotion over capitalism rather than Wang's
stress of the dictates of social ends over considerations of
conventionally 'immoral' means. Wang's companion Tiger and
the Ferryman die in the struggle – in turn hardening the resolves
of others – after the Ferryman has himself attained an 'all or
nothing' perspective on social change ('shouldn't we change our
lives so that we don't suffer? Or at least suffer only in changing
them?'[40]). Wang concludes the play reiterating the problem of
choice directly to the audience:

WANG *is alone on stage. As he speaks the lights begin to come up.*
WANG: We live in a time of great change. It is easy to find
monsters – and as easy to find heroes. To judge rightly what is
good – to choose between good and evil – that is all that it is to
be human.[41]

The images of *The Bundle* and the character of Wang are challenging in a way examined by Hay and Roberts:

> Bond makes the audience commit themselves emotionally before asking themselves to examine their response to what is happening on the stage.
>   It is a fundamental break with the Brechtian tradition of epic theatre, with which Bond's dramatic method has sometimes been compared. Like Brecht, Bond wants the audience to react analytically to the events he shows, but instead of seeking to distance the audience from the events by interrupting the action, Bond talks of the need to involve the audience by surprising and shocking them with images which are part of the continuing action: 'Alienation is vulnerable to the audience's decision about it. Sometimes it is necessary to emotionally commit the audience which is why I have aggro-effects'.[42]

Problems arise when the emotional response to an aggro-effect is isolated repulsion rather than continuous implication leading to a point of extremity. *The Bundle* may be more effective in this respect than *The Fool*, but may nevertheless remain problematic if Bond's revolutionary logic is *overruled* by an audience's immediate emotional response – say, to Wang's killing the baby or recommending rifles as the ultimate social panacea. However, *The Bundle* is at the very least a stimulating play in a Brechtian tradition forgotten by Hay and Roberts, namely the uncompromising examination of ideological implications afforded by *Lehrstücke* like *The Measures Taken* and *The Exception and the Rule*. As Bond says in his Note on Dramatic Method:

> Of course a dramatist can't prevent an audience from hardening its reaction. That's one reason why theatre can't by itself change the world. But if the audience decide that what we thought was true is false they will still have changed, not merely for themselves but for society. Their views will have been increasingly identified and defined. So theatre can co-operate with all those who are in any way involved in rationally changing society and evolving a new consciousness.[43]

Finally, *The Bundle* as a supportive examination of revolutionary socialism suffers by comparison to Brenton's *Thirteenth Night* because of the latter's more recognizably human and dramatically attractive protagonist Jack Beaty, whose self-criticisms alternate with his actions but nevertheless do not undermine his resolution, or by comparison to Peter Flannery's *Our Friends in the North* (1982) which has a more immediate setting in recent and contemporary Britain. Bond's subsequent attempt to write a contemporary 'answer play', *The Worlds* (1979), is highly disappointing. Although some debates feature stimulating attempted redefinitions of terms and concepts such as 'terrorist', 'law', 'common humanity' and 'morality', the plot is unconvincing. Trench is an attempt at another ideologically transitional figure like the Ferryman, and discovers for himself the ruthlessness of capitalism identified by his former captors, but his grievance seems inflated and his loyalty switch too fast and pat. Trench is really more of a political Timon of Athens (and holds a similar surprising banquet for his fair-weather friends), and his retreat into injured misanthropy sets him apart from the committed but shadowy figures of the activists. At the industrial dispute level, Ray is an appropriate foil for Terry, but the political morals can appear to come too quickly and easily. Bond's meditations, as charted in his prefaces, have arrived at the simple, pared-down principles of the activists after much developing thought, but *The Worlds* does not take its audience through this evolving subtext, only presents austere bluntness which anyone other than an already similarly committed audience will find difficult to endorse immediately. Bond seems to have fallen foul of the very fault he identified in his Note on Dramatic Method:

> merely recounting an event or telling a story on stage will not provide the opportunity for a correct interpretation of the event or story or the people involved. These things may be misinterpreted, and often will be, because many of the audience will not be politically conscious and so will not understand the event or story or even the moral content of the language in which it is described or played.[44]

In the poem-sequence 'The Art of the Audience', Bond writes:

> Who are our audience?
> We write for those who carry bricks
> Not for those who hire builders

The hirer's world is a dream that floats on painted clouds
We speak to him if he sits in our audience
But he's an onlooker
Only the others can judge[45]

Unfortunately, few brick-carriers currently frequent the Royal
Court Theatre, and Bond will have to keep a firm and realistic
notion of his venue, his immediate audience and the manner to
move them most effectively (without necessarily compromising
his own beliefs) if he intends to preach beyond the converted.
Recalling Sandy Craig's comparative definitions of political
drama and political theatre,[46] one might say that Arden's
ideological development has propelled his work from the sphere of
political drama to that of political theatre, in line with a strictly
Marxist analysis of society. In contrast, Bond has mainly
remained within the conventional arena of political drama, and
some of the weaknesses in his work spring from the contrary
tension of his ambition to speak to the potential audience of
political theatre. This is a debilitating tension rather than a
fruitful one and, whilst recognizing Bond's considerable contribution to British political drama, this flaw in several of his works
should be acknowledged.

Restoration (1981) is a funny set of politically conscious departures from the stock machinery of the Restoration comedy,
significantly dividing its attentions between the gentry and the
traditionally sketchy servants. The protagonists' ability to step
our of character and make a direct 'modern' statement in song is
an effective Brechtian touch, but it is unfortunate that the hero
Bob is so passive a victim whilst his aristocratic enemy Are is so
wittily engaging that the play's emotional and theatrical appeal is
out of balance with its bid to present a realistic dramatic account
of such moments in history. Even allowing for the lesson Rose
learns from Bob's fate, she is essentially powerless within the
framework of the play.

Summer (1982) is an unusually domestic play for Bond. Through
the friendship of two elderly women it dramatizes another
neo-Brechtian point, that kindness can be a mere cosmetic to
obscure and indirectly perpetuate injustice (as in *The Good Person
of Szechwan* and *The Bundle*). Marthe's rejection of her old friend
Xenia for her bourgeois individualism in wartime seems harsh –
Xenia has her attractive moments and is even amusing in her

fussiness – but Marthe emphasises that severity is necessary to bring the Xenias of this world (including any counterparts she may have in the audience) to full cognisance of their social role and guilt through its abuse, next to which their partially compensatory charm and selective benevolence are irrelevant. Bond seems here to have recognized some of the problems involved in presenting emotionally austere conclusions through the emotionally as well as intellectually engaging medium of drama, and one hopes he will continue to work towards an articulate and sympathetic exposition of why puritan ruthlessness sometimes has a valid place in the world of practical action.

7   Home Truths and Foreign Freedoms

PETER WEISS, TREVOR GRIFFITHS, ROBERT
BOLT, TOM STOPPARD, C. P. TAYLOR,
CHRISTOPHER HAMPTON, DAVID MERCER

I conclude there is an obligation, a human responsibility, to
fight against the State correctness. Unfortunately that is not a
safe conclusion.

Professional Foul[1]

How tiresome it must be to live in a country where human
rights are so respected that you must look elsewhere to justify
an otherwise futile sense of outrage.

Cousin Vladimir[2]

Just as Arden and D'Arcy identify and realise the potential of
setting political plays in non-contemporary historical periods,
other dramatists have fruitfully exploited conventional reactions
to foreign political regimes, sometimes to make an oblique
comment on matters 'closer to home', or alternatively to throw
into relief a general inadequacy of political response to anything
other than the immediate.

The experimental work performed by director Peter Brook
with the Royal Shakespeare Company in the 1960's produced two
outstanding examples of almost unbearably immediate audience
involvement in the problematic issues of freedom and justice as
presented by foreign or unfamiliar political regimes. Brook's
production of German playwright Peter Weiss's play *Marat/Sade*
in 1964 is a particularly rich example. The theatre audience is
required to play the part of a number of fashionable nineteenth-
century Parisian aristocrats witnessing one of the Marquis de
Sade's dramatic productions in the lunatic asylum of Charenton,

and on this occasion the play allows the individualist sexual revolutionary Sade to meet and debate with the socialist political revolutionary Marat (or at least an actor putting his case). Sade's play 'The Persecution and Assassination of Marat' has many Brechtian features of style, such as the choric Herald who addresses the audience and interrupts the play to remind the onlookers of its artificiality, the narration of events by songs, and the emphasis on debates and ideas. But Weiss's play in sum constitutes a more Artaudian, instinctive experience (as suggested by its performance in the RSC's 'Theatre of Cruelty' season) given its outer frame of performance by lunatics. The director of the asylum and self-styled 'voice of reason', Coulmier, ineffectually attempts to halt the play whenever its material becomes too inflammatory for the political or psychological climate, thus acting as an annoyingly complacent super-ego figure (and supposed representative of the audience's 'enlightened' values) against the patients' seething menace and insane passion, frequently erratic and barely suppressed. They form a sharp contrast to Coulmier's bland calmness and blind allegiance to Napoleon, prompting the question as to who is, in fact, mad – the socially unacceptable patients screaming for freedom through their roles as revolutionaries, or Coulmier attempting to suppress all volatile arguments with the privilege of his power. The climactic seconds of the play provide the audience with the simultaneously feared and wished-for breakdown of Coulmier's bids to organize the patients into placid conformity. The 'cast's' violent frenzy usurps the cold reason of the substitute 'audience' (Coulmier and his genteel family) whom they attack, their voices appropriately blurring 'Napoleon', 'Charenton', 'Revolution' and 'Copulation' as they run amok. But the effects of Weiss's play reverberate beyond their national and historical setting to question the definition and perpetuation of the terms 'freedom' and 'madness' in a given political context. Brook's collaborative effort with the same company, *US* (1966), provided a series of searching images to explore the immediacy of an audience's reactions to the contemporary American–Vietnamese war, concluding with the famous scene of an actor burning (apparent) butterflies until a member of the audience felt sufficiently moved to climb onto the stage to stop him.[3]

Trevor Griffiths's *Occupations* (1970) also deals with a geographically and historically distanced event – the brief and ill-fated seizure of Italian factories by their workers in 1920 – to present a more far-reaching, sympathetic but critical examination of the nature of revolutionary socialism. As Griffiths writes of the play in a prefatory essay:

> *What it asserts* is that courage and optimism do not, of themselves, ensure the success of revolutions, unless they are harnessed, disciplined, tightly organized; in a word, *led*.
>
> And what it *asks* – because it's a play that, characteristically, asks rather than asserts – is whether the courage and optimism aren't in some way necessarily damaged, distorted, in that disciplining process.[4]

Griffiths dramatizes this conflict of impulses in the meeting of Gramsci and Kabak, but not without unease about possible interpretations: 'I would support Gramsci's assertion that "It is a revolutionary duty to tell the truth" even where there is little comfort to be had from it'[5] (compare Wesker's belief that 'Optimism in art is the result not of happy endings and joyful exclamations but of the recognition of truths – secondary ones – whether the truth is a sad one or not'[6]). The essence of the conflict in *Occupations* and in other Griffiths plays is the tension between the viewpoint of the Soviet professional agitator Kabak ('You cannot *love* an army, comrade. An army is a machine. This one makes revolutions. If it breaks down, you get another one. Love has nothing to do with it'[7]) and that of the workers' spokesman Gramsci ('There is nothing in the world more relevant than love. . . . Treat the masses as expandable, as fodder, *during* the revolution, you will always treat them thus . . . if you see masses that way, there can be no revolution worth the blood it spills'[8]). In the background, Kabak's wife Angelica – like Weiss's Marat – acts as a personification of the internally rebellious country (a parallel more overt in Griffiths's original ending for the play). Whilst Gramsci comes to endorse Trotsky's maxim 'We shall not enter into the kingdom of socialism with white gloves on a polished floor',[9] Kabak remains sceptical about the spokesman's effectuality ('You still love them too much, comrade'). However, Scenes Three and Six give the audience, in the role of the factory workers, the chance to experience Gramsci's charismatic orations first-hand and gives the character an emotional attractiveness denied to Kabak by his rather warped private behaviour with his wife and maid. Thus, Gramsci's direct public expressions of integrity are poised against a keyhole view of Kabak's callousness in the confidential, domestic sphere, providing a significantly bad reflection on the latter's moral qualities.

Griffith's *The Party* (1973) also mobilises a variety of responses to a common political event, the French student revolution of 1968, but from an immediately contemporary series of English viewpoints. Those who gather in the Shawcross home in London SW7 share a concern about the events in France and a commitment to a revolutionary ideal for which no practical political party exists; but they share little else, as they demonstrate by their internal squabbles. It is left to the moribund Tagg to restore a note of harsh, almost brutal realism to what he diagnoses as vain intellectual self-indulgence and defeatism, and his speech will probably contain at least one valid criticism for ostensibly similarly committed audience members, already identified by the play's unsettling prologue address from Groucho (not Karl) Marx which ends in a film of Paris students marching with the caption 'Voilez Votre Alma Mater' (though Groucho also has some telling shafts for differently aligned audience members: 'Which reminds me, did you hear the one about the 150 000 supporters of De Gaulle who marched through the streets of Paris on 30 June 1968 shouting 'France aux français!' and 'Cohn-Bendit à Dachau'? You what? Oh, you were there. Well, well, well' and 'The bourgeoisie. . . . Wake up, madam, I'm talking about you. Give her a nudge, will you, sir? Thank you so much'[10]). The crux of Tagg's blunt message is that 'Suddenly you lose contact – not with abstractions, concepts, because they're after all your stock-in-trade. You lose contact with the moral tap-roots of socialism. . . . Finally you learn to enjoy your pain'[11]; or, more directly:

> The intellectual's problem is not vision, it's commitment. You enjoy biting the hand that feeds you, but you'll never bite it off. So those brave and foolish youths in Paris now will hold their heads out for the baton and shout their crazy slogans for the night. But it won't stop them from graduating and taking up their positions in the centres of ruling class power and privilege later on.[12]

The Party's image of the Left is, crucially, self-critical but not undercutting, through the very disparity of its spectrum of characters. As Edward Braun says of *Occupations*, 'the danger . . . is that the audience may see the two characters as representing an either/or choice, whereas with *The Party* the clear invitation is to pursue the argument in one's own mind and seek a fusion of ideas. In Griffith's next play for television, *All Good Men*, there is a similar presentation of alternatives',[13] as indeed there is in his next stage play *Comedians* (1975), to be discussed fully in the next chapter. *All Good Men* (1974) brings an aged compromiser into conflict with the more austere ideals of his son, anticipating the Waters-Price relationship in *Comedians* and pursuing the familiar Griffiths tactic of characters' mutual illumination and criticism in their respective paths to reform, producing a fruitful opposition to be synthesized by the audience.[14] Two other television plays by Griffiths are particularly noteworthy: *Through the Night* (1975) explores the problem of Gramsci's 'love' versus Kabak's 'army' as highlighted by the cold, inhuman treatment of a hospitalized woman by the social institution supposedly working for her welfare, whilst *Absolute Beginners* (shown in the series *Fall of Eagles*, 1974) returns to the style of *Occupations* to dramatize Lenin's rise to power in the London-based Bolshevik party, with particular attention to the shades of integrity and decisiveness embodied by the various members, and the problematic ruthlessness which Lenin is forced to adopt in his personal as well as public political dealings, demonstrating 'the classic dilemma of ends and means in terms of human, as well as political, behaviour'.[15] And Griffiths's 1982 film collaboration with Warren Beatty, *Reds*, shows the American journalist John Reed inspired by his witnessing of the Russian Revolution, and traces his subsequent problems when his left-wing faction of an American socialist organization is disowned by party right and centre, forcing him to fight for their official recognition by Soviet bureaucracy. An interesting contrast is afforded by Robert Bolt's stage play *State of Revolution* (1977) which also dramatizes the formative days of the Russian revolution but for different motives. Bolt seeks to demonstrate the gradual (and to him inevitable) divorce of state communism from its theoretical humanist roots. It is significant that the audience's guide through the events of the play is the ineffectual humanist Lunacharsky, who is made likeably forthcoming in marked contrast to the shadowy, ominous Stalin, and that Lenin is depicted as appalled by his loss of control over the would-be 'Bonaparte' Stalin. Bolt's basic dramatic tactic is common to many left-wing plays, namely the depiction of human tragedy which arises when the social status quo subverts its own ostensible ideals. However, Bolt's right-wing critique is not of the native capitalist society but of a foreign communist one with a view to vindicating Westetern society of comparative hypocrisy. But *State of Revolution* finally falls victim to a pitfall of historical political plays eluded better by *Occupations* and *Absolute Beginners*, namely the tendency to present politically important figures in personal terms too neatly analogous to their historical functions, producing a simplistic effect in their bald functionalism. In comparison with Griffiths, Bolt's ideological 'complexities' seem superficial as a result, particularly at the end of the First Act, when the sinister foreshadowing emphasis laid upon Stalin's entrance depends on the presumed extra-theatrical preconceptions of the audience; although *Occupations* also displays a tendency to the same failing by giving Kabak a private life which is negatively weighted in dramatic terms, when Gramsci is never shown in a domestic or 'off-guard' context.

Lenin also appears, albeit in a distinctly unconventional frame of presentation, in Tom Stoppard's *Travesties* (1974). Theories of art and politics are two of the witty farce's main themes, but they are handled unceremoniously by Stoppard's fast and freewheeling, often parodic, style, and are frequently present only to form the intellectual basis for more literate humour and self-delightingly idiosyncratic characterization. Cecily's lecture on Lenin, which imposes a critical form on the past for polemical purposes, involves the audience in a very different and markedly less entertaining relationship than that achieved by Carr's haphazard informal monologues; and Stoppard makes the intriguing contention that a taste for revolutionary politics and a taste for revolutionary art can be inimical, with Lenin as a case in point, as the Russian leader complains that hearing the music of Beethoven tends to mollify his resolution on short-term harshness in aid of long-term humanism. However, as Carr finally points out, wishing to be a revolutionary politician or a revolutionary artist are popular ambitions, and both categories of success claim their failed candidates from the other. *Travesties* is finally, like its literary progenitor, a very successful trivial comedy for serious people, but Stoppard's later works contain more ideological seriousness alongside their shimmering verbal wit. *Every Good Boy*

Deserves Favour (1977), the television play *Professional Foul* (1977) and *Dogg's Hamlet, Cahoot's Macbeth* (1979) are all concerned with personal freedom and freedom of speech as threatened 'behind the iron curtain' of Soviet control, whilst *Night and Day* (1978) pursues similar themes, with the foregrounded topic of British journalism, in a fictitious African site of revolution. *Every Good Boy* most resembles early Stoppard in its delight in formal parallels and verbal allusion, but also seeks to expose the totalitarian repression behind the benevolent facade of a society which deems dissidents mad and consigns them to long-term 'hospitalization', as well as charting the dilemma of Alexander, who is torn between rejoining his son and remaining true to his political beliefs. The interwoven themes of music, political integrity and geometrical imagery all meet in a mathematically neat formal conclusion when the Lady Bracknell-like eccentric *deus ex machina*, a KGB colonel, dispenses freedom on the basis of a mistaken speech act, a truly comic means of absolving all concerned from the rigidities of their positions. *Professional Foul* almost works in reverse order, as Anderson, a lecturer in philosophy and professional monitor of the verbal nuance, attends a conference in Prague with a detached, innocent frame of mind only to find himself implicated in the arrest of a former pupil on the grounds of the very academic investigations which hitherto seemed so distant from practical issues of state politics. The crux of Hollar's thesis – and Stoppard's – is that 'The ethics of the State must be judged against the fundamental ethic of the individual. The human being, not the citizen. I conclude there is an obligation, a human responsibility, to fight against the State correctness. Unfortunately that is not a safe conclusion'.[16] Anderson's apparently irrelevant professional ethic confers upon him the status of dangerous political activist when he attempts to repeat such conclusions at the conference, building up to the assertion that 'the implications are serious for a collective or State ethic which finds itself in conflict with individual rights, and seeks, in the name of the people, to impose its values on the very individuals who comprise the state'.[17] The fatal discrepancy between the interests of an institutionalized society and the citizens it ostensibly represents constitutes the fundamental pivot of all political drama, but, like Bolt in *State of Revolution*, Stoppard locates this conflict in a representative communist state. Griffiths's setting of *Occupations* in Italy is essentially different, as his investigation of separate paths to the common ideal of efficient socialism is intended to provide an informative parallel with similar objectives in Britain. Bolt and Stoppard do not use their foreign settings as a means to critical distance upon the general ideological thrust of their native society (for example, by drawing a parallel between Russian and British or Western threats to personal and/or political integrity), rather they are dramatizing objections to that foreign state as a manifestation of the ideological alternative to our own present one (an effect which Szanto's *Theater and Propaganda* would probably term 'integrationist'); in national terms, they are being critical rather than self-critical. *Cahoot's Macbeth* dramatizes Stoppard's concerns with even greater immediacy by placing the audience in the position of furtive witnesses of an illegal private performance of *Macbeth*. Like the actors, the audience become objects of the Inspector's bullying, but the closet performers subvert his killjoy authority by an excursion into private linguistic ingenuity to which *Dogg's Hamlet* has already made the audience familiar parties. The characterization of the Secret Policeman is interesting for its similarity to the neo-fascist 'bent copper' stereotype nurtured by Orton and subsequent agitprop and left-wing political dramatists (including Brenton and Keeffe), here deployed by Stoppard to fulfil the opposite ideological role to its more familiar one. Like *Every Good Boy*, *Cahoot's Macbeth* is a completely comic celebration of short-term victory over repressiveness, but *Night and Day* is more complex, comparing the controls on the presentation of information enforced by a budding revolutionary state and by a British union of newspaper workers, both of which are criticized for losing sight of immediate individual rights. The faith which Wagner places in the rigid institution of trades unions is mocked by its final block on his story in the name of solidarity – a principle which is further discredited as petty by association with the all-out guerilla war which claims the life of his opponent Milne. Stoppard's initial target, the tawdriness of competitive tabloid journalism, is an easy and accessible one, but he skilfully develops his points to make wider political statements. As in his other political plays, the organization and mechanisms of the (left-wing) social institution are identified as being at odds with the individual human interests they purport to represent. Whilst it would be churlish to deny the justice and seriousness of Stoppard's concern for Soviet dissidents, it is true that his plays aim to demonstrate the practical abuses of the theoretical alternatives to

Western capitalist society, thereby latently affirming the latter
and ultimately maintaining its conventional image of distance
from, and resistance to, the possibilities offered by alternative
criteria of social organization. In contrast, David Mercer's
comparative analyses of East and West are more challenging to
audience complacency in their equally witty, but more politically
complex, double-edged observations.

Oddly enough, *Every Good Boy*'s motif of an imaginary band also
occurs in C. P. Taylor's *Good* (1981), where the band – again
realised onstage – becomes a symptom of anxiety and its
attempted cauterization in the mind of John Halder, a German
lecturer witnessing the rise of Nazism in the 1930s. Halder makes
the audience his confidantes and jury as he describes his personal
psychological disintegration and the problems he has in linking it
with a national social and moral disintegration, where his mental
musical score to events might be 'A strategy for survival? Turning
the reality into fantasy?'[18] Even while his Jewish friend Maurice
expresses his fear of Hitler's anti-semitism, Halder characteristically tries to distance them both from the possible technicalities of
the Nazi programme and blames his unease on subjective sexual
neurosis. However, Halder's personal and professional circumstances pressurize him into joining the Nazis and adapting the
messages of his teaching and fiction writing to their ideological
flow. Taylor skilfully manages Halder's concessions to doubt and
expediency in order to maintain a sympathetic but critical
perspective on the character, and the nightmarish, fluid progression of events and speakers, in which even distinct identities break
down and Halder hears his own voice coming from Hitler, gives a
vivid impression of a time out of joint and control. Halder almost
hysterically manipulates arguments of ends and means in a bid to
remain productively indifferent to the fate of Maurice, who
continues to haunt Halder's waking nightmare as another voice in
his concerto of anxiety. Halder even desperately wonders if 'we
are allowing ourselves to be trapped by obvious, stock responses'
of primary morality, 'Instead of daring to confront ourselves with
reality maybe, Maurice, maybe. . . . It's the Jews' fault'; and
alternatively whether 'You think we might be having a nervous
breakdown. The whole thing is a national nervous breakdown?'[19]
But despite his mistress's comforting reassurances that 'we're
good people . . . both of us', Halder significantly finds his
imaginary distress signals realised when a group of prisoner

musicians greet him at Auschwitz, where he can have no doubt that 'The band was *real!*'[20] Halder is a sensitive man who, like some of David Hare's characters, finds his psychological health impaired by pressures to fit into a distorting social role, but Halder crucially refuses to recognize his problems in such terms, preferring private and subjective diagnoses which facilitate his public co-operation in social conformity, until his worst vague fears unavoidably and objectively come home to roost. Unfortunately, some of the play's intended power to alert audiences to what Taylor terms their 'peace crimes' to perpetuate daily 'Auschwitzes'[21] may be blurred by its close sympathetic involvement with Halder, whose latter-day Galy Gay-like adaptation to circumstances is delineated with so much sympathy as to make his co-operation seem almost necessary or unavoidable; but if the play's direction can establish its moral lessons beyond its protagonist's perspective and its particular historical setting, it provides a fine development of Galsworthy's 'liberal tragedies' by internally demonstrating the sometimes paralyzed practical position of the typical reasonable, broad-minded 'good' man – the target of Christopher Hampton's *Savages* (1973) which, like Stoppard's *Professional Foul*, has a particularly English, naïve central figure to act as repository for audience sympathy in that West and Anderson are evident representatives of the native audience's own nationality plunged into unfamiliar political intrigues on foreign soil, and these characters provide the unifying consciousness to act as a guide through events. But whereas Stoppard's Anderson became moved to a form of commitment and action through his own sense of implication, Hampton's West is a more unsettling and passive audience surrogate because it is he (not a friend or pupil) who is powerless under direct threat. Like the English soldier in Behan's *The Hostage* and Trench in Bond's *The Worlds*, West is held captive, but under the combined charges of both other characters; Leslie Williams's sense of national culpability was mocked by his class status, which he shared with many of the more engaging Irish low-lifers, but Bond's Trench is a hostage precisely on class terms; West is both English and privileged, and seeks in vain to protest on the very grounds of his nationality, reinforcing the role which also places him in danger. His rather prissy reliance on 'reasonableness' makes him a particularly apt figure for a harsh baptism into the world of cold political reality, of which he denies any part on first hearing Carlos's grievances:

WEST: It may be true or it may not be, and if it is I'm very sorry
about it, but it's nothing to do with me.
CARLOS: It is now.[22]

In fact, the flashback structure of *Savages* goes on to demolish
West's self-absolution from guilt. It transpires that West had, on
several occasions, been made aware of the Brazilian Indians'
plight (in the same way that the play now makes the audience
aware), and had even experienced revulsion at the blend of
capitalism and christianity being foisted upon them, but had
nevertheless failed to assume any personal responsibility – which
Carlos reintroduces in a particularly ruthless manner, neatly
circumventing West's objections (and the potential objections of
the audience):

CARLOS: You think that all's fair in love and commerce, but
some of us take it personally when our children starve to death
so that somebody in Detroit or Pittsburgh can buy themselves a
third car.
WEST: That's a ludicrously oversimplified way of putting it.
CARLOS: Well, as it so happens, it's a ludicrously oversimplified
process, starving. You don't get enough food to eat and, by an
absurdly oversimplified foible of nature, you die. . . . It can
be a terrible set back to your notions of international brotherhood . . .
   Don't think I'm so stupid as to be against them just because
they're Americans. . . . Before them it was you.
WEST: Me?
CARLOS: You. England.
   . . .
WEST: Well, it's hardly my fault.
CARLOS: That's it. Nothing's ever anyone's fault.[23]

The notion of Williams's responsibility and capture in *The Hostage*
was exposed as ludicrous, but Carlos's arguments have considerably more force and logic than the laughable Monsewer's,
mainly because West *is* a suitable representative of the class and
nationality at which Carlos wishes to strike back. The revolutionary's articulacy and wit are also valuable for bringing political
implication by silent consent into close, hard focus. He can
answer West's referral to democracy with 'Democracy is a luxury

for countries rich enough so it doesn't matter who they elect.'[24] West's interest in one facet of the Indians, the folklore which he previously detached from considerations of context, also acts as a documentary guide for the audience through the spiritual tenor of the Indians as they prepare the Quarup, so that the final intrusion of Western explosives is all the more shocking. West's presence in these intermittent scenes also leads the audience to expect that he will emerge safely from his ordeal, possibly repentant (as does the grudging mutual respect which grows between West and Carlos), so Carlos's apologetic but careful shooting of West is also unexpected. However, by placing scenes of the Indian massacre before and after that of West's death, Hampton mitigates the sense of injustice the audience may feel at his shooting – indeed, the shooting becomes firmly related by association to a chain of wider suffering. The play's refusal to accommodate any convincing reply from West to Carlos's penetrating allegations gives his relentless revolutionary logic an insistent refusal to be distanced, and the figure of West as mediator between the audience, Carlos and the Indians gives the exposition and conclusion of the play accessibility and power.

David Mercer is another playwright fascinated by responses to unfamiliar political settings and by characters who suffer in pursuing a maverick integrity in conflict with dominant social values, thus receiving or choosing the stigma of 'madness' through their refusal to submit to conventions. What John Russell Taylor describes as 'social alienation expressed in terms of psychological alienation'[25] forms the area of investigation in many of Mercer's plays, whether it takes the form of defeated regression as in *Ride a Cock Horse* (1965) and the television plays *The Birth of a Private Man* (1963) and *In Two Minds* (1967, filmed as *Family Life* in 1970) or reckless assertion of individuality, as in the television plays *For Tea on Sunday* (1963), *A Suitable Case for Treatment* (1962, filmed in 1965 as *Morgan*) and the stage play *Flint* (1970). Certainly characters like Morgan Delt or Ossian Flint have great dramatic vitality as paradoxically gleeful malcontents who score off their life-denying conventional foils like particularly anarchic versions of Shaw's heroes. Here Mercer is interested in madness and eccentricity as misunderstood but valid expressions of values and perceptions obscured or opposed by society, in order to shatter its conventional categorisations. The grip of the dominant social structure and its effect on the individual is also brought into focus by the international settings of some of Mercer's plays: The Berlin Wall in *Birth of a Private Man* (a particularly concrete image of social categorisation) and the colliding worlds of Bernard Link and Claire in *After Haggerty* (1970). On a lecture visit to Prague, the drama critic Link finds himself incapable of delivering his usual talk on the character of Jimmy Porter or defending his position as a comfortable Western Marxist. But this disquieting personal experience of political contradictions seems to focus his self-consciousness so that, by the end of the play, he can consign his stereotypical bluff North Country father to the dead world where he belongs; whereas the American Claire confirms her sense of her own integrity and capability in a foreign country, and her escape from a past world is similarly completed by the death of the elusive Haggerty. In psychological terms, the play is an examination of the characters' progress to individuation.

Cousin Vladimir (1978) works from an even more pointed sense of dislocated nationality and the sharp, unconventional focus of perception which this can yield. As its title suggests, the play also resembles a kind of tough, modern Chekhov in its vivid atmospheric evocation of British society as symbolized by the indulgence, aimlessness, sterility and self-absorption of a childish set of hardened drinkers. This unflattering reflection gains a counterpoint in the Russian emigres Katya and Valodya, with the latter initially appearing something of a reincarnation of Arden's seedy, unprincipled arch-survivor Krank, smug in the conviction (formulated in his thirties) that the Soviet Union is a failure because 'human species psychologically unfit to perform as theory requires'.[26] Throughout the play, Valodya and the Hard Core clique act as running checks to each other's national complacency, as when Valodya's identification of foreigners' hypocrisy goads Glenda into indicting the lack of principle beneath his critical standpoint:

VALODYA: They were ecstatic about social system they would not tolerate for one day at home. . . . The Cousin Vladimirs of this world stood by with frozen smiles, and incredulity in our hearts. Children, we thought . . .
. . .
GLENDA: What you mean is: the Cousin Vladimirs had one priority. To save their own necks. . . . And now a rat like you scuttles out, leaving better men and women to go to prison and into the mental hospitals for you.[27]

Parallels, as well as contrasts, serve Mercer sharp satirical barbs:

GORDON: Still. Doesn't seem to matter who's on top over there.
Does it? Gangsters one and all –
KATYA: Does it matter over here?[28]

Valodya gives an unsentimental account of the country he has
rejected, but nevertheless finds the smug condemnation of Russia
by the British an insufficient response ('How tiresome it must be
to live in a country where human rights are so respected that you
must look elsewhere to justify an otherwise futile sense of
outrage'[29]), typified by their simplistic reactions to Solzhenitsyn
('He is not just a flame burning brightly in the Bolshevik
storm. . . . Neither is he a coat-hanger for the self-righteous tatters
of your political system. . . . How corrupt you are!'[30]). The
appearance of national security pressure on Austin gives fuel to
Valodya's wry conclusion that the only thing distinguishing many
of Britain's national bureaucratic actions from those of Russia is
'English velvet glove'. The final revulsion of the sympathetic
Katya from the mordant spectacle of the flaccid Britons' tired
aping of the 'failed American dream' is predictable, but the
similar rejection by Valodya, who had previously made a
principle of uncommitment, is telling. Katya's assertion 'I think I
would rather fight on my knees, in Russia – than one day to die in
your kind of freedom. . . . Heartbroken'[31] is echoed by Valodya,
who recognizes the shabby part he and Austin play in their
respective shabby regimes ('Into what lie are you and I incorporated, in our different ways?'[32]), but adds 'From the little I
see in Europe, your freedom is something you do not know what to
do with'.[33]

Mercer's *The Monster of Karlovy Vary* (1979) is in many ways a
companion piece to *Cousin Vladimir*, but distinguished by its
hilarious farcical tone. In contrast to the cynical Valodya's
excursion into Europe, Mercer has Horatio Dander, self-styled
'worried armchair revolutionary' and Candide-like innocent
abroad, act as a very individual guide for the audience through
Prague. Dander goes to write screenplays and decide for himself
about the communist regime, primed with the conventional
Western 'impression the country was just one damn big prison',[34]
but his simple idealism is shown to be ludicrously self-
congratulatory. A brawl in a cellar club convinces him that he is

'At grips with brutal tyranny at last',[35] but this estimation is comically distorted when he meets one of the performers he believed arrested:

> DANDER: Mr Klumm it's an honour. You were terrific. Fantastic. I was so moved I nearly cried. How splendid that you got away.
>
> KLUMM: This the little dummkopf Hájek spoke about?
>
> . . .
>
> Dander. I work for the prison. We ain't started arresting each other yet. That's Stalinism.
>
> DANDER: (*to* JANA) How can I stay in the same room?[36]

A further ideological twist is added when Dander's father turns out to be a former member of the Luftwaffe, an allegation Dander receives with disbelief and embarrassment. Horatio shoots Klumm to strike 'a blow for humanism',[37] but the death is faked and constitutes a further undercutting of his grand aspirations. In one splendidly farcical scene, he remains oblivious to the way his unwitting listeners are being constantly 'disappeared' by overzealous secret service men, whilst he meditates in a park about political contradictions ('you'd say capitalism's all lies too. And you'd be right. . . . There's a very subtle moral line running through all this I'm sure. If I could only tease it out from the surrounding confusion'[38]). Eventually Dander is indeed allowed to penetrate into the heart of Soviet control to see the deceptions perpetrated under the excuse of 'What seems to keep everybody happy',[39] and he responds with a fatal gesture of resistance. The final scene is highly effective, as Klinka, the hitherto Valodya-like old cynic, is polarized by witnessing Dander's death to the point of producing underground resistance films instead of his usual fantastic romps. Dander is attributed with the heroic lines: 'Not only have our words but even our colours become your lies. You have torn the red flag from our hearts and unfurled it over imprisoned nations. . . . You have stolen the gentle black of peaceful anarchy and cut it into uniforms. . . . You have locked our human poetry in steel';[40] and the film concludes with a genuine mime of resistance to oppression. *The Monster of Karlovy. Vary*'s gradual modulation from very funny irony is highly skilful, as the audience is taken through Dander's initial glib anti-Soviet attitude to disillusionment to a critical perspective that he has genuinely earned and developed from experience – just as *Cousin Vladimir* discredits the easy criticisms of Eastern bloc communism and evolves a critical standpoint of greater integrity and originality to train on both Britain and Russia. In this respect, Mercer's plays contain a crucial additional perspective to those of Stoppard. Rather than run the risk of fuelling the self-righteous Dander perspective, Mercer makes the audience see their own national complacency in an alienated light as well as proceeding to a non-ironic, complex and unsettling recognition of injustice perpetrated in the name of state communism. On both fronts, Mercer makes the audience see that there are no easy answers, and produces political drama of complexity, wit and challenge in the process.

8 Cartoon Nightmares

HEATHCOTE WILLIAMS, TREVOR GRIFFITHS,
HOWARD BRENTON, HOWARD BARKER, BARRIE
KEEFFE

This is a nightmare. This doesn't happen in England.

Sus[1]

They want to make me into art, do you know why? 'Cos art
don't hurt. Look at Goya. His firing squad – I seen it on
stockbroker's walls! But I still hurt, see? I touch their little pink
nerve with my needle, like the frog's legs on the bench. I shock
their muscle and they TWITCH! They don't want to twitch,
see? They're so much happier lying dead! But I twitch 'em! I
SHOCK THE BASTARDS INTO LIFE!

No End of Blame[2]

Peter Ansorge, in *Disrupting the Spectacle*,[3] makes the overt critical
connection between the political plays which emerged in the
1970's and 'the obsessive, murderous plots and characters of the
late Jacobean dramatists', thus likening Brenton, Hare and Snoo
Wilson to modern versions of the 'sixteenth and early seventeenth
century "university wits" . . . who drew their inspiration from the
most violent and scandalous events of their own epoch, which
proved the most vital in our dramatic history'. The thematic and
stylistic correspondence now verges on being a critical cliché, and
requires both expansion and qualification.

In my Introduction, I described the clash of the dislocated,
unconventional moral spokesman with the ostensible but failed
representatives of social morality – as exemplified by Jacobean
tragedy – and the broad, cynical, satirical anatomy of an amoral
society – as exemplified by Jacobean city comedy – as two of the
most potent structural models for producing engaging, vital
drama. The Jacobean malcontent, who both impels and comments on the action of the first, will be a man of high principles

134

now disillusioned, if not deranged, by their lack of congruence
with the society he now perceives (and particularly by the lack of
congruence between the supposed morality of public office and
the true morality of private behaviour as discerned in the
hypocritical activities of the representatives of authority). He may
flirt with a cynical self-identification with these amoral times, but
can finally emerge as an unlikely moral agent through making a
negative stand against the utter corruption of a society which can
offer no untainted mechanism of justice to which he may appeal.
The malcontent's witty disgust at, and trickery of, the self-
indulgent and self-congratulatory dullards who control society
from the inside affords opportunities for the exposure of discrepancy between principle and action to pungent effect. The
audience may vicariously enjoy an exposure of their social
superiors' weaknesses and a gesture of revolt against them. The
final re-emergence of the conventional wheel of social morality, as
in *The Revenger's Tragedy*, is a placatory but petty check to the
malcontent's moral autonomy, and may even serve as a further
wry indictment of this form of 'justice', but does nothing to
diminish his dramatic authority (the final victory of the comparatively colourless may throw it into sharper relief). But if most of
the audience sympathies are accorded to the frenzied logic of the
malcontent, the 'court' in which the plays are performed may also
recognize aspects of themselves in his targets, making for a
literally offensive dramatic experience.[4] No less discomforting is
the complementary dramatic form, the satirical anatomy, in
which the moral dimension to social dealings is conspicuous by its
absence; rather, the dramatist presents an intensified mirror-
image social panorama with particular attention to corruption,
hypocrisy, greed and materialism – 'see what you have become' –
and the hero is likely to identify himself completely with his social
environment and be distinguished principally by his greater
efficiency in crime than his contemporaries, until the eradication
of morality reaches such a point that the cheerful villain has no
place to hide and is hoist by his own petard. Again, his
punishment, if it comes, will be more of a testimony to society's
double standards than to its moral efficacy; he acts on the
connections between society and corruption which the audience
may only suspect, but his revolt will be individualistic and
self-interested whereas the malcontent's will be ultimately moral
and socially existential.

This admittedly lengthy exposition should recall dramatic patterns familiar from plays already discussed. Shaw's 'higher evolutionary man' who scores points off his more conventional foils is a comic adaptation of the malcontent's moral and theatrical energy, and we may also think of Jimmy Porter's confused but abrasive moral tirades and Serjeant Musgrave's infectious 'madness'. However, the work of Williams, Brenton, Barker and Keeffe constitutes an unprecedented return to the violence and immediacy of the Jacobean dramatist's satirical attack upon his own society. The danger in stating this proposition is that the new dramatists concerned may initially be construed as imitating a familiar literary form or style, and thus may be packaged away under a neat critical wrapping. In fact, their affinities with a previous style of drama may not be conscious (although Brenton's *Revenge*, *Thirteenth Night* and Keeffe's *A Mad World, My Masters* twist a self-conscious resemblance to additional pointed effect), let alone slavish imitations. Rather, the plays of Brenton et al are remarkable as redefinitions of the Jacobean style of play in all its otherwise unequalled violent, urgent intensity. The point of the modern neoromantic political play is not its resemblance to an existing literary model, and hence the danger of a critical over-eagerness to label and dismiss it as such; the point is its contemporary urgency and immediacy, sometimes feeding off the gaudy scandal exposé flavour of the tabloid press or horror, rock and film 'trash culture'. Even the original Jacobean tragedies were required to displace their disclosed political iniquities to a corrupt foreign, often Italian, court, whereas the kind of play which has recently been presented at the RSC's Warehouse Theatre, or perhaps the Royal Court, is unflinchingly overt in its address to recognizable modern British society and the tenuous facade which it believes masks its widespread corruption, and equally unflinching in the dramatic weight it places behind direct violent attacks designed to burst through this facade. In the process, they are likely to polarize their predominantly middle-class audiences into the allocation of sympathy to underdog or reactionary in a particularly extreme and discomforting way. In this respect, the plays of Arden and D'Arcy and Bond share some qualities with the dramatists discussed here, but their differences are also significant. Whereas Arden and D'Arcy have moved out of the bourgeois legitimate theatre in search of what they consider a more fertile audience, Brenton, Hare, Edgar and others have tended to shift their attentions to larger, subsidised theatres in order to engage larger and often less politically sympathetic audiences, which in turn gives the plays added edge in their manipulations of audience response. And Bond's politically serious but essentially earnestly poetic plays often lack the malicious humour and black wit which give Brenton and Barker their characteristic theatrical vitality with which to lace their equally serious dramatic objectives.

Neither should the identifiable neo-Jacobean note in these plays blind us to other characteristics or influences. The ironic, grotesque parade of social caricatures owes as much to the modern cartoon as to the Jacobean city comedy for its immediate familiarity, and Sandy Craig has written well on the cartoon elements in alternative theatre:

> [The establishment] claim that this new theatre is 'cartoon' theatre, implying that it is superficial, brutal and one-dimensional. Cartoons were originally a narrative form of visual art and certainly alternative theatre . . . is cartoon theatre in the sense that its narrative style is imbued with a visual consciousness. However, the metaphor can be extended. Theatre naturalism is like a Constable painting, complete and detailed, and forcing on its audience – composed ideally of separate individuals – an attitude of reflection and contemplation, a contemplation of its details, its wholeness, its uniqueness . . .
>
> Naturalism perceives the world, and its relation to the world, as one in which 'everything connects like a never-ending Victorian novel'. There is no doubt that the other-worldly narrator is objective, real, true. The cartoon theatre rejects this . . . but in its reflection splits into two forms. Either it projects dreams and fantasies onto the audience, or it deconstructs the world and in this process shows the audience that the world can be changed.[5]

The debt to Brecht's epic theatre is large and obvious, and it is worth emphasising the almost unanimous apprenticeship served by recent dramatists with alternative fringe theatre groups, so that the residues of this dramatic style have continued into their work for more conventional theatre audiences and venues. However, the climactic effect is more likely to be shock and

polarization than the ostensible Brechtian goal of alienated
detachment, and it is also important to establish the innovatory
contribution of Joe Orton, whose irreverent iconoclasm and
elegant descriptions of manifold brutality combined to leave a
series of cynical black farces which finally deny their protagonists
any escape from their nightmare worlds of predatory corruption.
Katharine J. Worth links the gleefully anarchic dark fantasies of
Orton with Beckett, Barnes and Heathcote Williams for their
common interest in 'ecstatic or demonic states of being'[6] as
expressed in plays which assimilate aspects of absurdism and
expressionism to produce intense, savage comedy, 'confronting
and exploring madness and its relation to ecstasy and enlighten-
ment'.[7] This is another line of descent which may owe something
to the dislocated mind of the Jacobean malcontent but should not
be expressly identified with its direct influence. The political
playwrights emergent in the 1970's certainly share a fascination
with characters who slip their socio-psychological leash to
become, intermittently or permanently, a force of naked, gleeful,
destructive energy, impressing their individuality and defiance on
an indifferent, sham or malevolent social environment. Shaw's
life-force visionaries were the only sane people in an insane world,
Jimmy Porter's harangues sprang from a partly-acknowledged
but ultimately private neurosis, Bond reinvented one of the oldest
literary models of the 'mad' social critic in Lear, and Mercer's
Morgan and Flint asserted their individuality in passionate,
volatile and 'anti-social' ways. However, the revolts of Maurice
and Perowne, Gethin Price, Jed, Jack Beaty, Cargill, Claw,
Gocher, Kid and Buddy are altogether less comfortable or
ironically distanced eruptions of violence in response to their
society, where the rejection of conventional social role and
psychological restraint seem synonymous, liberating, simplifying
and productive in terms of the opportunities for defiance suddenly
made available (Hare's Susan Traherne is another such figure,
and the more qualified viewpoints of the patients in Edgar's *Mary
Barnes* are also relevant; whilst two separate characters in
Flannery's *Our Friends in the North* have their perceptions of
corruption dismissed as 'paranoia'). Their sudden reaction to a
gradual build-up of social pressure takes the form of a powerful
explosion of nervous energy and self-expression aimed at the
representatives, on or beyond the stage, of a conventional social
hegemony which has been identified as one enormous confidence

trick perpetuated equally by controllers and controlled. To quote William S. Burroughs (a considerable influence on Heathcote Williams):

> To conceal the bankruptcy of the reality studio it is essential that no one should be in a position to set up another reality set. The reality film has now become an instrument and weapon of monopoly. The full weight of the film is directed against anyone who calls the film into question, with particular attention to writers or artists. Work for the reality studios or else. Or else you will find out how it feels to be *outside the film*.[8]

Heathcote Williams's *AC/DC* (1970) is a seminal work, depicting the attempts of a group of characters to disentangle themselves from the 'reality film' and strike back at it (Worth highlights its Artaudian qualities at the expense of its political import[9]). *AC/DC* builds up a persuasive socially deterministic view of man with particular regard to the media's imposition of standards and personalities, identified as 'psychic capitalism'. The play's main strength is in its cumulative force and imaginative intensity in drawing the audience into a state of mind rather than presenting them with a particularly rational debate; certainly in live performance the characters can generate an atmosphere of psychological hyperactivity and criteria for imaginative revolt which are infectious, almost intoxicating. Sadie leaves her friends Gary and Melody, with their fundamentally conventional interest in 'ego loss', for the oddly symbiotic duo Maurice and Perowne who are engaged in disconnecting themselves from the barrage of media standards and even gaining revenge through sufficient generation of 'psychic static', or realisation of unconventional states of mind. The characters' identification of so many 'FAmous people' as fundamentally anonymous facets of a psychological conspiracy to steal the individual's instinctual patterns is an intensified version of an increasingly convincing truth; as for their revolt, Melody's shocked allegation that Sadie is 'really Evil' draws the response (oddly satisfying in this context) 'Better than being a TV set',[10] and much of the play's shock value, as well as authority, comes from its identification of such familiar personalities as Mick Jagger, Ian Smith, Ronald Reagan, the Beatles and Timothy Leary as 'media turds' looking for someone to 'chew their clitoris', culminating in Maurice's reported slashing of

newscaster Reginald Bosanquet and Perowne's confrontation
with his appalled wife to justify the attack:

> Your husband's altering the shape of my face . . . currently
> posing as my phantom limb, and trying to flatter me by asking
> me whether he can work the seams in my head which consist
> entirely of his own waste products.
> . . .
> All he's ever said to me is: This is the semantic stratum in
> which you shall live, move and have your being, and if you
> move out of it, what means have I got to report your death?[11]

AC/DC accurately captures a great deal of late-1960s sense of
protest and shares its weaknesses, in that Perowne, Maurice and
Sadie are in continuous danger of forsaking external action and
meaning in favour of a retreat into a vague private cosmology, and
their protest finally ends in immolation of the self for the personal
high rather than assertion of the self in and for a public sphere of
reference. Nevertheless, they attain a radical perspective which
an audience is likely to find haunting and to some extent
persuasive.

A more conventional but equally forceful work is Trevor
Griffiths's *Comedians* (1975), which like Osborne's *The Entertainer*
(1957) uses the comedian's relationship with his audience as a
metaphorical index to the state of British society, but with
important departures. The comedians' tutor, Eddie Waters, has
the music-hall background and ideal of dialogue with an audience
that recall Archie Rice and his final crushing failure to achieve
reciprocity with his public. Both Waters and his pupil Gethin
Price are ideologically opposed to the recipe for easy success
advanced by the London agent Challenor, who prescribes
complete subservience to an audience's tastes and prejudices with
the common aim of 'escape'. Waters has contrastingly taught his
pupils that a real comedian

> *dares* to see what his listeners shy away from, fear to express.
> And what he sees is a sort of truth, about people, about their
> situation, about what hurts or terrifies them, about what's
> hard, above all, what they *want* . . . a true joke, a comedian's
> joke, has to do more than release tension, it has to *liberate* the
> will and desire, it has to *change the situation.*[12]

Similarly, he asserts that 'Comedy is medecine. Not coloured sweeties to rot their teeth with',[13] a claim that his creator might advance for the theatre as a whole. But in his programme for 'changing the situation', Waters resembles the recurrent Griffiths humanitarian (compare Gramsci, Waite) who is complemented by the similarly dissatisfied but less sentimental activist – Kabak, William, Lenin, in this case Gethin Price – who questions the efficacy of the more traditional paths to change. Price is edgy, volatile and brilliant, with the rebellious determination 'I stand in no line. I refuse my consent',[14] and characteristically presents *his* view of society's prejudices through his act rather than Challenor's view, or even Waters's. Price's turn requires the theatre audience to enact the role of the working men's club audience and endure the baiting and ultimate violence to which he subjects two incommunicative dummies, '*well-dressed beautiful people, a faint, unselfconscious arrogance in their carriage . . . perhaps waiting for a cab to show after the theatre*'.[15] The savagery of Price's chilling, flawless demonstration of class hatred is likely to be too naked and accurate to suit the patrons of the working mens' club, let alone the safe, majority hostilities Challenor wants endorsed or the peace of mind of the actual middle-class theatre audience who recognize the dummies as their own representatives in this disastrous lack of communicative reciprocity (particularly when Price falls back on the tribal self-reassurance 'we're coming up *there* where we can gerrat yer'[16]). Mocked by the lack of response, his bovver boy clown explains 'There's people'd call this *envy*, you know, it's not, it's hate',[17] and desperately escalates his attempts to crack the cold veneer of their silence, ending in a horrific image of violence when he pins a rose to the female dummy's dress – which is quickly stained by a crawl of blood from a pierced vein beneath. Eddie berates his tactics, if not his objectives, for being 'ugly. It was drowning in hate. You can't change tomorrow on that basis. You forget a thing called . . . the truth'; 'We gotta get deeper than hate.'[18] Gethin counters 'You think the truth is *beautiful*? You've forgotten what it's *like*'; 'I can't paint your pictures. (*Points to eyes*) These see.'[19] The respect but separation of Waters and Price is a rich dramatic metaphor for many schisms, between generations, comedians, politicians and playwrights, yet perfectly enclosed within the play's naturalistic framework. But the unforgettable image which the audience will retain from the play is bound to be that of Price, the chilling clown veering off the

conventional rails to present his own forceful warning image of
class violence and later exulting 'It was all ice out there tonight. I
loved it. I felt . . . expressed.'[20] Thus, in the words of Griffiths
himself, he 'smashes the categories' of convention, remains
'unremittingly hard and decisive, discovers himself and takes the
first steps towards repossessing himself'[21] (and Price's fierce
integrity in defiance of potential commercial patronage recurs in
Finn, a skinhead in Griffiths's 1982 play *Oi for England* who
smashes his band's equipment rather than let them be used and
sponsored by an extremist right-wing group).

Howard Brenton began writing cruel, black, vital cartoon-like
plays for the touring Portable Theatre group in the late 1960s and
early 1970s. David Hare, one of the founders of the group, has
claimed that many of the Portable shows depicted 'tightly knit
social situations in extreme decay',[22] and this is certainly a
common theme throughout Brenton's work, but so is a concern
with the (de)mythologizing of heroism. Just as Arden and D'Arcy
were concerned to explore the political and social myths of the
establishment and expose them as sentimental (self-)deceptions
in *The Hero Rises Up* (1968) and *The Island of the Mighty* (1972) and
Bond presented a deliberately surprising perspective on Shakespeare in *Bingo* (1974), Brenton showed an early interest in
depicting the internal confusion and defeat of supposedly exemplary historical figures – with all due consequences for the society
whose finest ponts they are held to embody – in *Wesley* (1970), *Scott
of the Antarctic* (1971) and later Churchill in *The Churchill Play*
(1974). These deconstructions of conventional heroes are
interestingly balanced by the protagonists of Brenton's other
early plays, Christie in *Christie in Love* (1969), Hans in *Hitler Dances*
(1972) and Jed in *Magnificence* (1973), savage homicidal figures
who make unlikely vehicles for widespread sympathy because of
their extreme divergence from conventional norms of behaviour
and belief; nevertheless, Brenton is careful to demonstrate their
humanity, especially compared to the self-styled guardians of
order who shrink from extending sympathy or understanding,
with the result that these deviants become, to some extent, almost
Everyman figures. Christie's brand of 'love' exposes a double
standard in a society whose moral guardians believe in conventional sickly-romantic notions of love but also amuse themselves
with sexually antagonistic limericks and urge Christie to re-enact
his crimes with almost voyeuristic glee, but also so that they can

brand him a demi-devil and dissociate themselves from him. Hans, the dead Nazi soldier of *Hitler Dances*, is both hapless victim and inner demon of a repressive, depersonalizing society – a human 'dog beneath the skin' who represents the violence still haunting the politics of Europe and an errily fascinating spirit of cruelty crouching in many a psychic recess. Jed in *Magnificence* is a true modern malcontent, but, importantly, only emerges as such at the end of the first half of the play. The first three scenes take pains to demonstrate the humanity, idealism and powerlessness of the activist squatters to an audience who may not initially feel much kinship with them. The change in Jed is then established as a warped expression of these qualities against a warped society that has been shown as brutal and denying any real possibility of peaceful change. Brenton has stated 'I'm very interested in people who could be called saints, perverse saints, who try to drive a straight line through very complex situations, and usually become honed down to the point of death.'[23] Jed, like Gethin Price, is a splendidly theatrical example of the uncompromising individual who is determined to assert his ideals and repossess his individuality with an almost manic concentration of purpose and unflinchingly direct action, 'Honed down. Pure, Angry.'[24] However, Jed's companions, once 'Diamond at the core', have become softened and conventional, and the theories of Lenin which once inspired now seem to have little relevance to comfortable, resilient British society. Like Gethin in his determination to wrench some sort of reaction out of his dummies and audience, Jed is principally concerned to register his own destructive protest against the apathetic complacency of society's calm facade (which also constituted a maddening taunt for Maurice and Perowne): 'Right through their silver screen. Disrupt the spectacle. The obscene parade, bring it to a halt! Scatter the dolly girls, let advertisements bleed. . . . Bomb 'em, again and again!'[25] The Tory MP Alice is identified as a suitable incarnation of respectability and complacency to serve Jed's purposes as a target:

JED: It would be magnificent to have you bleeding on the lawn.
ALICE: I can't understand that. Dear God. How can any human being understand that?
JED: No, I do. Late, late summer, musky smell from the FUCKING RHODODENDRONS. An English garden with its Englishman. Done at last. DONE. Oh Mr I am deeply in

contempt of you. All of you. Bubbles, is it, in the muscle? Your nails, hair, little bits. And your mind. I am deeply in contempt of your English mind. There is BLAME THERE. That wrinkled stuff with the picture of English Life in its pink, rotten meat. In your head. And the nasty tubes to your eyes that drip Englishness over everything you see. The cool, glycerine humanity of your tears that smarms our ANGER. I am deeply in contempt of your FUCKING HUMANITY. The goo, the sticky mess of your English humanity that gums up our ears to your lies, our eyes to your crimes . . . I dunno, I dunno, what can a. . . . Do? to get it real. And get it real to you. And get at you, Mr English Public Man, with oh yeh the spectacle, the splendour of you magnificently ablaze for the delight and encouragement of all your enemies. . . . A little danger. Into our sad.[26]

Audience members who are unwilling to submit to Jed's angry dramatic logic, preferring Alice's placatory conventional social logic, run the risk of joining Alice as targets of Jed's abrasive contempt. Cliff adds some safer, more democratically socialist moralizing over Jed's corpse, which may assuage the intellect, but even in death the self-consuming Jed should retain his malcontent's grip on the emotions despite this 'disclaimer' (and Brenton's choice of epigraph from Brecht's *The Measures Taken* seems to support the more dangerous, white-hot revolutionary). Brenton's *Revenge* (1969) and his collaboration with David Hare, *Brassneck* (1973), are more savagely humorous works in the style of Jacobean city comedies, but fiercely contemporary in their identifications of public greed and corruption. The two extremes of *Revenge*'s society, old lag Hepple and MacLeish of the Yard – significantly played by the same actor – view themselves as grand revengers locked in a titanic feud, which their author prefers to play in an ironic, mock-heroic profusion of crooks and more stupid crooks. The simplistic brutality of the policeman strikes a particularly Ortonian note, and the relationship of Hepple and MacLeish is a comic anticipation of that of Byrne and Paisley in McGrath and Boyle's *The Hard Man* (1977). But Hepple finally has a nightmare which ends his inflated view of their struggle as well as Brenton's ironically cartoon-like account of their adventures:

Funny. My dreams of a criminal England, it's all come true

with the 1980's. The casino towns, the brothel villages, the cities red with blood and pleasure. Public life the turn of the card the fall of a dice. The whole country on the fiddle, the gamble, the open snatch, the bit on the side . . .

We need not have bothered. Ours weren't such a cosmic struggle, were it, after all.[27]

Society has made even Hepple and MacLeish outdated by virtue of their black-and-white perceptions of it, and the final image of a society too indiscriminately criminal even for them ends the play on a challengingly cynical note. *Brassneck* uses the same amoral zest to hoist society by its own petard of corruption, as Alfred Bagley, like Jonson's *Volpone*, uses the bait of his own wealth to attract and exploit a less intelligent gallery of grotesque gulls. *Brassneck* has a panoramic breadth in its perceptive assembly of would-be leading social types and almost recognizable political personalities, all set to the counterpoint of various social rituals, from familial to national, which have become further tools in the monopoly game of social advancement, 'human pomp and fine displays' concealing 'splendid plans that never tally' while the 'dinosaurs' of the old order like Bagley and Roderick fade away.[28] In their place emerges Sidney Bagley, who takes his uncle's ruthless teachings to their logical extreme and moves into organized crime, strip clubs and ultimately drug dealing, demonstrating the thin line between socially approved exploitation and the less respectable variety. Whilst Alfred seemed partially motivated by disillusion and revenge against the upper classes, Sidney is a mere unscrupulous crook; all the other characters, even the supposed left-wing politicians, compromise themselves to the point of ineffectuality and only remain as the grist to the Bagley's mill, a comically handled diagnosis of Britain in 'The last days of capitalism'.

Like the *Marat/Sade* and *Comedians*, *The Churchill Play* (1974) makes the theatre audience party to a self-conscious performance for which a particularly bemused or shocked group of spectators is stipulated to be present on the outskirts of the stage, providing the audience with an exaggeratedly scandalized model of conventional repulsion at the plays' subject matter, as well as the chance to see the plays strike home and catch the consciences of the spectators. This is another polarizing device, in that the theatre audience will be mindful of the personified forces of decorum

which the performers should view as a constraint, but prefer to
treat as a target, as they play 'To them. At them.'[29] To react like
the surrogate audience is to lay oneself open to the same charges
that are levelled at the surrogate audience (snobbery, complacency, complicity in social repression, self-congratulatory class-
consciousness), whereas to sympathize with the performers'
aggressive efforts is to side with a subversive force. In *The Churchill
Play*, Captain Thompson and his wife provide an apparently
convenient 'middle ground' repository for audience sympathy,
being discontented with their assigned roles in Camp Churchill –
particularly Thompson, who attempts to check the overt brutality
of his subordinates and effect a liberal humanistic reconciliation
with the imprisoned 'subversives'. This may seem an unlikely
juncture at which to introduce a comparison with Galsworthy,
but it is informative to consider the earlier dramatist's treatment
of the liberal conscience alongside Brenton's. Barthwick in *The
Silver Box* is, like Thompson, worried by his complicity in a
repressive social system, but their senses of guilt are no help in
bringing them to decisive plans of remedial action. Galsworthy's
attitude to Barthwick remains sympathetic even in his moral
paralysis, whereas Brenton's attitude to Thompson is scarcely
less contemptuous than that of the fascist Sergeant Baxter, who is
worth comparing to Lemmy in *The Foundations*. Lemmy's experience of the First World War gave a keen threatening edge to his
radicalism; once the Englishman is trained to shed blood, he
claimed, he will continue mechanically, 'Conservative by nature'.
Brenton's Sergeant similarly elects to come in from the cold war,
but with the opposite ideological conclusions.

SERGEANT: Ten years the ordinary soldier has scrubbed your
bedpan. That you may not smell the terrorist in the street.
Soldier Tom doorway to doorway, bullet in the jugular bullet in
the crotch. Ten years down Ulster then English streets. Then
the late seventies and the laws against industrial unrest. Soldier
boy at the picket line, working men 'is own kind comin' at 'im
yellin' Scab Scab. (*Scoffs*) I went down a mine, a corporal then,
in the strike o' nineteen eighty. The miners o' that pit tried to
kill us, y'know that? Only time I've ever been in Wales.
'Women spit very hard. At Corporals anyway. (*Formal again*)
The British Army's got politicized, y'see, Sir. You should be
very glad we've not gone red.

THOMPSON: What have you gone? Black?
SERGEANT: Way o' putting it, Sir.[30]

At least Serjeant Musgrave brought his madness back to his own
doorstep out of a sense of compassionate outrage. Brenton, like
McGrath and Boyle in *The Hard Man*, sees an even less palatable
possibility, namely that liberal society will someday have to face
the brutalization of the 'refuse system' it depends on but prefers
not to acknowledge. Brenton is ready to give dramatic weight to
Baxter's opinion in one matter: that Thompson's fence-sitting
earns him (and all who identify with him) the title of 'fucking
namby pamby Sunday School do-gooder fucking lily-white
bleeding heart'.[31] Caroline Thompson's ideal is not to find the
strength to intervene in the brutalization of Camp Churchill, but
to move away from and forget it; but she is faced with the
consequences of her irresponsibly individualistic priorities in the
prisoners' armed insurrection:

> CAROLINE: (*at* JIMMY) A house. Why do you sneer at that? . . .
> Not wrong to want that. In peace. Grow the vegetables.
> Recycle. Save the heat of your own body. Sunlight for power. A
> glass roof, and plants growing, under the eaves. Yes. And
> children in bright clothes. On the swing. On the lawn. That's
> what I want. That's not obscene, is it? The house. The lawn.
> The plants. The children playing . . . that's not obscene . . .
> JIMMY: Want a house do you, lady? What, with a garden? Yeah,
> are barbed wire round t'stop dirty animals like me getting in?
> Oh Lady, Neo-Luddites'll come out a the dark. Right through
> plate glass window of your house. Kick in your three-D colour
> telly. And paraffin on your fancy furniture. And burn you, burn
> you bright.
> CAROLINE: What have I ever done to you?
> JIMMY: You put me in 'ere, Lady.[32]

Brenton and Jimmy's slash through Caroline's bourgeois idealism is harshly ideological – unlike the primarily moral puncturing
of the smug families in *The Silver Box*, *The Foundations* or *An Inspector
Calls* – and in this unremitting vision of class culpability, even
Wesker's Dave and Ada Simmonds might be branded as the
enemy. Brenton's crisis-ridden prophecy of political extremism is
a fiercely effective dramatization of the 'all or nothing' criterion of

political sympathy. The Second World War and its hero Churchill are identified as a further symptom of the continuing class war under Brenton's Marxist analysis, and the mythical reply of the war-stricken common people, 'We can take it, guv, give it 'em back', is exposed as the crucially different 'We can take it. . . . But we might just give it back to you one day.'[33] Brenton's extrapolation of contemporary political tendencies to this bleak nightmare vision challenges the audience to prevent it being born, highlighting how 'We are all caught up in some vast conspiracy of obedience. Who is responsible? None of us, all of us',[34] but also demonstrating how the recognition of this is not, alone, sufficient. This is also the main theme of the subsequent short play *The Saliva Milkshake* (1975) in which Martin, 'not a political person', is appalled by Joan's revolutionary determination and reports her to the forces of 'order' for a more recognizable and placid England, only to have Joan's diagnoses of its fundamental brutalities confirmed. Martin, the informant, is judged a dangerous threat to his country as 'like many a Liberal Conscience you dallied that night, you. . . . swung on a hair's breadth'; and Martin's horrified reaction 'This is England, England. Not a police state' earns the reply 'That. . . . depends on who you are.'[35] Martin is finally maimed, caught between forces he failed to comprehend, in a concise exposition of the weaknesses of what Bela in Howard Barker's *No End of Blame* identifies as 'The Woods Option'.

Brenton's next play, *Weapons of Happiness* (1976), depicts the collision of the worlds of Josef Frank, a Czechoslovakian veteran of Stalinist purges, and a group of striking South Londoners, crystallized by the surprisingly Ossian Flint-like romance between Frank and enthusiastic young activist Janice. The interplay of generations and experiences produces no striking conclusion to match Griffiths's *Comedians*; in fact *Weapons of Happiness* is closer to *The Party* in its concentration on the tangles in the heritage and activities of the Left, lamenting the lack of a conscious and coherent tradition of revolt in the general consciousness. *Epsom Downs* (1977) is a return to the social panorama with many echoes of Jonson's *Bartholomew Fair* in its massive tapestry of holiday characters, unusually light-hearted for Brenton yet still socially perceptive and vitally pungent. The darkest note is when the Ghost of Emily Davidson appears to the modern housewife Margaret as a personification of a tradition of revolt, not unlike

Josef Frank, and urges Margaret to cut loose from the prevailing jolly mediocrity and assert her protest, as Jed wished to:

> GHOST: It's only a white rail. You could jump. Push the copper over. Crack the windscreen with your knife.
> MARGARET: It's got butter on. Be blood and Anchor butter, all over the place.
> GHOST: England at peace on Derby day. It is just a picture, thin as paint. Slash it.
> MARGARET: What's the point? They're bound to have a spare Queen in the boot.
> GHOST: See the dirty wall behind.[36]

However, their debate is resolved in a festive moment of mutual sympathy, a harmonious comic variation on the subsequent savagery of *Sore Throats* (1979) in which an oppressed wife, Judy, succeeds in breaking through the violent prison hidden beneath her conventional marriage and repossesses herself through grim, gruelling defiance. Brenton's collaboration with Tony Howard, *A Short Sharp Shock!* (1980) is a grotesque cartoon caricature of the contemporary Conservative government's rise to power, a broad if unpretentious slice of agitprop which ends with the Prime Minister challenging the audience:

> MARGARET: And you know, though I be small-minded, ignorant, and the ruin of you, you will vote for me in 1984.
>   Or the British will have to make Socialism work. And you daren't, dare you?
> *She points at her buttocks.*
>   Kiss![37]

Contrastingly, *The Romans in Britain* (1980) has an ambitious epic sweep, for which the Preface to Arden and D'Arcy's *The Hero Rises Up* might have furnished a very relevant epigraph:

> When the Romans came to Britain, they came as a determinedly 'rectilinear' people of very *progressive* inclinations. Everything in this *conservative* 'curvilinear' island was to be IMPROVED . . . with symmetry and efficiency, and, above all, *done properly*. The native Celts never entirely submitted.[38]

Arden and D'Arcy's *The Island of the Mighty* also sounds echoes of possible influence in *The Romans in Britain*, particularly with regard to the cool, ironic characterization of the latter play's numerous characters. In fact, the first half of *The Romans* has a sometimes scrappy quality from the violent mobilization of so many characters, hardly any of whom manage to establish any authority or focal role before their deaths. No doubt this is a deliberate effect, but the consequent apparent shapelessness hinders audience attempts to perceive its narrative direction; the pattern only emerges at the end of Part One, when the Britons' talk of resistance gains increasing parallels with current civilian resistance to the British Army's presence in Northern Ireland, and these parallels are made overt with the entrance of Caesar and his troops in modern battledress. The second part of the play is more successful, as the modern English undercover agent Chichester hallucinates a flashback to 515 AD and the passing of the Roman order. Placing contemporary British military activity in Northern Ireland in a tradition of Roman–Celtic struggles had a disorienting effect for the National Theatre audience, as it re-established the fact that the original Britons were, in fact, the Celts, and the invading Romans the forebears of the English race, which has surprising consequences for national mythology, as Chichester points out:

> King Arthur! Celtic warlord. Who fought twelve great battles against the Anglo-Saxons. That is, us.
>
> Ha! Very fashionable, the Celts, with the arty-crafty. Ley-lines. Druids. But show them the real thing – an Irishman with a gun, or under a blanket in an H-block and they run a mile.
>
> If King Arthur walked out of those trees, now – know what he'd look like to us? One more fucking mick.[39]

However, Chichester's cover blends with his real personality and he suffers from the growing gnawing conviction that 'I am the great wrong in Ireland', which he dies lamenting ('Because in my hand there's a Roman spear. A Saxon axe. A British Army machine gun / The weapons of Rome, invaders, Empire'[40]). This grim self-accusation dies with him, but the contrapuntal Saxon episodes provide a more optimistic recipe for progress, as Corda and Morgana reject their Celtic father's pagan superstition and the two English cooks renounce their allegiance to their moribund Roman mistress, and the four join in a fruitful alliance freed from the oppressive weight of their heritage of hostility. Whereas *The Island of the Mighty* was a complete demythologization of the Arthurian legend, *The Romans in Britain* leaves the legend, if not the historical period, as a lyrical ideal, invented by the quartet to symbolize an age of peace 'lost and yet to come'. Despite its sharper second half, *The Romans in Britain* forms an oddly undigested whole, as if not all its ideas were expressed with Brenton's usual clarity and force, but *Thirteenth Night* (1981) avoids any such objections. Sub-titled 'A Dream Play', it combines speculation on the viability of socialist ideals in future British government with a compelling thriller quality in a witty parallel to *Macbeth*, as is indicated by the name of the protagonist, Jack Beaty. Injured in a scuffle following a local Labour Party meeting, Beaty suffers an hallucination which gives him the chance to fulfil his ideal of contesting for power as a truly socialist force in British party politics. Three anarchists, Rose, Cygna and Joan, fill the roles of the Wierd Sisters to tell how power can be Beaty's if he takes advantage of the current government's distance from the popular voice, and his ruthless mistress Jenny Gaze encourages his ambitions. But as well as realising the initial plot-lines of *Macbeth* in modern terms, *Thirteenth Night* presents a perceptive view of the British political machinery and the difficulties it poses for any attempt at effective radical change – the reigning Prime Minister Bill Dunn being a complacent social democrat as ill-equipped for strong leadership as Chavender in Shaw's *On the Rocks*. Having given the audience some of his persuasive oratory (like Gramsci in *Occupations*), Beaty is driven to bear comparisons with Stalin and Cromwell by personally leading a revolution with the aid of Ross, chief of police, only to find that the maintenance of an effective regime necessitates further violence, hardness and gradual isolation. His final reflection on the partiality of his success recalls Andy Cobham's embittered review of the 'patchwork' accomplished in *Their Very Own and Golden City* (Beaty addresses the audience directly, asking 'But what do you expect? Someone must take it up. Authority, the banner, the will. . . . You're going to have blood on your hands. You're going to have your dead. Eh, comrades?'[41]). But Beaty's growing necessary detachment from his former electorate has provoked the wrath of Rose, Cygna and Joan. The *Macbeth* parallel forms the basis of a surprising departure when Ross appeals for aid against Beaty from the exiled Murgatroyd, and adds the report of the death of Murgatroyd's family; however, Murgatroyd does *not* prove to be the Macduff *ex machina*, but thwarts the audience's literary and conventional expectations by drowning. Returned to everyday consciousness, Beaty speaks of a cautionary vision of an ideologically 'successful' future which turned repulsive. However, given the political climate which confronts Beaty and the results he achieves – a truly socialist Britain, withdrawn from Ireland and independent of a satellite role to either America or Russia – his 'embraces of the butcher' seem necessary acts, and present a grimly realistic assessment of the machinery of power rather than a liberal shrinking from their consequences. The final destructive intervention of the anarchists seems irresponsible, an interesting progression on Brenton's part from his early anarchic anger to a more reasoned if equally determined consideration of the path to consistent socialist government. *Thirteenth Night*'s investigation of the ethics of revolt effectively answers the criticism of Brenton and his peers that they can only make negative or destructive responses.

Brenton's adaptation of Brecht's *The Life of Galileo* for the National Theatre in 1980 informs his next original play, *The Genius* (1983), almost as much as *Macbeth* does *Thirteenth Night*. Acerbic American mathematician Leo Lehrer is exiled to an English Midlands university for trying to influence the use of his own theories of nuclear physics, only to encounter student Gilly, who has arrived at similar theories independently. Gilly's sense of study and ideas as apolitical may be shared by the audience, but Leo demonstrates otherwise, replacing the intellectual thrill of Galileo's lessons for Andrea with her grim baptism into a spiral of apocalyptic terror. Their attempt at what the Vice-Chancellor dismisses as 'CND street theatre' fails to dent the poise of an end-of-term garden party, even when Gilly arrives in the guise of a flashburn victim (a dislocating moment of pretence akin to the wounded Dervish who tears off his own arm in *The Churchill Play*). As in *The Saliva Milkshake*, the tidy inertia of English life turns out to mask a web of Kafkaesque political crosscurrents; and, as in Shaw's *Major Barbara*, society's power structures are shown to converge inexorably on the arms race, with liberal humanist notions (in this case, university arts studies and 'academic freedom') rendered pathetically irrelevant. Like Galileo, Leo falls to the temptation of despair, recantation and, in this case, cocaine; but Gilly galvanizes her tutor in malcontented political awareness so that he joins the women characters' protest at a Greenham-like arms base, after they have attempted to strike a blow against 'Father Death' by delivering the new wave of secrets to the Russian embassy to preserve a balance of power ('There was a cat sitting up in the ivy, by the steps. She blinked at me and said "Meow! What have you done?" "Done something at least, my dear" I said'[42]). The open ending, reminiscent of *The Churchill Play*, initially feels unsatisfying, and the embrace of Gilly and Leo seems impractically cosy when their comrades are storming the wire fence against a barrage of police. Nevertheless, the play's terrible sense of its (and our) potential ending can hit the audience with fierce starkness, and suggest that the only hope lies with the example provided by the likes of Gilly and Leo – a new form of 'genius' in the sense of guiding figures who will take arms against the mutations of scientific knowledge, not shy away from their implications in comfortable ivory towers. The play's hope (and, it suggests, the world's), however tenuous, lies with those prepared to do 'something, at least'.

The television play *Desert of Lies* (1984) juxtaposes two expeditions into the Kalahari desert, fuelled respectively by the missionary zeal of an English puritan family and journalist Sue's hunger for experience, and a tale of 'hope and violence' for her newspaper. Both attitudes are identified as forms of misplaced idealism and perceptual imperialism which Europe seeks to impose on Africa, and both expeditions break down into internal dissent and fatality. Only Sue survives, with experience more immediate and challenging than she bargained for. She returns to London with first-hand knowledge of bush life and a half-caste child, crucially outside the European-designed 'reality film' image of Africa and refusing to perpetuate it through her projected articles: 'I just got lost in the desert. Why tell lies about it?'. Brenton blends the nightmarish desert raptures of both parties in a witty and powerful image of (self-)deceptive global mythologies and personal extremity which smashes social categorization.

Howard Barker's plays have a similar witty, violent astringency to those of Brenton. Although Barker's intense images of conflict may not have the consistency of Brenton's, they can spangle with an even more successful black humour, and proceed from a wry perception of society as a tissue of legitimate or non-legitimate crime, expressed here by Udy in *The Hang of the Gaol*:

> It came to pass, in this unspecific time I am referring to, that a sufficient number of English yobbos, weary of endless slash and chivvy, agreed to offer up their rights to one sole ruler who would adjudicate and carry out the GBH on their behalf, when this happened, we don't know. In the darkest crevice of the past. But it happened and we got THE LAW.[43]

Given this vision of society as a predatory jungle, Barker's characters tend to be either those who perceive the pattern and identify with it overtly in acts of crime and exploitation, moral compromisers who perpetuate it beneath a hypocritical facade, or those who remain on the respectable side of society but turn it to their advantage, having learnt 'the hang of the gaol'. Amongst all this, any character attempting to find firm moral ground is apt to become confused and disillusioned even to the point of dementia; as Barker claims, 'The theme of moral exhaustion is a major one in my plays'.[44] Like Brenton, Barker has no sympathy for those who coast along, however guiltily, on top of a corrupt society, but sympathizes with those who, despite massive opposition, attempt to strike a blow for personal and political integrity in the dark fantastic cartoon-like odysseys they are made to endure. The title character of *Stripwell* (1975) is an admittedly jaded and weary guardian of the law, brought into sharp confrontation with basic human issues when an offender, Cargill, threatens revenge. The judge's secret liaison with a stripper and his supposedly socialist wife's lack of consistent principle combine to create an atmosphere of privileged decadence which son Tim takes to its logical conclusion, like Sidney Bagley in *Brassneck*: his naked self-interest finds perfect expression in heroin smuggling, an essential distillation of corruption outdating Stripwell and his kind. The judge at least becomes increasingly aware that something is rotten, an insight the other characters are unable or unwilling to attain. He concludes 'there is no public morality without a corresponding private one. And there is no change without indignation'[45] and shops his son. But this moral stand comes too late to be effective beyond Stripwell's immediate family, and Cargill, the man imprisoned for asserting 'an ill-defined sense of grievance and social injustice', appears for revenge on Stripwell and his passing order. Like Jed in *Magnificence*, Cargill is almost dissuaded from his course by the articulateness of his prospective victim, but his final 'No!' is a belated answer to Stripwell's plea for a separation between gut feeling and practical action, the divorce on which his kind have hitherto prospered.

The highly original hero of *Claw* (1975), otherwise known as Noel Biledew, is a fiercely unglamorous, bathetic avenger who forms a sharp and telling contract to the almost compensatory social attractiveness or sexual potency many previous dramatists have granted their disillusioned rebels (from John Tanner and Ayamonn Breydon to Jimmy Porter, Pip Thompson and John Clare). This gives Noel's exploits a splendidly comic, mock-heroic edge, but also gives the character a final sense of sympathetic vulnerability. Noel's youthful unpopularity soon sets him apart from society, and the teachings of his communist father are uncertainly assimilated (trying to sell a comrade to a policeman has a comic distance from the 'carrying anthrax' into the 'woolly nests' of the bourgeoisie he thinks it constitutes), but further humiliation turns Noel into an amusingly parodic, but fundamentally sincere version of the malcontent. His reading of Marx goes a step further than his father's; rather than stand against the surrounding decadence, Noel determines to aid and identify with the corruption in order to hasten the fall of capitalism and procure a little worldly success in the process. Noel's rise brings him into contact with an expanse of corruption headed by Clapcott, where Noel feels 'on the inside. The filth confronting the filth'.[46] But his self-identification with society's worst excesses proves morally untenable even for him, and his abortive attempt to register a 'No!' and kill Clapcott only brings him imprisonment, where the teachings of his more principled father ('I tried to tell you, keep your anger for your class'[47]) assume their full weight. Noel tries to win the support of his gaolers with a crucial re-write of his previous declaration of ruthless individualism. Nevertheless, at the instigation of the safe and respectable Clapcott, they do not defend him, but calmly murder him. The audience's repulsion at this chilling image reflects well onto the authority of Noel's plea, as the play's predominant ironic comedy ends in a skilful transition to haunting political immediacy.

The comic inventiveness of *Claw* is also present in the haunting, more dream-like *Fair Slaughter* (1977), which begins with Old

Gocher succeeding where Claw failed, by winning the sympathy
and co-operation of his gaoler, Leary. Carrying the icon of
communist resistance in the unlikely form of Trotsky's engine
driver's severed hand, Gocher recounts his past life in a series of
picaresque conflicts with various national institutions and political forces and running battles with arch-capitalist Staveley. At
one point, he makes his living from a music-hall act which grows
in resemblance to that of Gethin Price:

> (*Suddenly he brings his banjo down onto the floor with a tremendous
> smash. Pause. He looks around the audience.*) I have shit on you. You
> have paid to come here, and I have shit on you. No, don't laugh
> missus, I'm not ill. Stop smiling, it's not funny. It's a fucking
> tragedy. You and your wonderful good humour, your British
> talent for seeing it through, CHRIST! You would have your
> daughters in a brothel and still not lift a finger! I tell you it's not
> funny! It is not funny that we are here to laugh at our communal
> bloody misery, it is a sin![48]

Stavely naturally thinks this is a denial of Gocher's role as escapist
entertainer: 'He hates the people who come to see him. He
despises the audience who love him, and I think that's vile. I think
that's a disgusting attitude for an entertainer to adopt.'[49] Gocher
counters that 'There are times for action, and times for entertainment. And there are times when entertainment is a crime. THIS
IS ONE OF THEM.'[50] He remains unswerving in his principles
when teaching his young daughter about reality in the world
outside: 'The thing we keep bumping into, and which is never
really very nice, which is awful in fact. Despite those whoppers
they tell us, we see it and it isn't very nice'.[51] Not surprisingly, this
conviction gnaws at Gocher until he is driven to an outburst of
defiant self-assertion:

> LOOK WHAT THEY HAVE DONE TO ME BECAUSE I
> WOULD NOT PLAY THE BANJO TO THEIR BLOODY
> LIES! A FATHER AND A CHILD IN THIS DISGUSTING
> ROOM! LOOK AT THE FILTH THEY FLING US IN,
> THE BASTARDS, THE PARASITIC BASTARDS, THEY
> DRINK OUR BLOOD! I WILL KILL THEM, I WILL
> KILL THEIR BABIES, IT WILL BE A SLAUGHTER
> WHEN WE'VE FINISHED, A FAIR BLOODY
> SLAUGHTER, LET ME, GOD![52]

Gocher's attempt to ensure there are 'No more Staveleys in the world'[53] counts as 'fair slaughter', a ruthless but necessary act; but when Gocher and Leary meet Staveley again many years later, Gocher cannot repeat his homicidal resolve. Leary orders ruthlessness, but Gocher is aware it was 'humanity' which resulted in his own freedom, and capitulates to 'pity and tolerance' that he had always reviled. Whatever the ideology, Gocher urges 'Criticize. Always criticize',[54] and his stimulating impulse is later reincarnated by Barker in Bela Veracek and Galactia.

Barker's next trio of plays, *That Good Between Us* (1977), *The Hang of the Gaol* (1978) and *The Love of a Good Man* (1978), seem slightly less successful than *Claw* or *Fair Slaughter*. *That Good Between Us* has a by now familiar basis in a nightmare vision of a repressive future, where the Home Secretary has been granted unconditional power. The uniform corruption of the self-interested characters recalls the first half of *The Romans in Britain* in that no character of any great dramatic or moral authority is allowed to emerged for the audience to refer to as a point of stability. McPhee has vitality but remains oblivious to the import of much that he is involved in; and Godber resembles a non-comic version of the early Claw, willing to identify himself completely with the system he serves in order to make himself a 'star' on its own terms – but he fails to make Claw's final growth to moral insight. McPhee survives principally because of his innocence, but this seems tenuous protection for the future against such a climate of unscrupulous egoists whose mutual extermination fails to generate much of a coherent pattern, let alone reassurance. Neither does *That Good Between Us* explain the transition from the current situation to the future nightmare as pointedly as *The Churchill Play*. *The Hang of the Gaol* depicts official whitewashing and impotent democratic socialism, to the point that a young government investigator Ponting is driven mad by the decadence he witnesses, only to return and reassume his 'dangerous' position inside the system, like Godber. As in *That Good*, the characters are generally powerless in a society careering uncontrollably into greater and greater decay, with the result that much of the dramatic conflict can be insufficiently substantial. *The Love of a Good Man* is more effective, a savage black comedy on profiteering from the immediate legacy of the First World War. The Prince of Wales's embarrassment at the suffering concerned does little to help the dead or redeem him, as it goes untranslated into any practical action, although the contractor-undertaker Hacker comes to a form of self-awareness. *The Loud Boy's Life* (1980) traces the rise of an Enoch Powell-like politician whose questionable rise to power nevertheless marks him as an individual symptomatic of his times – his apparent appeal being that 'He is, for an ashamed people, The Man Who Is Not Ashamed.'[55]

No End of Blame returns more to the style of *Fair Slaughter*, and is probably Barker's best play to date. Sub-titled 'Scenes of Overcoming', it traces the international pilgrimage and political development of Bela Veracek as *Fair Slaughter* did of Gocher, both of whom are artists concerned to hold a responsible mirror up to society. *No End of Blame* gains considerable effect from the running contrast of Bela to his friend Grigor; when the play opens on a First World War battlefield, Bela has attained a characteristic Barker insight into the flimsiness of 'official' morality, how given the atrocities they are required to commit in national service 'I do not understand a morality which says we have to draw a line at petty theft.'[56] Grigor, in contrast, is loath to endorse even the radical 'fair slaughter' of an officer who has just threatened the duo's lives. The temperamental gap between them continues into their studies at Budapest Institute of Fine Art, where Bela, like Gethin Price, literally cannot draw his tutor's visions, or follow the order to 'look for beauty everywhere' and become 'a high priest in the temple art';[57] neither can Bela be interested in still life like Grigor, to whom emotion and animation are disruptive anathema; instead, Bela prefers the harsh didactic shock of the less pretty and durable but more instant and widely-seen cartoon ('I don't want to be a painter. I hate oils, studios, manipulating colours inches thick. Give me ink, which dries quick, speaks quick, hurts') and his test of art is 'I STIRRED THE POLICE, THEREFORE, I TOUCHED THE TRUTH.'[58] They forsake their studies for Russia, in the shared company of fellow student Ilona, only for Bela's published work to bring him into conflict with 'the line that Comrade Lenin is advancing'. The tribunal scene is a familiar device for heightened political self-justification in the face of oppressive conformity, from *Saint Joan* and *The Life of Galileo* to *Every Good Boy Deserves Favour*, and Barker adds the first of two witty and effective additions to the list, with Bela scoring dramatically off his over-eager, petty 'judges':

SECOND COMRADE: We say an artist is only free if his society is free. He cannot be free AGAINST the freedom of his society. Can he? That is intellectual sickness. (*Pause*) Isn't it? *Pause*.
BELA *stares ahead*.
BELA: I am not a good intellectual.[59]

Meanwhile, Grigor and Ilona's radicalism has evaporated leaving them longing for 'The Woods Option', the liberal dream of self-realisation through supposedly apolitical withdrawal and isolation expressed by Brenton's Caroline Thompson amongst others, and sharply demolished by Bela:

> But I don't believe, in all honesty, given the complexity of the present social and industrial machine, the woods option is a wholly satisfactory response, since the deliberate rejection of experience contributes nothing to the alleviation of human pain, nor relieves you from its consequences, or to put it brutally. . . . You don't miss the bullets by shutting your eyes![60]

Bela claims the real fight is 'against worship, it's against the surrender of your self!'[61] and asserts his passionate belief by destroying a floral tribute to Russian communism, a form of art he rejects as secular idolatry. The continuous back projections of Bela's cartoons and Grigor's drawings which punctuate the play's scenes provide a striking mutual contrast but also a visual guide, in the case of the cartoons, to the historical background of the play, such as Bela's vivid Hitlerine bat on the eve of the Second World War. Now exiled in England, Bela clings to his conviction 'I believe the cartoon to be the lowest form of art. I also believe it to be the most important form of art'; 'The cartoon changes the world. The painting changes the artist. I long to change the world. I hate the world.'[62] In return, his RAF camp audience gives Bela the injunction to tackle moral contradictions head-on and expose the unglamorous truths of war, the sort revealed by the internees' 'Churchill Play':

> Draw the real war. Not Hitler. Easy hating Hitler. Too easy for a man like you. Draw the real war, will you? The war which goes on beneath the war? The long war of the English people.[63]

The result is that Bela finds himself before a second tribunal for criticizing the line that Mr Churchill is advancing, and, despite

Bela's claim that 'My politics are to look for the truth, and when you find it, shout it',[64] a second compromise is enforced. By means of counterpoint, Grigor is shown re-emerged in London, housed, fed and clothed by the council and tamely passing the time doing paintings-by-numbers of Windsor Castle and Yankee Winjammers, whilst Bela's job on a national paper is re-allocated to an ideological puppet whose zenith of insight is that 'life's a non-stop comedy show'. In the face of such grounds for pessimism, Bela's nihilism and scathing denunciations of British society (which carry a force equal to Mercer's in *Cousin Vladimir*) seem bleakly inevitable, climaxing in a humorously hindered suicide attempt and a final senile depression in a mental hospital, familiar repository of the impotent idealist. When Grigor's latest form of 'worship' – psychic powers – seems confirmed, Bela is even ready to surrender his self-respect and condemn himself as mad. At this point, *No End of Blame* looks set to finish on what has become a clichéd image in the political play: the rebellious protagonist, tragically crushed and demented by the contradictions of his continued life in society. However, Barker upends the formula to rescue Bela from the ranks of Maugham's Eva, Mercer's Kate, Bond's Shakespeare and Clare, Brenton's Skinny Spew et al. As Glasson says:

> That isn't it. Don't give in to that. (*Pause*) You build your little temple, somewhere in the bottom of your brain, put brass doors on it, and great big hinges, burn your little flame of truth and genius and worship it, WHAT ABOUT US? (*She points to the cartoon*) ['*They grew tired of thought*'] THAT DON'T 'ELP US! (*Pause*) Assign the blame. (*Pause*) It's madness if yer don't. Cos that's how we go on, blame this, blame that, get it wrong sometimes of course, but never say we're barmy, or we will be . . .[65]

Glasson's withering of the temptations of despair gives Bela the strength to end the play on a stirringly resilient appeal to the audience:

> BELA: Give us a pencil . . . somebody . . . . (*He staggers out of the chair, advances towards audience*) Give us a pencil . . . give us a pencil . . . give us a pencil . . .
> *Fade to black*.[66]

No End of Blame manages to be inspirational without sentimentality, and its focus on the art of the cartoon simultaneously provides a powerful justification of the dramatic style of Barker and his contemporaries, to which many critics have been disappointingly, conventionally unsympathetic. *No End of Blame* itself defiantly demontrates the remarkable theatrical impact of which such a style can be capable.

Victory (1983) begins a sequence of plays set in, and concerned with, history, tracing characters' 'Choices in Reaction' to an England in revolutionary upheaval and the ravages of civil war. *Victory* shows widow Bradshaw's dogged persistence in reassembling her dismembered husband's 'bits' amidst the human flotsam of Restoration England, clinging to life and dignity like an ancestor of McPhee, but able to achieve little else. *Pity in History* (1984) is slightly more hopeful for its downtrodden characters. Set in a cathedral in 1644, it depicts the struggles of a laconic mason, Gaukroger, and his dissatisfied apprentice, Pool, who find their professional commission to carve a monument to a dead landowner becomes the pivot of violent action and impassioned debate amidst the skirmishes between an unlikely crew of down-at-heel puritan soldiers and the landowner's ruthless widow, Venables. The army captain tries to educate his cluster of bedraggled youths into a sense of class struggle, but the chaplain teaches that 'Property is the basis of all order.' Only the indignantly moribund cook Murgatroyd and the fatalist Gaukroger can cut through their inclusive philosophies to the underlying bathos, but Pool is lured by the decisive involvement of a military life, and joins up. History seems a decadent or destructive force; the captain laments that it 'comes into the quiet man's drawing room and goes barmy in his china'; Venables sees it as a disruptive 'storm' to be weathered by the conservatives who can 'keep their feet', though her property's survival is grounded on the corpse of the cook; and Gaukroger sees it as a phenomenon external to much human activity, 'we heard the cannonade and I knew, this was History coming over the hill', finally inimical to the permanence of his work, or indeed any human endeavour. But Pool deserts and rejoins Gaukroger, attempting to rouse the mason from despair by proposing a new art born of one's faith and the other's craft:

POOL: GEDDUP, GAUKROGER. . . . Find the language.

Find the style. New manner for new situation. When in doubt, invent. Cheat a little bit. Get by.

GAUKROGER: He lectures me . . .

POOL: Calamity, all right, bowled over, flat on yer back, smash-up, looks bad, admitted, but not fatal, still got 'ands, still got eye –

GAUKROGER: He exhorteth me . . .

POOL: STICK WITH IT, MICHAEL, EH?   (Scene 16)

This injunction, like Glasson's to Bela in *No End of Blame*, dredges Gaukroger back to endeavour, as the duo prepare to seek something 'real' to replace the former 'dead art'. Their relationship recalls that of Waters and Price in Griffiths's *Comedians*, but the skill of the old order is here finally reconciled with the harsher political awareness of the new, creating a further, literally progressive sense of 'history' to jostle against its other invocations. It also provides an organic development of Barker's theme of artistic style, and the need to find 'New manner for new situation'.

Scenes from an Execution (1984) continues this theme of artistic representation from *No End* and *Pity*, as Venetian artist Galactia paints the battle of Lepanto, but not from a glorifying point of view as her commission presumes. Rather she insists on stressing the unjust waste of war, like Murgatroyd in *Pity*, locating blame in the egoism of the powerful. Her untidy, passionate, painful style brings her revilement and imprisonment, then repressive tolerance which makes her, like Bela, scared of being flattened into the art of a nation concerned to demonstrate its broadmindedness. She is initially enraged that the authorities have 'SMOTHERED MY DANGER' – 'One hundred feet of pain and you LICKED IT SMOOTH' – but her painting moves the public, to whose judgement she consigns it, in at least partial acceptance of the contradictions of her role as a political artist.

Barrie Keeffe is another playwright interested in the political force of violent outburst by the socially dispossessed, although his two trilogies *Gimme Shelter* (1977) and *Barbarians* (1977) have less of the black fantastic flavour of Brenton and Barker's work. In *Gimme Shelter*, *Gem* and *Getaway* more easily fit the description of social tragedies in their portrayals of young people moving into deadeningly conventional lives without expressing, much less defeating, their innate isolation. The danger in presenting less articulate or politically conscious characters in a socially critical framework is that their protest may go insufficiently articulated to give the play a true political cutting edge; this is true to a certain extent of *Gem*, if taken in isolation, when it appears a deft piece of social naturalism. The Kid's protest in *Gotcha* has more potency as an image – holding his insensitive teachers hostage with a cigarette over a motorcycle petrol tank – and has a fantastic power and logic, whilst *Getaway* brings together both sets of characters to chart their pressurized choices of submissive existences, their emotional sense of aching isolation being a common, but unexpressed, deformation as a result of their environments. *Barbarians* traces the progress of three unemployed youths, Paul, Jan and Louis, through three separate playlets which gather a cumulative force which climaxes in the almost symbolic violence of *In the City*, where the boys' quests for solidarity and tribal security have been absorbed by the British Army and the National Front, which channel their anger at the loss of self against conveniently identifiable scapegoats such as the Irish and blacks. Paul and Jan's final attack on Louis is prepared for naturalistically, but also has an emblematic force in its departure from their previous alliance against the respectable world. The final tableau, in which Jan reluctantly beats up his friend to get himself arrested and avoid a posting to Northern Ireland, has a powerful immediacy the equal of *Gotcha* when Jan's pleading forces the audience into sharp, uncomfortable awareness of their own role in the play, which suddenly emerges after the exclusive dwelling on Paul, Jan and Louis's isolation:

JAN *kicks* LOUIS *savagely.*
LOUIS: He's only kicking me so you won't let him kill someone else.
JAN: See, I did it all. I'm a trained killer. Lock me up. To protect myself . . . and society from everything you've done to me. 'Cause, 'cause . . . otherwise I'll do it back. To you. Worse.[67]

A Mad World, My Masters (1977) is a conscious attempt to write a modern Jacobean-style city comedy and succeeds with comic gusto. A complex network of numerous vivid characters enact a plot of cheeky knavery and corruption in high places, more concerned to expose wide-spread criminal folly in every corner of society than chasten specific vices or classes. *Frozen Assets* (1978) is an interesting if inconsistent work in which, by almost a willed act of fantasy, Keeffe enables one of his volatile young victims to confront 'the people who had created the life he endured and would have to go on enduring. The hero finally met the enemy face to face'.[68] To appreciate its full force in these terms, however, requires a familiarity with Keeffe's previous work or a similar political commitment before the play begins – which cannot always be guaranteed. Nevertheless, Buddy's picaresque journey through the strata of society is highly effective when he is allowed to function as a touchstone jester, like Barker's Claw, exposing the ways in which 'Anyone with bread like this, they ain't got it legal'[69] or the ways in which the law can be manipulated from the inside – whilst he remains trapped on the outside. Keeffe's lack of authorial distance from Buddy results in some sentimental characterization, with the young refugee's final scene with Sammy becoming downright mawkish, and elsewhere the play wavers uneasily between being a grotesque comedy of modern gulls and cony-catchers or the vengeful rampage of a serious but tainted malcontent through the homes and values of those who would prefer not to acknowledge his existence (whose ranks may include the theatre audience). The contradictory impulses under-cut, rather than complement, each other, but individual scenes retain an impressive symbolic and emotional power. *Sus* (1979) is a sharp, compact, hard-hitting little play focussed at reforming a specific social iniquity, namely the 'sus' law of detention of suspects, allowing the audience to experience the unfamiliar and intensely horrific viewpoint of an interrogated suspect through the eyes of black Leon Delroy, whose growing agitation and political indignation increase alongside the policemen's anticipa-tion of a new dawn of further power. The result is an almost documentary piece of powerful agitprop, trained on a particular detail of violent hypocrisy in the legal system. Not only is Delroy's nightmare of England real, but Keeffe shows the way it could intensify in line with the policemen's chilling prophecy.

Howard Barker has justifiably expressed his concern about the 'tremendous pressure on writers to "mature" ' and the apparent reluctance of many established newspaper and literary critics to give him and his peers 'houseroom unless we develop in conventional ways (show more detachment)';[70] correspondingly, the writers in question have exhibited a distrust of many supposed artistic criteria, fearing the insulating, anaesthetizing effect of being absorbed by what they view as a fundamentally repressive tolerance. Like Bela Veracek, they prefer short-term effects, cartoon pungency and the capacity to 'hurt' in an immediately political, non-literary manner. A more constructive criticism for their future work might take the form of Orbison's words to her daughter in *That Good Between Us*: 'You have to be careful with disgust. It is so deceptive, it often tricks you into thinking it is radical. When all the time it is some strangled cry for feeling at any price. Which is not the same thing, is it?.'[71] But the considerable achievements of their dramatic power must be acknowledged, partially for their determination to 'paint their own pictures', which have often echoed Gethin Price's charge 'You think the truth is *beautiful*? You've forgotten what it's *like*', but principally for their relentless questioning, like that of the Jacobean dramatists, of the problematic potential of 'fair slaughter' – a brutally realistic critique of murder-endorsing *and* ostensibly murder-condemning social moralities. They have also been united in their demonstration that expedient self-identification with a corrupt and predatory social system might bring its short-term success to the plastic egoists who submit to it, but also how 'individualist daydreams lead only to the pit of self-disgust', if not self-immolation.[72] Accordingly, they have presented compelling and sympathetic studies of socially dislocated figures, psychologically 'honed down' but existentially authentic, bent on realizing the Burroughs goal of 'storming the reality studio' in necessary conflict with – and sometimes in open defiance of – an audience's conventional presumptions. Barker has claimed that his approach to work is 'to employ imagination to dislocate the expectations of an audience, to continually surprise them and in so doing make them confront reality with different eyes'.[73] His plays, and those of Williams, Griffiths, Brenton and Keeffe, stand as powerful realizations of the 'cartoon nightmare's' dramatic potential; and if our dramatic 'National Gallery' cannot grant due credit and exposure to 'cartoons' like *AC/DC*, *Comedians*, *Thirteenth Night* and *No End of Blame*, then it is time for its policy to be reviewed.

9 Earning a Place in the Story

DAVID HARE, DAVID EDGAR

> I have to believe there's someone, you see. Somebody else who's been living like me.
>
> *Plenty*[1]

> And I abhor apartheid's cunning. What it's done to me, by splitting me from my comrades, isolating me. Removing me from that collective strength, that stops me being just a white man with an upset conscience, places me in history, and gives my conscience scale.
>
> *The Jail Diary of Albie Sachs*[2]

As previously noted, Howard Brenton has perceived that in previous theatre, 'things would bind the audience and the performers together', things such as religion, patriotism or a sense of elegance; but in contemporary Britain 'the only thing that binds us together today is profound unease, and laughter is the language of that unease'.[3] Accordingly, Griffiths, Brenton, Barker and Keeffe have written disquieting comedies which reflect and express this sense of social disintegration to the point of locating it within the theatre audience itself and polarizing the audience with a particularly pointed demonstration of the consequence scornful or hostile energy that can ensue from this situation.

In contrast, Hare and Edgar are concerned to perceive a sense of history which can provide a sense of causality, continuity and inspiration behind the disparate, initially bemusing pattern of 'isolation in a crowd' which is the only socially sanctioned image of so much daily life. This is not to be confused with Osborne's sentimental longings for an Edwardian age he never knew, nor with Arden and D'Arcy's deconstructions of the official national

166

mythology; rather it owes more to Wesker's goal 'only connect' –
perceiving the causes of increasing social and human fragmentation – and, when necessary, to Brenton's consequent longing for a
tradition of revolt to afford encouragement towards the changing
of this situation. As Hare claims:

> We are living through a great, groaning, yawling festival of
> change – but because this is England it is not always seen on the
> streets. In my view it is seen in the extraordinary intensity of
> peoples' personal despair, and it is to that despair that as a
> historical writer I choose to address myself time and time again.
> . . .
> We are drawing close, I think, to what I hope a playwright can
> do. He can put people's suffering in a historical context; and by
> doing that, he can help to explain their pain.[4]

Hare has written a series of plays to demonstrate that the personal
is political, or that private existence is not separate from, but
profoundly influenced by, public life. Edgar has similarly noted
that 'we live in an age *defined* by a lack of any shared philosophical,
religious and artistic assumptions' which therefore lacks 'any
sense of history, of changing social circumstances, of political
developments':

> Culturally, you can see it most clearly in American television
> soap opera, a continuous series of similar domestic events,
> occurring independently of the outside world, endlessly re-
> peated situations, like the interlocking wheels and cogs of a clock,
> permanently moving round, but never moving forward. It is my
> belief that life is not like soap opera, that history does move, and
> that human behaviour is best understood not just in personal
> but also in political terms.[5]

Both playwrights view their relationships with their audiences in
complex, sophisticated but realistic terms. Hare has described the
theatre as offering 'a unique suitability to displaying an age in
which mens' ideals and men's practice bear no relation to each
other',[6] exposing and enacting the discrepancy for public judgement, remembering that 'As you can't control people's reactions
to your plays, your duty is also not to reduce people's reactions,
not to give them easy handles with which they can pigeon-hole

you, and come to comfortable terms with what you are saying';[7] whilst Edgar is particularly adept at confronting the audience 'with their own emotional response . . . to a point that I call dynamic ambiguity',[8a] which is designed to stimulate and challenge rather than offer the comparatively easy options of simple identification, dissociation, facile optimism or tragic resignation, yet still advance a consistent and persuasive response to events which is strengthened, rather than undermined, by modulations of alienation and self-criticism, the final aim being 'to present recognizable reality within a context which makes clear its place in history'.[8b]

   In Hare's first trio of major plays, *Slag* (1970), *The Great Exhibition* (1972) and *Knuckle* (1974), the translation of political and moral principles into action is conspicuous by its absence. The resultant wry, ironic satirizing of supposedly radical elements in the predominant social sterility can give the impression that the author enjoys the grist they provide for his sharp, polished comedy, to the point where the dominant tone is that of comedy of manners rather than political critique. *Slag* demonstrates how a feminist retreat from a hostile hegemony can lead to an ineffectual, self-insulating isolation rather than a discovery of individual and collective identity, as demonstrated by three teachers' loss of their pupils in their bid to maintain an austerely pure ideal. *The Great Exhibition* pointedly divides its similar acts under the headings 'Public Life' and 'Private Life' and couples jaded Labour politician Charlie Hammett with his actress wife Maud in a series of worldly-wise observations on the similarities of their professions. *Knuckle* is a more distinctive and successful tour behind the scenes of capitalism, principally because of the addition of Curly Delafield as unlikely but engaging guide who stands outside the satirized areas of society. In the pagaent of exploitation identified as Britain, Curly is the ambiguous malcontent-trickster who wavers between protest, self-identification with his environment's most reductive processes, and extrapolation of these processes into a less respectable but more honest line of commerce. As a seedy ascetic avenger with a 'smudge of indignation' he resembles Barker's Claw, but his calculatedly shocking observations in his professional role as gun-runner have an impact reminiscent of Andrew Undershaft's unsentimental embarrassments of capitalist discretion. Curly admits that his work was, as 'the noisiest profession I could find',[9]

a response to the 'silent indolence' of his father's speculating
activities but without the hypocritical charade of club-like
camaraderie and the quiet refuge of self-reassurance afforded by
private hours with Henry James. Curley's perceptions are as
unflinching as the shots he fires into the imaginary target in the
front stalls (Part One, scene three); but, like Brenton's Hepple, he
finds himself almost redundant in modern Britain:

> When I got back I found this country was a jampot for
> swindlers and cons and racketeers. Not just property. . . .
> Boarding-houses and bordellos and night-clubs and crooked
> charter flights, private clinics, horse-hair wigs and tin-can
> motor cars, venereal cafés with ice-cream made from whale
> blubber and sausages full of sawdust.[10]

The Micky Spillane/Len Deighton styled thriller form is used
skilfully in its comic transference to Guildford and its final
revelation that the 'victim' is probably alive, having contrived the
whole convoluted scheme to expose the trail of exploitation and
violence stemming from a stockbroker's readiness to swindle his
own mother in a property deal. The unglamorous realistic
departures from the conventional romantic plot model are as
important as the engaging comic familiarity produced by its
evocation. However, there is a sense that Curly and his author are
cracking black aphorisms into the moral void in a barely
successful bid to avoid being swallowed by its nihilistic despair.
Fortunately, Hare's introduction to his next play *Fanshen* (1975)
shows a consciousness of this problem:

> Nearly every outstanding piece of writing since 1900 belongs to
> a culture of dissent. Writers have been trapped in negatives,
> forced back into sniping and objection, or into the lurid colours
> of their private imaginations. At some stage they will have to
> offer positive models for change, or their function will decay as
> irrevocably as the society they seek to describe.[11]

Hare's adaptation of William Hinton's book 'seeks to explain to
an audience who have no real experience of change what exactly
that change might involve and how it can in practice be
effected',[12] and a principal strength of the play is its grounding in
real and recent events – a point which will be expanded when

discussing Edgar's adaptations. Indeed, Hare specifies that one of the actors in the Prologue should stress the book and play's common status as 'a record of one village's life between 1945 and 1949' and the fact that 'Many of the characters are still alive'.[13] The play's Chinese village setting and the cool, episodic simplicity with which its transition to communism is narrated give the play a strong Brechtian flavour which should not detract from its successful individuality. Hare is faced with the rarely-confronted problem of demonstrating the development of a collective ethic, to which intransigent individuals have to submit for the common good, and investing it with dramatic vitality – Western theatre being considerably more accustomed to responding to the reckless energy of the rebellious individual dissociating himself from a prevalent conformist mediocrity. C. W.E. Bigsby views *Fanshen* as an inadvertant critique of the collective spirit,[14] just as Martin Esslin claims that Brecht's mid-period *Lehrstücke* portray the unacceptable face of communism;[15] however, *Fanshen* in sympathetic performance can generate a genuine if unconventional compulsion. Given the requisite production style of pure clarity, the alienation to which the villagers subject their previously unquestioned world-views can produce an infectious enthusiasm and childlike satisfaction in the development of understanding and experimentation. First, the villagers have to accept the individuation of decisive autonomy, then review their own situation and discover their independence from their landlords ('What can they do which we can't? Nothing. What can we do which they can't? We can work. Our labour transforms their land. . . . They depend on us'[16]). It is also crucial that the concept of *fanshen* remains dynamic, open and self-critical; first the land reform is inconsistently applied, then an excess of zeal produces an unrealistic leftist bias, leaving the delegates to return and attempt a just synthesis of previous experiments, ending the play in a progressive spirit. Neither does the play minimize the apathy, selfishness and exhaustion against which the various reformers have to maintain a determined face, even within themselves; but their spiritual readiness to confront and overcome these problems strengthens the importance and urgency of their resolve:

> Why do we live in this world? Is it just to eat and sleep and lead a worthless life? That is the landlord and rich peasant point of view. Enjoy life, waste food and clothes, have children. But a

Communist works not only for his own life: he has offered everything to the service of his class. If he finds one poor brother suffering from hunger and cold, he has not done his duty. Comrade.[17]

The moments when *Fanshen* successfully dramatizes this trancendence of self-interest far outweigh its occasional faults, and the way that a relatively small nucleus of actors is required to play a multitude of characters aids the impression of collective effort and purpose.

Teeth'n'Smiles (1975) has more affinities with the pre-*Fanshen* trio in its unsentimental, almost pessimistic view of a supposedly revolutionary force, this time rock music as brought into conflict with the world of the Cambridge May Ball. The play's chronological setting of 1969 emphasises the dissipation of rebellious potential, and the band's cool, embittered wisecracks set much of the tone, as they retreat into private disillusionment or experience-seeking. Given its basic premise of colliding worlds, *Teeth'n'Smiles* seems oddly predictable, even anti-climactic, as Maggie's explosive impulses find only a minor outlet in an ineffectual moment of petty arson. No doubt Hare would counter that the historical impression recorded was precisely that of anti-climax enlivened mainly by the cynical self-mockery in which Arthur excels, and the title refers to this surface of detached, ironic cool over a hidden despair being a counterpoint to the superficial forced jollity of the stage performer.

Plenty (1978) has considerably more cutting edge by virtue of its meticulously assembled eighteen-year European historical panorama and the capabilities of perception and revolt in the heroine, Susan Traherne. Susan is a vivid creation, a volatile knot of energy who walks the tightrope of conventional propriety with deliberate and pointed inefficiency. The edge and aggression encouraged and channelled by Susan's wartime service of the Allied Resistance leaves her ill-equipped for the placid subservience expected of her as a woman in peacetime, a contradiction which unbalances her mind (in this way she embodies Hare's conviction that 'people go clinically mad if what they believe bears no relation to how they live'[18]). As a courier for the Resistance in 1943, Susan experiences natural tension, isolation and absence of reciprocity in her furtive, dangerous activities, but fondly remembers the encouragement and inspiration afforded by fellow-agent Lazar. Back in the 'peace and plenty' supposedly afforded by peacetime Britain, her ideological isolation returns and her taut energy remains, but with no opportunity of sublimation except the conventional pursuit of meek self-interest afforded by the professional world of commerce – in her case, advertising. As she says, 'Those of us who went through this kind of war, I think we do have something in common. It's a kind of impatience, we're rather intolerant, we don't suffer fools. And so we get rather restless back in England, the people who stayed behind seem childish and a little silly.'[19] But although she shares this edgy integrity with her fellow agents, neither are they 'clubbable' thanks to the harsh self-reliance that they cultivated as a necessary characteristic and the equally necessary ignorance of each other's private names, details and natures. Susan's alienated view of post-war Britain's puerile self-indulgences resembles the biting insights of Mercer's Cousin Vladimir and Barker's Bela Veracek, whilst the violent nervous energy she barely keeps in check gives her the dangerous, honed-down fascination of Brenton's Jed or Griffiths's Gethin Price ('I feel I'm usually holding myself in for fear of literally blowing them out of the room'[20]). Her potential for destruction is symbolized by the wartime revolver she keeps, and her refusal to endure polite diplomatic hedging on the Suez crisis leads her to dislocate the tactfully frivolous atmosphere of a foreign office dinner party with careful indiscretion. However, the targets of this latter discomfiture, her husband Brock and his professional superior Darwin, do at least acknowledge an uneasy tension between their public roles and private convictions ('Mostly we do what we think people expect of us. Mostly it's wrong'[21]) for which they are later penalized by successors. Nevertheless, the declining Brock fails to accept the full ramifications of Susan's extreme perceptions and actions; and his protests have some validity when he says: 'You claim to be protecting some personal ideal, always at a cost of almost infinite pain to everyone around you. You are selfish, brutal, unkind. Jealous of other people's happiness as well, determined to destroy other ways of happiness they find.'[22] But Brock's conditions for progress whereby Susan forfeits her essential values ('in the life you have led you have utterly failed, failed in the very, very heart of your life. Admit it. Then perhaps you might really move on'[23]) reveal that his 'compromise' is tantamount to mindless self-annihilation, and provoke Susan's departure. Reunited with her former fellow-agent Lazar, she can be herself, with all the mixed blessings that involves, such as antagonism ('I like to lose control'), and existential self-isolation ('I've stripped away everything, everything I've known. There's only one kind of dignity, that's in living alone. The clothes you stand up in, the world you can see'[24]), but also a human need for reciprocity and encouragement ('I have to believe that there's someone, you see. Somebody else who's been living like me'[25]). But all Lazar can offer is an isolated evening of doped sex, remaining unsurprisingly cagey about his real name and background ('I gave in. Always. All along the line. Suburb. Wife. Hell. I work in a corporate bureaucracy as well'[25]); and the play ends with a contrasting, ironic echo of the optimistic certainty and comradeship which inspired Susan during her youth in France. Susan's training gives her the strength and intelligence to expose her country's decline into shabby, materialistic expediency, but the hardness necessary to the preservation of integrity seems to leave her trapped in a void of isolation, offering scant comfort to an audience convinced by the considerable passion and logic of her stand. Therefore, it is the actual writing and performance of her life story which confers upon it a communicated value of which the character herself remains unconscious, awarding her the 'place in history' for political–existential resolve which the recipient rarely lives to be aware of, let alone derive solace from.

Two subsequent excellent television plays, *Licking Hitler* (1978) and *Dreams of Leaving* (1980), seem partially to grow out of *Plenty;* *Licking Hitler* also takes up *The Great Exhibition*'s equation of public life and playacting to more serious and powerful effect, as it focusses on the efforts of a British propaganda unit set up in the Second World War to unsettle German morale with simulated 'private' broadcasts. The situation is rife with incongruities and ironies. Archie Maclean, an ex-Clydeside journalist with a gift for vituperation, leads the production of a kind of state-endorsed agitprop directed at a rival country in a bid to 'drive a wedge between the Party and the people'.[26] Like Munro's *The Rumour*, the play affords a 'backstage' glance at the processes of manipulation for supposedly long-term national interests and their immediate short-term human damage. Archie's ruthlessly efficient double-bluff to brand Nazi dissenters as Bolsheviks so that 'Millions die' represents a devious twist previously overlooked but immediately instigated ('if it means covering the whole continent in obloquy and filth . . . then that is what we shall do'[27]). However, the 'corrosive national habit of lying'[28a] overspills into Archie's private life, infecting his view of human relationships with a bitter reductivity that drives him to lie about his lover-secretary Anna and bring about her dismissal. Even more than Susan Traherne in her resistance activities, the propaganda unit is isolated, with no idea of its effect and no coherent sense of its moral roots ('whereas we knew exactly what we were fighting against, none of us had the whisper of an idea as to what we were fighting for'[28b]). The consequent need for liberal and metaphorical human contact felt amongst its employees is just as necessarily warped and strangled, stranding its victims in an embittered vacuum. In peacetime, Anna at least attempts to remain true to the 'shame and anger' she felt gave Archie a sense of integrity. She withdraws like Susan Traherne from the intrinsic dishonesties of her marriage and career in advertising, but Archie writes and directs sentimental escapist films obscuring the truth about the background which once fuelled his aggression. He never replies to her challenge of his activities or proffered affection; even more than Susan and Lazar, his personality is distorted by the contradictions of 'war' and 'peace' to the point where it is 'unclubbable'. *Dreams of Leaving* also deals with interpersonal inspiration and the hazards of isolated standards, but in an early 1970s setting. William is content with his profession of journalism in which the house-style is self-consciously 'absolute rubbish' until he encounters the fiercely independent and uncompromising standards of Caroline. In a way, the play offers us a chronologically-transplanted Brock's-eye-view of Susan Traherne (Susan, Anna and Caroline all being played by the actress Kate Nelligan in the original productions of the plays). William feels the compulsion of Caroline's unconventional will and tries to live up to her existential standards in his daily professional grappling with the cynical propaganda of integration. Whether as an unconscious sexual tactic or out of a genuine desire for encouragement, he relates his stand to her, only to be met with scorn for expecting a 'reward' in an 'unjust . . . hell of a world'.[29] Caroline remains true to her personal lesson of existential independence perhaps too austerely, as the effect is to shut her up permanently inside her own head, driven mad by the strain and confusion of trying to retain her integrity amongst the day-to-day kaleidoscopic erosion of a mystifying, superficial society. Like Brock, William retreats into the reassuring opportunity to dissociate himself from Caroline and her principles: 'I'd always believed the things that she told me, everything she'd said about how one should live. . . . Now it turned out . . . well I was grateful . . . that's what I felt. Thank God she was mad.'[30] This observation leaves him free to assume a safe, comfortable, conventional but secretly defeatist bourgeois existence and leaves Caroline alone and disowned in a psychiatric hospital – which could almost provide the starting point for Edgar's *Mary Barnes*.

Hare's recent work has continued this line of interweaving history play and love story. *A Map of the World* (1982) shows two men, an author and a journalist, attending a United Nations conference out of what they come to recognize as a need for human contact, and holding an ideological debate initially for the sexual favours of a young American woman. The television film *Saigon: Year of the Cat* (1983) shows the relationship between a CIA agent and a British woman who works in a bank in Vietnam in 1974. Like Hare's other women characters, she awakens his conscience and attempts to provide him with a standard of behaviour; but the execution of her ideals, and the relationship, are both smudged away in the American evacuation from the country.

Edgar's early plays for touring groups sometimes evoked established popular or literary models in order to provide a basis of shared experience which could then be developed in less familiar, more challenging directions; notably in the use of thriller conventions in *Operation Iskra* (1973) and the presentation of the Watergate scandal in parodic Shakespearian history terms for *Dick Deterred* (1974). Edgar's work has also shown a similar efficiency in plays written for West End theatre and small touring groups, and a clear-eyed view of the challenges represented by each:

> Theatrical and cultural developments since 1956 have produced a more heterogenous potential audience and you have to think who you're playing to in terms of the language, references and conventions you employ; I'm interested in arguing with the audience, and if you're writing a play attempting to analyze and combat racism you are going to address yourself to different elements of the argument if you are writing, as I did with *Destiny* and *Our Own People*, a play to play to the liberal intelligentsia on the one hand and a play to play to a

non-theatre circuit on the other. The danger in writing for
specific audiences is that you may get into a mechanical frame
of mind predicting audience responses, but within a broad
framework you may have to emphasise difference parts of a
consistent perspective.[31]

Edgar agrees with Hare's formulation that a play's potential
power 'is not going to be in the things you are saying; it is in the
interaction of what you are saying and what the audience is
thinking'.[32] *Destiny* (1976) is a highly successful response to this
recognition in its direct approach to emergent British fascism, its
attraction and its hideous results. It gains immediacy from its
contemporary setting but also from Edgar's prefatory establishment of the historical processes creating the modern situation.
The play's opening in India demonstrates how certain attitudes,
beliefs and behaviour were legitimized, even encouraged, in
certain characters by supposed national interests (like Archie's
insidious skills in *Licking Hitler*) and how the maintenance of the
British Empire manipulated and geographically distanced fascis-
tic impulses. Without this clear outlet, the middle-ranked and
middle-class Turner is taught by the stronger members of a
British Nazi party to redirect his aggression, born of his uncer-
tainty, into the service of their group in a local election. Another
strength of the play is the broad political and social spectrum
established around the local election in Taddley Heath and the
fascinations and weaknesses given to the very human faces which
collectively constitute this panorama, as befits Edgar's intention
'to create characters that the audience could relate to and in a way
that they could confront in themselves' whilst always maintaining
the firm objective 'to put the frighteners on the conventional
play-going audience – people who might be attracted in the
direction of fascism'.[33] Certainly the unease and fear of the people
on which Nation Forward builds its support are depicted with due
sympathy and complexity, making their allegiance to the party all
the more disturbing when we are made witness to the backstage
manipulations of its leaders, who are themselves divided by their
degrees of extremism. But the ignorance, bigotry and self-interest
of the group do not in themselves allow the other characters or the
audience to dissociate themselves completely from their sources,
or dismiss them as the fuel of a cranky, peripheral phenomenon.
This is particularly well dramatized in the emotions of the

Conservative candidate Crosby, and the changing reactions of his friend Platt, as Crosby recounts his meeting with the Nation Forward group at their office:

CROSBY (*to* PLATT): And it was very strange, when talking to these people; thought, oh, no, they can't be, with their grisly xenophobia, they can't, or are they, our creation, Demons. Alter-ego. Somehow. (PLATT *smiles*) And I remembered being small, the Coronation, and the climbing of Mount Everest, a kind of homely patriotism, sort of, harmless, slightly precious self-content. A dainty, water-coloured world, you know. (PLATT *looks embarrassed*) And then, their monstrous chauvinism. Dark, desire for something. . . . Kind of, something dark and nasty in the soul.
Pause. PLATT *has a little cough.*
Felt out of time.
PLATT: Beg pardon? Out of what?
CROSBY: I'm scared.[34]

Similarly, the Labour candidate Clifton's simplistic response to the problems constituted by Nation Forward is rebuffed by his social worker wife Sandy, who deals practically with the ordinary human beings he discusses in generalized terms; and Clifton's intendedly realistic compromises join in a mutual critique with Paul's clearer, harder socialism which denounces Clifton for his ineffectuality. Characters who might have remained ciphers in a social spectrum are given rounded, humanized viewpoints in a comprehension which even extends to several of the fascist spokesmen; however, *Destiny* is not paralyzed by its widespread understanding of characters, as are Galsworthy's attempts at political plays. Edgar:

The machinery by which an analysis should convince theatrically is by confronting the audience, by saying 'How far are you really away from this?' *Destiny* was accused of trying to be sympathetic as a kind of virtue in itself, showing how liberal I was from a great height. I didn't want to do that, I wanted to confront the audience by saying 'Have you ever felt like this?' rather than join with the audience in a patronising way, which is why some characters didn't have any domestic life which might have provided an excuse for their actions. Those moments of surprise and shock about a transfer of sympathy and emotion were very much the dramatic technique I was using.[35]

Easy responses and identifications were anticipated and criticized, forcing the audience to reassess their personal attitudes to the play's themes in a fresh, urgent, alienated light; which is not to say that such attitudes were left in disrupted stasis. Having met and accommodated conventional, partial responses to Nation Forward, *Destiny* ends with a dramatically striking confluence of their theory and practice: Turner's conspiring exploiters are revealed as the corporations which provide support for his political party, leaving the final word to a *'gentle, quiet, insistent'* voice over the final tableau:

> Only one thing could have stopped our Movement: if our adversaries had understood its principle, and had smashed, with the utmost brutality, the nucleus of our new Movement. *Slight Pause.*
> Hitler. Nuremberg. Third of September, 1933.
> *Blackout.*[36]

Thus the quotation is offered for the digestion and response of the audience a crucial moment before disclosing its source, which provokes a more easy and instant response, then leaves the attributed phrase and its author to acquire a more urgent and relevant import in relation to the preceding events of the play, and ends it on a typically well-crafted and effective note.

Wreckers (1977) presents Edgar's treatment of a favourite Barker theme, the incongruities of the law, and takes its impetus from the lively backdrop of the East End of London – 'on one hand, an area of great working-class solidarity, and, on the other hand, an area in which people are very proud of their individuality, and one element of that is an involvement in fiddles of various types'.[37] Hudi stands at the core of this contradiction as an individualistic, *Daily Express*-reading lorry driver, but, like Turner, he finds himself the pawn of more powerful forces. Hudi's confrontation with friend Micky at a dockers' picket line, where both are intent on safeguarding what they view as their respective professional interests, has an emblematic, ironic power; as does a corresponding scene in the second half when Hudi, recommitted to a collective ideology, and a social democrat of a Labour MP find themselves twin sacrificial victims to the 'myth' of a united Labour party. However, the comparison of Hudi with the MP is established only to be negated from another standpoint: unlike Hudi, the MP supports the rule of government which renders his attempts at reform ineffectual, whilst Hudi's 'fiddles' and the clandestine arson performed on behalf of a large company are identified as separated only by a dubious line of legality which takes scant notice of scale and respective environmental experience. *Teendreams* (1979), a collaboration with Susan Todd, interweaves the socialist idealism of student Frances with the contrasting hopes and pressures of romantic wish-fulfilment instilled in the girls she later teaches. Frances's attempts to be sympathetic, raise consciousness and offer guidance appear to be ill-judged when one of the girls, Trisha, attempts suicide, and Frances withdraws, defeated, to her parents' comfortable house; but the skilful integration of mutually critical viewpoints found in *Destiny* also appears in *Teendreams* to administer checks to the viewpoints of both naïve and pessimistic characters, extending the dramatic focus to a determination to resolve such complexities:

> We wanted to take the model of youthful idealism turning into middle-aged cynicism and despair, a very hoary old plot model, and to turn it round. By starting the play with the suicide and repeating the second speech of the play, we intended the audience to assume that was going to be the last scene, and that we were doing that plot model of disillusionment; but then have the characters actually coping in a way which was perhaps more realistic than the heights of idealistic revolutionism and, in a sense, beyond it, a progression. That was an attempt to *go through* an argument which has been formulated in terms of a dramatic convention, set up a theatrical expectation and then deny it. In taking the conventional theatrical form of a conventional ideological model, using it and disrupting it – not merely disrupting the audience as an end in itself – we attempted to provide a critique of that plot device's ideological basis and function.[38]

The most successful modulations of sympathy in *Teendreams* include the rebuke of Frances by her reductive colleague Brewer,

who is then rebuked for his complacency by Frances's friend
Rosie; and Frances's wry tag of 'Peter Pan' for Colin in his
apparently innocent ideological impetus, which he neatly reverses
to ask 'If I am Peter Pan. Who have I come to visit, in her Wendy
House'[39] of her parents' comfortable surroundings. Along with
her memory of her own youthful resolve, this prompts Frances to
the recognition: 'I've passed the point, of no return. The Wendy
House was smashed, oh, long ago. . . . So. Back. To all the mess
and muck and guilt and failure and missed opportunity. Remembering, perhaps, occasionally, what all the pain is for. So what else
can I do?.[40] The accommodation and transcendence of the
disillusionment plot motif strengthens the thrust of *Teendreams* and
makes its principal characters earn the approbation of the
audience; just as, in *Destiny*, dramatic symmetry is evoked to
undercut the associations of ideological symmetry when the
young boys Paul and Tony confront each other in the cell. Both
explain their respective beliefs and fire off their contrasting
slogans, with the crucial distinction that Paul is genuinely
concerned about Tony's welfare.

   Mary Barnes (1978) and *The Jail Diary of Albie Sachs* (1978) are
both adaptations of autobiographies by the name characters to
which the added dimension of dynamic historical process is
brought. Like Hare's *Fanshen*, they derive added import from the
factual basis of their events and the continued existence of the
actual protagonists, which thus removes the hard-won but
optimistic endings from any charge of facile sentimentality, of
which the fictional but downbeat *Plenty* and *Dreams of Leaving* may
have been wary. Edgar acknowledges that *Mary Barnes*'s opening
scene of a psychiatric lecture had its genesis in the desire to
continue from the closing scene of Mercer's *Family Life* and
present a contrasting, sympathetic view of progressive psychiatric
theory,[41] as opposed to Mercer's description of an individual
disintegrating under repressive social pressures of which
psychiatric 'care' merely represents a self-perpetuating extension.
In this way, *Mary Barnes*, like the final scene of Barker's *No End of
Blame*, evokes but redresses the now-familiar social tragedy plot
device of psychological destruction as seen in *Dreams of Leaving*,
The Fool, and many others. Like *Teendreams* and other Edgar plays,
Mary Barnes also takes account of the complex problems encountered by its radical idealists, preventing their ultimate victories
from being simplistic or utopian and engaging the audience's

sympathetic will towards the fruition of their efforts (an effect most remarkably achieved in *The Life and Adventures of Nicholas Nickleby*). However, if *Mary Barnes* refrains from the same conclusion as *Plenty* and *Dreams of Leaving*, it establishes with similar conviction the link between public irrationality and private psychological suffering. Mary's regressive nightmare is that 'the bomb's inside her. She has swallowed it, can't spew it up, or shit it out. It's going to explode',[42] to the point where she takes on the evils of the world, Christ-like, in psychological self-isolation; and Angie suffers from the more familiar, but nevertheless real, psychological tension produced by the discrepant values and viewpoints of her family and boyfriend. Together they provide mutual support and justification which allows them to work through their mental crises and reassume an integrity symbolized by Mary's regained ability to individualize herself, add surname to forename, and reply to Eddie's 'knock, knock, who's there' linguistic convention 'IT'S MARY BARNES!'.[43] Mary's renewed ability to assert her complete identity from that point confers upon her a form of historical status, demonstrated by the inspirational model she proves to others and symbolized by Keith's final echo of Eddie's small but significant reciprocal game:

KEITH: That's Mary.
ANGIE: Mary who?
KEITH: That's Mary Barnes.[44]

Thus Mary and the others attain the goal of the psychiatric centre as expressed by Brenda, the holistic perception of oneself in a social and historical context: 'We didn't build the future. But we are no longer, other, to ourselves'.[45] *The Jail Diary of Albie Sachs* also deals with a form of isolated regression and psychological ordeal, and with the torturous but finally triumphant forging of a historicized integrity. But Albie lacks the aid afforded to Mary, as he laments his separation from 'that collective strength, that stops me being just a white man with an upset conscience, places me in history, gives my conscience scale';[46] his isolation has to become his route to victory as well as his penalty. Initially, he has the support of his whistling fellow-prisoner who turns 'me into we',[47] but also the audience is encouraged to feel themselves filling the void when they are made party to Albie's narration of his daily tasks, complaints, and the practising of his joke and its effect on the guard. Albie says, sublimating his loneliness into planning a play:

> the real problem is to show just what it's like, in isolation, the disintegration, and the horror of it all, to people who are not alone, because they are together, watching, as an audience, my play.
> And then, I think.
> Perhaps the best thing is, not in the play, but in the audience, for them to see, for me to come out, to the audience, and say, my day is staring at a wall, now I am going to make you sit and stare, you mustn't talk, or read your programmes, look at other people. For three minutes, you must sit and stare. And then perhaps they'd know.
> Just what it's like.
> (*Pause.*
> *For about 15 seconds.*
> *Then* ALBIE *goes to his bunk.*
> *He lies down.*
> *Another three-quarters of a minute.*
> ALBIE *puts his forearms across his face.*
> *He does not move, for another minute and a half.*
> *Then he puts his arms by his side.*
> *Another half a minute.*
> *Then he swings his legs out, stands.*
> *He speaks, not to the* AUDIENCE, *briskly, as he walks out, through the fourth wall of the cell.*)
> When this is over, I will leave South Africa. I owe that thing to me.
> (ALBIE *walks off the set, off the stage.*)[48]

This forces the audience into a heightened awareness of their own situation and role in a communal event, then pointedly contrasts this awareness with an experience of Albie's *lack* of communication and focus in his situation. After this, Albie becomes more distant, both to his captors and the audience, and his struggle becomes grimmer, particularly with Freeman. The need for contact that has previously united even Albie and Snyman, despite the ideological gulf between them, now takes second place to the illegal means to grind Albie down and the withdrawn determination with which he fights back, 'a little core, as hard as steel, quite pure. But rather cold',[49] best symbolized by the way he shuts off his mind into concentration on trivia even when there are sounds of a vicious caning taking place outside (Act Two, scene three). He is now motivated more directly by an intellectual concept of his political and historical, rather than merely human status; but at the same time, suffers an emotional distancing from this role, leaving him, when he is released, with 'a kind of fatalism. Crippled spirit'.[50] Nevertheless, his former fellow prisoner Danny is swift to stress that it is Albie's public status, and the authenticity it implies, that has a reach and effectiveness beyond the inevitable strains that have occurred within Albie Sachs as private individual:

DANNY: They won't forget.
Oh no. They'll still say, Albie Sachs. The one locked up alone for all those days, who ran off to the sea.
ALBIE: And Albie Sachs, the one who –
DANNY: (*Interrupts, an order*) They'll still say, Albie Sachs. That one, the one locked up alone for all those days, who ran off to the sea.
(*Pause.*)
ALBIE: You're right. That is the one. They must remember.[51]

'Albie Sachs', like 'Mary Barnes', has even within the play ceased to be merely an individual's name and acquired public associations of inspirational qualities through reaction to the political and historical processes of his or her time and environment. *The Jail Diary of Albie Sachs* and *Mary Barnes* can, as semi-documentary plays, accommodate within themselves a uniquely historical response to their subject matter through an external perspective necessarily denied to the earlier, autobiographical works, thus generalizing their effect, as Edgar has recognized:

So what was written as a specific story for a specific time becomes, I think, a play not just about psychiatric theory but also about building alternative cultures, about how to create collective communities, about the relationship of politics to personal life. It is for this reason that in both plays I have a last scene which is set some time after the main story, to throw the events of the story into relief, to help the audience to think historically about them.[52]

Indeed, we move out a further historical dimension with the possibilities of an audience's reflexive and self-defining response to the plays' meshed viewpoints; thus the audience extends the process which the plays describe. Edgar managed to bring a similar complex and dynamic charge to *The Life and Adventures of Nicholas Nickleby* (1980), his adaptation of the Dickens novel for the Royal Shakespeare Company. Leon Rubin's book *The Nicholas Nickleby Story* (London, 1981) describes the evolution of the production and the very considerable contributions of directors Trevor Nunn, John Caird, Rubin and the Company members to *Nickleby*'s great success, but *The Life and Adventures* also importantly represents the continuation and development of Edgar's characteristic strengths. The term 'melodrama' has acquired many derogatory associations, mainly through its connections with the espousal of what are now identified as destructive Victorian morals, most glaringly in the areas of society, the family and femininity; but a pure theatrical melodramatic charge, when caught, can engage and unite an audience in a collective, vital emotionality in a basic and probably unique way. In addition, Dickens's plot for the novel *Nicholas Nickleby* represents a remarkable series of explorations of the emotional 'breaking point', in which characters submit for a while to situations and duties against the grain of their beliefs, only to throw off the yoke of mounting tension in fierce explosions of energy and action, having already reached the point of co-operation or implication beyond which they *refuse* to go (such characters obviously include Nicholas, Kate, Newman Noggs, Verisopht and the pupils of Dotheboys Hall – but also John Browdie, Madeleine Bray, Madame Mantolini, Walter Bray, Peg Sliderskew, Frank Cheeryble, the Muffin Boys, even Ralph Nickleby). These build-ups and explosions provided excellent opportunities for Edgar's skills in engaging sympathy for the individual under stress, presenting a clear view of the complexities impeding the triumph of their principles, but then achieving a convincing and heartily anticipated refutation of their opposition and assertion of the pressurized character's uncompromised values. Such tensions and resolutions are perhaps best exemplified by Nicholas's hatred of himself for the role he plays in the continuance of Squeers's regime at Dotheboys Hall, and his final defiant resolve to interrupt and return the punishment meted out by the hateful schoolmaster; in this case, Nicholas's gauche innocence, even obtuseness, produces a delay in his reaction but compounds the audience's desire to see wrongs redressed – and a huge sense of relief and accord when this is realised. As Newman Noggs remarked of Nicholas at one point: 'He is a violent man, he has a violent streak, but he has cause, I like him for it.' For the audience, as for Newman, Nicholas became an assertive projection of moral strength which is frequently envied or willed but rarely achieved, particularly in the unavoidable conflicts between the irreconcileable viewpoints represented by Nicholas and by Sir Matthew Pupker/Gregsbury, Squeers, Ralph, Sir Mulberry Hawk or Arthur Gride, for whom, nevertheless, 'Everything is on their side – law, money.' Indeed, the presence or absence of money is a crucial factor in almost every scene, with Nicholas always championing the underdog against his vengeful enemies (Ralph swore to strike back at Nicholas with the conviction 'If he so despises the power of money, then I must teach him what it can do'). The end result was an entertaining and moving, but relentlessly muscular and never escapist, picaresque epic which spanned all strata of Victorian society and evoked quite passionate audience involvement in the fortunes of the characters. But perhaps the most telling, inventive and successful theatrical addition by Edgar to the Dickens novel came with the final scene; Dickens's blatantly and precariously idyllic conclusion in which the protagonists withdraw into a freeze-frame of domestic bliss was interrupted by the plaintive singing of a Smike-like refugee from Dotheboys Hall, which Nicholas initially ignored; but again, the tension became unbearable, and Nicholas stepped out of the ensemble of harmonious couples to take up the boy in an active and literally appealing gesture of practical companionship, symbolizing the continuance of cruelty and despair and the need to take action against them. The attempt was not to undermine the ending of Dickens's original, rather to demonstrate the true essence of the whole 'in such a way that revealed not only the material, but also the complexities and ambiguities of Dickens's attitude to it, and the complexities and ambiguities of our response to that as well'.[53] The effect was an apt, unsentimental, challenging and involving final image on which to conclude the marathon production, refracting back to the audience the real, urgent responsibilities of the continuation of the intense involvement and sympathy they had accorded to the dramatic pilgrimage over some nine hours.

Maydays (1983) moves from 1945 to the early 1980's through England, Hungary, America and Russia, an ambitious epic which traces and interweaves the political fates and reactions of Crowther, a working-class communist, Glass, a middle-class Trotskyist, Lermontov, a Russian army officer, and Amanda, an unmarried mother. The play takes the audience through Crowther's dissaffection and relocation on the political spectrum of the 'malcontents' he sides with, whilst Glass's commitment breaks down under strain, and the two former disputants within the left become jointly involved in the creation of a party on the hard right. As in *Destiny*, these right-wingers' modulations of thought and experience are depicted sympathetically but criti- cally. The American, Weiner, gives a persuasive and understand- able account of his grief and confusion following the death of his son, like Rolfe in *Destiny*, but it is startling to see the political allegiance to which this leads him. Weiner joins the right-wing party of Crowther and Glass, who also try to use Lermontov (now a dissident) as the guest of honour at their banquet. In this key scene, Weiner expresses his new-found conviction.

> To affirm that agitation's agitation, even if it's published quarterly in learned periodicals, and that subversion is subver- sion, even if the subverters of our culture are distinguished film directors, poets and musicians. And that treachery is treachery, even if the traitors to our country have no need of telephoto lens, tape-machines and microfilm, but ply their trade as smart left lawyers, clever linguists, and conscience-stricken academics.[54]

Lermontov deviates from the speech written for him, which also denounces 'subversives', and instead draws upon his prison camp experiences with fellow 'agitators'

> Who up until their sentences were teachers, physicists, academicians and administrators. Writers and poets. Actors, film directors and musicians. Workers and trade union officials. Linguists and lawyers. Publishers. Professors.
> *Pause.*
> People who, resist.[55]

Lermontov's little political drama, concluded by his refusal of the party's presentation, involves the audience in the thrill and unease of his stand, as he indicts them, in the role of the dinner guests, as 'Faces who have forgotten, if they ever knew, the superhuman things that human beings can accomplish, when for a moment they themselves forget what they've been told they are'.[56] Amanda also reappears to demonstrate a rearguard against Glass and his kind, when they confront each other at the wire perimeter of a Greenham-like American arms base, where, like Gilly and Leo in Brenton's *The Genius*, Amanda is involved in a protest 'which can only be accounted for by something in the nature of our species which resents, rejects and ultimately will resist a world that is demonstrably and in this case dramatically wrong and mad and unjust and unfair',[57] something Glass can no longer remember. The closing moments of *Maydays* provide a delicate balance of inspirational endeavour and imminent disaster. At the première production at the Barbican theatre, the voices of the nameless women peace camp protestors spoke to Glass from different points in the auditorium, aligning the audience with their range and size, before we were made party to a terrifying demonstration of strength from the weapons base, all troops and hardware put on full alert. It is left to Lermontov's prison camp friend, Korolenko, to provide a final small-scale demonstration of resilient resistance, passing on documents like Andrea in Brecht's *The Life of Galileo*, with the codeword 'Maydays' used to signify a recognition of history's constant movement and a determination to involve oneself in that movement at whatever price.

Edgar doubts whether he will ever return to 'the holy simplicities of the early 1970's, either politically or dramatically, and suggests that *Nickleby*'s success is a symbol of the sparse, cool tone which dominated so much of the new drama of that period; but he adds that 'it would be sad to lose that aggression', compromising and inhibiting energy whilst endeavouring to create more complex and convincing plays, and that 'You can get too "responsible" as you increasingly realize what the theatre can do.'[58] Certainly Edgar and Hare have demonstrated their ability to write plays that are rich but incompromising, self-critical and thereby more realistic and confident in their assertions. They have also managed to create political drama which, in its quite unforgettable images of isolated pain and collective strength, forces its audience to confront the cost and value of an active role in history, and thereby reassess their own role in the perception and dynamic of that history.

10   Past Imperfects and Present Indicatives

BRIAN FRIEL, MARTIN LYNCH, PETER WHELAN, CARYL CHURCHILL, STEPHEN POLIAKOFF, PETER FLANNERY, NIGEL WILLIAMS

> it is not the literal past, the 'facts' of history, that shape us, but images of the past embodied in language . . . we must never cease renewing those images; because once we do, we fossilise.
>
> *Translations*[1]

> If we had really cared enough would places like this exist?
>
> *Savage Amusement*[2]

As John Berger and others write in *Ways of Seeing* (London 1972, p. 11):

> History always constitutes the relation between a present and its past. Consequently fear of the present leads to mystifications of the past. The past is not for living in; it is a well of conclusions from which we draw in order to act. Cultural mystification of the past entails a double loss. Works of art are made unnecessarily remote. And the past offers us fewer conclusions to complete in action.

In reaction against this mystification, many political dramatists seek to regain and revitalize images of (and from) history. The playwrights considered in this chapter attempt to use the parallels afforded by the past, or the warnings arising from a heightened sense of the present or near-future, to make their political points.

Several plays by Brian Friel question the mechanics of historical definition, the way that people, places and events are commonly and inalterably fixed in an 'official' reading of them, and the power of the artist's imagination to present a provocative alternative, as recognized by David Hare ('Our lives must be refreshed with images which are not official, not approved; that break what Orwell called "the Geneva conventions of the mind" '[3]). In *The Freedom of the City* (1973), Friel's audience is called on by a judge to act as tribunal in determining the enquiry result on three civil rights marchers, who were shot by troops when emerging from Derry Town Hall, which they were 'occupying'. In fact, the audience is invited by Friel to judge the various counsels for prosecution and defence who so earnestly attempt to impose their various inflated and mutually exclusive patterns of perception onto the trio's rather pathetic actions – to which the audience is made sole witness. The Judge's professed interest in 'facts' and warning against 'moral judgements' is a sure indication of his ill-concealed partiality; the lecture by American sociologist Dodds is informative as a frame of reference, but too simplistic and cerebral in its neat pigeonholing; one priest's attempt to heroize the three pawns is ludicrously over-inflated, another priest's view of them as hapless tools of a communist conspiracy is little better, the media's interpretation inaccurate, the ballad-singer's new ditty glib and opportunistic, and the reaction of the 'peace-keeping forces' absurdly trigger-happy. The concurrent glimpses of the figures at the nucleus of the furore increasingly ironizes and discredits all these assessments, as their general unwittingness and fallible humanity prevent them from according with each other's assessments (or lack of them) of political status and responsibility, let alone with images of ruthless terrorists or inhuman statistics which the official voices alternately attempt to confer upon them. Dodd's patronizing address to 'Middle-class people – with deference, people like you and me'[4] is complacent and condescending in its diagnosis of people like the luckless trio and 'the rigid caste that encases their minds and bodies',[5] when his own perceptions are smug and inadequate compared to the shades of opinion voices amongst the three victims; and the Judge's identification of his mistaken conclusion as the only one 'consistent with the facts'[6] mocks the validity of his procedure, and lends a frightening edge to the conclusions he receives and imposes. In contrast to all of this, Friel shows his central figures in generally socialist, but fundamentally humanistic terms, as confused, frightened and high-spirited human beings who will always be denied 'the freedom of the city' or the luxurious surroundings they have accidentally blundered into. Friel's presentation recalls that of O'Casey's Dublin Trilogy, with its tone of lament for humble innocents caught in the crossfire of more powerful but less human partisan forces. The almost ridiculously inappropriate potential for danger attributed to Friel's trio by surrounding opinions is particularly reminiscent of Davoren's misinterpretation by his fellows in *The Shadow of a Gunman*, except that the trio significantly do nothing to encourage mistaken impressions. The basic situation of sympathetic, all-too-human figures trapped with their backs to the wall in a wry and tragic *impasse* recurs in *Volunteers* (1975), in which a group of political internees help on a archaeological dig with the grim background knowledge that, on their return to prison, they are to be killed by their fellow prisoners. The only protest they can register – Butt's deliberate destruction of an ancient vase – is petty (like Skinner's defacement of the Mayor's desk with a cigar in *The Freedom of the City*), but again their variety and humour falsifies any dogmatically political, negative assessment of their human worth, not least in the way that they spin stories around the central motif of Leif the skeleton, 'a tangible précis of the story of Irish man',[7] and always characterized as 'a victim of his society',[8] the closest thing to historical self-awareness that the dig can afford them.

Friel's *Translations* (1980) unites the themes of his earlier plays in historical parable form – the setting is an Irish hedge-school in 1833 – which maintains a highly effective and pertinent parallel with present-day Anglo-Irish relations. The 'civilized' qualities which Owen has made his memories of the hedge-school are sketched before the condescending voice of English 'officialdom' comes to standardize and anglicize local place-names for a map; but Friel ingeniously involves the audience in both communities by enabling them to understand the language of both, as does Owen. This makes for some humorous and poignant effects when understanding breaks down, as Owen and the audience are forced into an almost agonizing awareness of both what separates and what unites the two cultural groups. The romance of Maire and Yolland is a familiar Romeo-and-Juliet motif given added theatrical possibilities by their mutual misunderstandings and the quite classically comic higher awareness granted to the audience; but the audience, like Yolland and Owen, becomes aware of the derivations of the original Irish place-names they are changing, and thus the sense of 'erosion' in which they are co-operating. The common humanity of Friel's characters emphasises the divisiveness of this linguistic imperialism even further; instead of learning each other's languages and natures with the aim of mutual appreciation, the two sides become hostile and chauvinistic. But the idea of an all-encompassing understanding is not a vague utopian ideal, because Friel *makes the audience experience it* within the play – but with tragic exclusiveness. Owen, the pivotal figure whose sense of expediency even permits his name to be changed to Roland, experiences a growing appreciation of his native lore as manifested in the place-names; and when the English Captain Lancey issues his violent ultimatums to the village, Owen is shocked into charging his translation of Lancey's cold formal message with indignant horror – just as he had previously attempted to add courtesy and benevolence to Lancey's equally mechanical initial statement of purpose. The final entrance of Owen's drunken schoolmaster father Hugh and his rambling elderly pupil Jimmy Jack forms a striking parallel to the final appearance of Boyle and Joxer in O'Casey's *Juno and the Paycock*. But unlike those irresponsible wastrels, Hugh and Jimmy can struggle to articulate a conscious gloss on the problem at the core of the play through a classical aphorism bordering on epiphany: 'I am a barbarian in this place because I am not understood by anyone'.[9] Jimmy's own problem is that he lacks 'someone to talk to',[10] and is aware that his idyllic plan to overcome this by marrying the Greek goddess Athene is marred by a crucial problem:

> Do you know the Greek word *endogamein*? It means to marry within the tribe. And the word *exogamein* means to marry outside the tribe. And you don't cross those borders casually – both sides get very angry. Now the problem is this: Is Athene sufficiently mortal or am I sufficiently godlike for the marriage to be acceptable to her people and to my people? You think about that.[11]

But Hugh's response is to begin the recitation of another classical fable in which a beloved city is overthrown by a people 'proud in war', as is 'ordained by fate', a less optimistic parallel to events than that established by Jimmy. Thus the play ends on a finely poised balance of alternative possibilities, and it is thoroughly appropriate that a play, predominantly wary of the wedges that an official and exclusive sense of history can drive between peoples, should end on a duly qualified semi-visionary glance towards future potentialities.

Belfast's Martin Lynch has made effective reassessments of Northern Ireland's more recent past in his collaborations with the Charabanc Theatre Company, *Lay Up Your Ends* (1983), on the necessary growth of trades unionism amongst the Belfast women mill workers in 1911, and *Oul Delf and False Teeth* (1984), set during the Northern Irish election on 1949, charting the problems of autonomy for characters planning their futures with British state aid. Lynch's own plays are more powerful and modern in their settings. His characteristic ear for the resilient humour of the North also informs *The Interrogation of Ambrose Fogarty* (1982) and *Castles in the Air* (1983), but it has to battle against the impingement of grim realities. *Ambrose Fogarty*, like Keeffe's *Sus*, involves the audience in a first-hand account of detention and the physical and verbal violence involved. Lynch effectively crosscuts between the work and banter of a West Belfast police station and the ordeal and powerless, politicized rage of Fogarty at the treatment to which he is subjected (even more ruthlessly than that depicted in *The Jail Diary of Albie Sachs*, and with a more geographically immediate setting). *Castles in the Air* is a searing demonstration of Belfast's housing problem and its disintegrating effect on a family. The slim hope represented by spirited but feckless builders, exchanging jokes and discovering the work of Brecht, is offset by the increasing claustrophobic hopelessness facing Mary Fullerton and her family. Lynch again crosscuts between the tragically polarized characters to end on an unforgettable shock image of Mary's horrific but understandable suicide. The unevenness of Lynch's writing is balanced by his blend of humorous vitality and appalling events, which suggests he is the Irish political dramatist with the strongest potential for dramatizing its social problems. It is to be hoped that his reputation grows further beyond his native land.

Peter Whelan, in *Captain Swing* (1978), turns to the peasant uprisings of the early nineteenth century – like Bond in *The Fool* – in order to discover a tradition of revolt which may have parallels in modern industrial situations; thus, Whelan and Bond try to give dramatic expression to scenes from an 'alternative history', instead of the imperialist or aristocratic affairs which constitute much of 'official history' and are inverted by Arden and D'Arcy in plays like *The Hero Rises Up*. *Captain Swing*'s vitality springs from Whelan's vivid nightmarish dramatizations of the Corn-men (lurking spirits of violence) and Swing (a 'people's monster' forged in the imaginations of the labourers and projected onto an unwitting, fatally ill merchant's traveller) and the pivotal figure of Mathew Hardeness. Mathew is an effective repository for audience sympathy, experiencing the crisis at the labourers' level yet holding back from unlawful conduct in the name of 'reason'. But Mathew's growing involvement in the situation forces him into making emotional commitments: first to a peaceful humanistic 'reassertion of the law' against its ostensible agents and guardians; then to a fearful rejection of his fellows' violent intoxication by the 'spook' of Swing, which drives him to kill Farquarson, the vehicle of their passion; and finally to an angry disillusionment which makes Mathew regret the latter action, as Swing 'was the only power they knew we possessed. Yet we killed him. No! The meek shall not inherit the earth. . . . What is this law the people keep . . . if they kill Swing. . . . And those who govern break us?' [12] Mathew's progression through his ordeals of experience and conscience are likely to make him a more widely sympathetic figure than Bond's Clare, which in turn gives more weight to his final, radically questioning position. Whelan's next play, *The Accrington Pals* (1981), continues *Swing*'s strengths in realising a historical period and situation with present-day relevances and shooting it through with powerful seams of visionary nightmarishness, but *The Accrington Pals*, with its tale of a locally-raised First World War battalion and the women they leave behind, has dramatic antecedants in the plays of C. K. Munro and O'Casey's *The Silver Tassie*; Whelan, like the two earlier dramatists, is concerned to show the pressure and misdirected glory which encourage men to go to war, poignantly deflated by a dream-sequence in which May hallucinates that she trains a rifle on her former sweetheart Tom, now a bitterly resentful corpse. Perhaps the play misses some cutting edge by failing to depict its latent unsympathetic figures, the predators who batten on its carefully described victims.

Caryl Churchill's *Light Shining in Buckinghamshire* and *Vinegar Tom* (both 1976) return, like Bond and Whelan, to earlier times of social crises and upheavals. *Light* gives an unusual episodic account of religious radicalism in a seventeenth-century community. Churchill outlines her subject matter in a Preface:

> The simple 'Cavaliers and Roundheads' history taught at
> school hides the complexity of the aims and conflicts of those to
> the left of Parliament. We are told of a step forward to today's
> democracy but not of a revolution that didn't happen; we are
> told of Charles and Cromwell but not of the thousands of men
> and women who tried to change their lives. Though nobody
> now expects Christ to make heaven on earth, their voices are
> surprisingly close to us.[13]

Light has a particularly pointed parallel with modern events in its
description of English troops being sent to Ireland, announced
directly to the audience in one character's urgent pacifistic
outburst; whilst *Vinegar Tom* shows how seventeenth-century
witchhunts provided the community with convenient scapegoats,
and uses songs which emphasise present-day parallels of male
domination. Perhaps the most memorable scene in *Light* is the
penultimate one, 'The Meeting', in which the friendless vagrant
Brotherton is coaxed out of her feelings of shame and inadequacy
and into an acceptance of her womanhood and humanity in a
christian community. The immediately subsequent final scene
then strikes a particularly rueful note in its accounts of how the
characters all lost or missed the opportunities afforded by their
revolutionary spirit and collective strength. *Cloud Nine* (1979) is a
farce linking imperialism and sexual oppression, and treats
history in a particularly idiosyncratic way: the first act lampoons
a British outpost in Africa during Victorian times, then the second
act moves to present-day London, but with a time passage of only
twenty-five years for the recurrent characters. In addition, male
roles are played by women and vice versa. The resultant
confusion of impressions and broad comedy which characterize
the first act give an appropriate sense of conflict with rigid
disharmony when the protagonists are attempting to escape from
their social and sexual restrictions. The second act is a less savage
look at the modern, comparatively liberal sexual climate, which
nevertheless still contains many characters struggling towards
self-fulfilment with little support or confidence. The first half's
climate of distorting colonial conformity finds a modern parallel
in the ghost of an uncomprehending young British soldier who
died in Northern Ireland. The whole is resolved through an image

reminiscent of Brenton's *Epsom Downs*, in which the Victorian and modern Bettys appear together and embrace in self-acceptance – an image given wider resonances by the homogeneous sexuality of the characters (or versions of the character) but the heterogeneous sexuality of the players involved in the separate acts. Churchill's television play *Crimes* (1982) projects a sense of social disintegration into the future and sets the action in the early twenty-first century, where a warden/therapist plays through video recordings of his deviant prisoner/patients. The most obvious potential effects of such a setting are geared towards providing an alienated, extrapolated view of the present – characters speak of being a child of the '80's depression, refer to the '2 million employed' and find petrol fumes more familiar than country air – but Churchill attains a particularly inspired reflection back onto current trends with one prisoner's tale of how his neighbour was imprisoned under the Prevention of Terrorism Act for opening her front door, thereby breaking a curfew and witnessing police conduct during a riot. The black prisoner explains the sudden sympathy between himself and his elderly, white, respectable neighbour, who, when confronted with such tortuous *Exception and the Rule*-style judgements, comes to the conclusion 'What is wrong with being a criminal with the country in the state it is now?'.

Churchill's *Top Girls* (1982) sets modern executive Marlene amongst a group of historical and literary 'exemplary women' for a dinner party, then concentrates on her relationship with her sister Joyce, who brought up Marlene's baby at the cost of her own so that Marlene would be able to pursue her career. The play ends with a political argument between the sisters, and Joyce – like Matti in Brecht's *Puntila* – comes to an unsentimentally critical view of Marlene as her class enemy, sister or not. *Fen* (1983) is an account of foreign exploitation, frustration and despair in a rural East Anglian community. *Softcops* (1984) returns to the themes of *Crimes*: 'There is a constant attempt by governments to depoliticise illegal acts, to make criminals a separate class from the rest of society so that subversion will not be general, and part of this process is the invention of the detective and the criminal, the cop and the robber'.[14] Accordingly, *Softcops* shows the pagaent of justice disrupted when Lafayette rouses the crowd, intended to observe his execution as a moral lesson, to recognize their similarities to him and start a riot, whereby he escapes. Further examples from nineteenth-century France demonstrate that the *perception* of criminality is an integrating, even vicariously fascinating, force for 'orderly citizens' (mainly privileged), and is the main sense of oppression and degradation for the isolated offender. Pierre ponders new methods of reinforcing the divisions between deviancy and conformity, and inadvertantly but tellingly garbles his programme:

> The criminals are supervised. The insane are cured. The sick are normalised. The workers are registered. The unemployed are educated. The ignorant are punished. No. I'll need to rehearse this a little. The ignorant are normalised. Right. The sick are punished. The insane are educated. The workers are cured. The criminals are cured. The unemployed are punished. The criminals are normalised. Something along those lines.[15]

By exposing and demonstrating these institutional blurs, *Softcops* deconstructs the society of spectacle and its latent oppression of its members into legitimized forms of association.

As *Crimes* shows, contemporary society can provide the fulcrum for fictitious excursions into the future as well as into the past, and Stephen Poliakoff, Peter Flannery and Nigel Williams have created haunting visions of imminent social breakdowns. Flannery sets his prophetic play *Savage Amusement* (1978) four years beyond its first staging, but Poliakoff specifies 'The present' and Williams gives no guidance. The latter two playwrights depict a heightened present only just out of sight, describing contemporary disintegrations or crises which are felt to be symptomatic of more widespread future crises. In Poliakoff's *Hitting Town* (1975), Clare and Ralph take a joyless, futile wander through the sterile urban wasteland of Leicester, and Ralph seems horribly fascinated by the recent IRA bombings he has barely avoided in Birmingham. His simultaneously fearful and tantalized vision of future similar social disruptions meets with no reaction from his sister or from their general environment, and Ralph identifies himself with this very process of moral and emotional entropy; but the more distant Clare is aware of the futility of his petty rebellions like the embarrassment of local disc-jockey Len Brazil on a phone-in broadcast. The companion play, *City Sugar* (1975), shows Brazil himself becoming nauseated by the sickly odes to conformity and escapism which he is employed to dispense, just as Susan Traherne in Hare's *Plenty* finds her rather less convincing choice of an advertising career to be a series of exercise in deadening integration (as Barthes claims, 'the mythologist cuts himself off from all the myth-consumers, and this is no small matter'[16]). Brazil's taunting bids – half contemptuous, half fascinated – to understand a girl who enters one of his competitions reveal a slow loss of control over his role and materials, as suggested by the nightmare associations he fires off as part of a quiz question. Brazil's job of perpetuating consumer passivity has left him in need of an outlet for his aggression, whilst Nicola, the contestant, experiences the fragility of Brazil's world and realizes his listeners could 'TEAR THROUGH IT IF WE WANTED. (*Pause*) But it's not worth it really'.[17] *City Sugar* ends on a deliberate note of unresolved tension for both characters, but its social observation and provocative juxtaposition of disintegration and equally chilling integration recur in more directly political form in *Strawberry Fields* (1977). The enigmatic and eccentric Kevin and Charlotte seem to be correct in some of their descriptions of their disgusting environment, with its crumbling motorways, sticky cafés and acrid junk food, but what they construe as a stand against the predominant entropy – their service of an extremist right-wing group – is in fact a 'shabby, vicious, second-hand' continuance of this very entropy into moral and political terms. Nick serves as an effective representative of the audience in his involvement with Kevin and Charlotte, first adopting a wry but fascinated condescension but then experiencing a loss of control and increasing unease amidst the cold apathy of apparently dried-up English ghost towns. Nick teases out various clues in a bid to define and dismiss Kevin and Charlotte as ineffectual cranks, but their supposedly impossible nightmare vision is confirmed as real and dangerous when Charlotte coolly and methodically shoots a policeman. From then on, Nick feels growing horror as they produce their warped diagnoses of contemporary ills and expound their determination to act violently on these initially laughable, now chilling convictions. They are also secure in their belief that they are the vanguards of a larger future reaction: 'There's a civil war coming . . . In eighteen months, two years. I don't want it to happen, but I can see it coming'.[18] The second act ends with another *coup de théâtre* when Nick thinks he is free, only to be shot by a poised and controlled Charlotte; thus Poliakoff establishes with frightening immediacy the dangers of underestimating the threat Charlotte and Kevin represent. *Shout Across the River* (1978) returns to the more symptomatic, social metaphor style of *Hitting Town* and *City Sugar*, in which individual crises crystallize larger tendencies of social decay. Christine, a volatile schoolgirl isolated as a neurotic rebel, organizes an idiosyncratic course in a form of existential psychiatry for her mother, who is almost a reversed-mirror-image of conformist anxiety. After a Ralph-like rampage of fleetingly exhilerating but ultimately squandered energy, used in petty social disobedience, Christine collapses in a spasm of exhausted nihilism. Mrs Forsythe is right to applaud her daughter's 'black rage' and energy, but denounce its dissipation into such petty avenues. Her assertion to Christine, 'you just have to use all that power in there. . . . And there'd be no stopping you',[19] seems a little too neat amongst the characteristic Poliakoff terrain of social distortion and arid pointlessness, but nevertheless remains an important qualification of her daughter's viewpoint and indicates the articulateness, autonomy and authenticity which she herself has recently rediscovered, grounds for optimism in themselves.

Sherman, the record company executive in Poliakoff's *American Days* (1979), is a development of Len Brazil: the confident but narcissistic, glamorous but hollow 'constant' who remains in the music business whilst the artists, upon whom he is parasitic, arrive, depart and have their originality or energy packaged into some pre-existent, toothless form. If the Blues speak of resilience under pressure, Rock is generally a musical expression of revolt, and the hopeful auditionees of *American Days* see it as a chance to effect an additional personal liberation from their backgrounds (just as commercial compromise can facilitate individual success within the system's terms for Griffiths's comedians). Poliakoff's third incarnation of the slick, bright, modern leech is Nigel in *The Summer Party* (1980), the promoter of a rock festival which acts as a metaphor of repressive tolerance in what may be Poliakoff's most resonant and haunting play to date. The executives and artists at the festival are significantly kept in pampered separation from the thousands of spectators who 'have come to this glittering occasion to prove to themselves they're still alive',[20] and the child star Mister David is an effectively tawdry figurehead-sop to the crowd, breaking consumer objects with fraudulent 'magic' whilst providing a comment, through his true child's petulance, on the childish egocentricity of his elders. The presiding Chief Constable of Police, Kramer, is established as a reasonable, even ascetic, representative of his profession, particularly astute and sympathetic when compared to the surrounding characters. When Kramer steps up onto the stage to address the festival (and theatre) audience and prevent a riot, he unites them in a carefully delivered, almost mystical, heightened common experience of sunrise. With the situation saved, Kramer is suddenly revealed as the most dangerous magician when he exercises a Brazil- and Sherman-like sadistic control over a girl, to the point of becoming as childishly egoistic as Mister David. Kramer's awareness also extends to his own powers, and an unhealthy enjoyment of their exercise:

> For I have this power . . . to make people feel less. I have seen violent things in my whole life, things you cannot imagine, and now they have no effect on me at all . . . I meet people all the time as I work – I *know* what they want.
> . . .
> They want a few certainties again, to feel safe. . . . To be told things won't change any more, to be able to believe there's a God in heaven again. To be protected.
> . . .
> It doesn't have to be real. It's the way it's done . . . the right tone of voice. They all want to be reassured now –[21]

The effectiveness of Kramer's transition depends on his earlier impression of humanity and authority amongst the more voluble but less practical whizz-kids. Once granted this sympathy, he can then shock the audience by emerging as a menacing figure akin to Kevin and Charlotte of *Strawberry Fields*, but with a more dangerous blend of stealth, charisma and legitimized power. His final control of the 'party' represents a challenging, powerful final image, not least because the audience may well have co-operated in willing him towards this position. *Favourite Nights* (1981) shows Catherine in her adopted landscape of London casinos, gambling to forget her inability to make any contribution to society after her hard work and qualifications, trying to 'skim across depression' on adrenalin and self-consuming proud independence. Her sister Sarah recognizes Catherine's potentially suicidal honing-down, but has to acknowledge that 'everything is luck now' and seems

critique of Nicky's conventional internal channels of reform, but comes as the climax of a highly logical, persuasive series of economic and emotional developments, ending the play on a provocative but convincing note.

The energy, resilience and determination of Flannery's defiant human flotsam are also important ingredients in Nigel Williams's tenacious underdog characters, and the plays to which they bring such ferocious wit. Williams specializes in sustaining the challenges of his characters through their own articulateness, complexity and self-parody, recognizing like Poliakoff and Kevin in *Strawberry Fields* that 'People want superficial reasons for things. . . . *So then they can dismiss them.* They want easy, obvious answers for things.'[25] Williams's protagonists, on the other hand, refuse to let themselves be reduced to identifiable ciphers and thereby to have the aggression of their threats mitigated; and, like Kevin and Charlotte in Poliakoff's play, they are all the more haunting because of this. For example, the problem schoolboys of *Class Enemy* (1978) are quick to predict and devalue any patronizing pseudo-liberal expressions of sociological determinism or condescending sympathy from their prospective teachers (or audiences):

> IRON: Sent us unuvver Russian. Anuvver Red fuckin' Russian.
> NIPPER: 'How do you feel that your environment affects you?'
> IRON: Ai don't know sah.
> NIPPER: 'Do you feel that the urban environment situation leads to poverty and despair in the Inner City?'
> IRON: I feel that you are a cunt in glasses.
> NIPPER *laughs. Quite sycophantic.*
> NIPPER: 'Great. Great.'
> IRON: I feel it'd take fifteen years an' 'arf a' British Leyland 'fore your cock so much as started the long climb upwards.
> NIPPER: 'Oh chriffic young man.'
> IRON: I feel, really sah, that ve on'y fing ter do wiv you is ter fill yore arse wiv smarties an' flog you ter the Arabs.
> NIPPER: 'Yeah. Do you feel that you are radicalised?'
> IRON: FUCK OFF![26]

Iron berates the other boys for their inability to make political connections when he himself is identified and fuelled by a scorching and persuasive class hatred. Nipper's bid to emulate

Iron's confident aggression is distorted when he is reduced to mouthing the clichés of a fascist conspiracy theory against blacks; compared to him, Iron's hostility seems relatively accurate in sociological terms. However, like McGrath and Boyle's *The Hard Man*, *Class Enemy* gives an audience no opportunity to sentimentalize or distance violent hatred, particularly when Iron voices the determination to 'GO OVER VER RIVER AN' WE'RE GONNA SMASH AN' BREAK AN' BURN AN' KILL EV'RY RICH CUNT WE FIND WE'RE GONNA BE SO FUCKIN' DANGEROUS VEY WON'T KNOW WOT 'IT 'EM.'[27] Even an audience which prides itself on its political 'progressiveness' can feel little comfort in the company of such rage. The more patient and humanistic Sky-Light begins to seem realistic in his assessment of Iron as 'twisted', making 'every fuckin' fing into a sob story', and even enjoying a scapegoat for his personal peevishness like the universally condemned Nipper, when in fact, however frugal, 'iss *livin'* innit? Iss better'n bein' dead fer a start'.[28] Iron's fierceness and energy give him great dramatic vitality, but Sky-Light makes some valid points about Iron's class hatred, the convenience and simplicity and legitimization of insensitive, violent, puritanical egocentricity which it comfortingly provides; to this extent, Sky-Light wins the argument when Iron ruthlessly beats him up, as this very ruthlessness makes the other boys reject Iron. But Iron is certainly more intelligent than the others, and Sky-Light's humanism can frequently sound bland or unworldly. The only viewpoint conclusively refuted is that of the Master who rejects them all as 'Savages'. In this and *Sugar and Spice*, Williams's structural strategy recalls that of William Golding's novels: the author mobilises thesis and antithesis, leaving the audience or reader to attempt a satisfactory non-reductive synthesis.

Williams's *Trial Run* (1980) shows two black youths, Billy and Gange, holding some white hostages in a Woolworth's basement, ostensibly to protest against the conduct of a particular policeman. But whilst Gange is primarily motivated by simple personal revenge on the policeman Evans, Billy's flair for self-dramatization and self-parody are used to prevent the white hostages from minimizing the issues at stake or dissociating themselves from their captors' grievances:

JOHN: They're political. I told you they was political.

SPIT AT REASON 'COS REASON IS WHY WE'RE ON THE
WRONG SIDE A' THE ROAD!',[37]) Foreman deflects the attacks
on the pickets' morale and launches his own assault on Private
Tanner, dividing the troops against themselves and wrecking
their standard military patterns of analysis and reaction ('it ain't
a decent old-fashioned clean-cut war like you joined up for din't
yer you Scotch git'[38]). Foreman, the sharp-tongued agitator,
manages to agitate the troops against their own leaders, and Sam
follows in his own way with a characteristically humanistic appeal
('I'M LOOKIN' DOWN A RIFLE BUT I CAN SEE A FACE
ON VE SIDE O.K.?'[39]), but the decisive component of the line,
the self-deprecating Chaser, stops crucially short of co-operation
with a sympathetically expressed loss of stomach for the fight; the
final tableau, in which he sinks down into the 'middle ground' of
which Foreman had previously denied the existence, ends the
play on a mutually questioning note for the audience to resolve
in their own sympathies.

Sugar and Spice (1980) switches from industrial to sexual politics
with equal effectiveness and perhaps even more searing theatrical
intensity. A group of girls led by Sharon begin a session of
self-intoxication under the roof and auspices of aging model Suze,
whose essentially patronizing and conventional attempt at rebel
camaraderie dissolves into hysterical shock as the girls prove her
to be increasingly out of her depth. The appearance of a male
'hostage', Steve, gives Sharon ammunition for invective, particularly when Steve attempts a stereotypically vain and mechanical
pick-up with another of the girls, Carol. Like Billy and Foreman,
Sharon is sharply skilful at defusing conventional criticisms of her
discontent through witty parody:

> No. I tell a lie. I am not able to 'ave a child on account my womb
> is situated be'ind my right ear 'ole an' every time a sperm gets
> near it it goes inter terminal shock. No. I tell a lie. I am un'appy
> becos I am all 'orrible an' ugly an' cannot wear partyjresses like
> ve ovver girls an' 'ave ter walk arahnd in a suit of armour ter get
> people ter whistle at me. No. I tell a lie. Women are known ter
> be inconsistent. I am jealous of my lovely young friend 'ere,
> Carol, on account she gets all ver boys and I end up wiv ver
> bridge rolls. No. I tell a lie. She ends up wiv ver boys *an'* ver
> fuckin' bridge roll. No. I tell a –[40]

Sharon's vitriolic verbal energy perhaps scores more points in the auditorium than on the stage, where, like Iron in *Class Enemy*, she finds her friends slow learners, if not downright intransigent ('SOMEONE'S CHRYIN' TER GIVE YOO AN EJUCATION 'ERE BUCH YOO AIN'T LISTENIN' ARE YER?'[41]). But her puncturing of conventionally sexist attitudes amongst her accompanying characters and in her environment has a Shavian critical vitality which an audience, perhaps considering itself more enlightened than the girls, will probably recognize, support and enjoy. However, Sharon's attacks on Steve move from the verbal to the directly physical. She is accused by Carol of being a neurotic killjoy imposing her own equally distorted views and relentless hatred on others (as was Iron by Sky-Light); and the hostage, Steve, tries to absolve himself from personal responsibility much in the manner of Billy's captives in *Trial Run*:

> STEVE: We ain't all bastards you know. Some of us are quite recognisable 'uman –
> SHARON: I DON' WANNA 'EAR ABAHT YORE RECORD FER GOOD BE'AVIOUR SONNY. I AM REALLY NOT INCHERESTED! YOU 'EAR?[42]

Sharon's rejoinder has its validity considering the way Steve began by behaving, but the subsequent threatening of his naked genitals with a broken bottle has, like Iron's rage, a riveting but profoundly discomforting force which becomes increasingly difficult to condone, whether or not a reaction against a manifestly oppressive social system. But the intrusion of Steve's friends John and Leroy interrupts the action and initiates an almost symbolically symmetrical expression of anger in the play's second half. John's inventive but simmeringly dangerous bursts of misogyny contain some perceptive critiques of conventional social attitudes and expectations (interestingly drawing from Sharon the very charge of homosexuality she was forced to dodge), but they quickly descend into a grubby violent hatred in the name of defiant independence, mirroring Sharon's misanthropy and concluding in an identical image of insupportable hostility as he holds the same broken bottle at Carol's crotch. Like Iron, John appears to burn himself out in a welter of hatred, after wounding Steve; but the final tableau of crossfire victims, Steve and Carol, seems a provocative oversimplification, like Sky-Light's humanism.

Carol's distracted advice 'Don' listen ter no-one Stevie not either side a' the fuckin' fence. You foller 'oo you like' has its merits, and Tracy's interjection 'WELL CARM ON FER FUCK'S SAKE! DON' ANYBODY FUCKIN' CARE?'[43] instigates a long over-due mobilization of assistance for Steve; but the image of an isolated sexual utopia with which Carol comforts Steve is unlikely to last long outside the room or the play. Again, Williams forces the audience to attempt a synthesis of the mutually critical, theatrically exhilerating, but ultimately over-reductive energies he so powerfully expresses.

Williams's fifth full-length play, *W.C.P.C.* (1982) is a lighter piece, in which the problems of analysis and reaction find expression in the farcical tale of an innocent young police constable who discovers that the Metropolitan Police's Vice Squad is rife with ebullient homosexuality, but also finds that there is no uninvolved figure of authority to whom he can appeal, and therefore no coherent or effective protest he can make, amidst the prevalent gleeful deviance. Williams's ability to justify and dramatize extreme possible reactions against social conformity is complemented by a readiness to arrange even these counter-entropic vitalities in a mutually questioning pattern, leaving the audience with a stark, rich and irreducible theatrical experience which anticipates and cuts through almost all barriers of compla-cency whilst demanding a coherent response. His verbal intensity and inventiveness, allied to his balanced structural sophistica-tion, make him one of the most complete and exciting of recent dramatists.

Conclusions

RHODA: Their decency, their reasonableness – their CUL-TURE! (*Pause*) At university – I was at university – we started a theatre and we had this show – this amazing show we took on tour – in which at one point we dragged a man from the front row – physically dragged him by his arms and legs – and robbed him in the middle of the stage. We are committing an offence, we said. We are robbing him. And they sat there, his friends, and he laughed very weakly, all embarrassed, while we actually mugged him and undressed him and actually roughed him up a bit. And then we shoved him back in his seat and chucked his clothes at him, and he sat there pulling on his trousers almost secretly in case the actors were DISTURBED! And when the show was over, they all clapped, including him, and we all waited for him to ask for his money back. But he didn't. He left the pigskin wallet with the money in. And I thought that was very, very decadent. I thought that was VILE, STINKING DECENCY on his part. I said we had to go on from there and actually maim someone. Do someone an injury. Really FUCK THEM UP a bit!

GODBER *watches her, bemused.*

GODBER: You university wits. With your funny little appetites . . . *Fade to black.*

That Good Between Us[1]

Rhoda's taste for 'chaos' turns out to be yet another form of decadence; but her creator, Howard Barker, has almost certainly shared her initial indignant impulse. As Jonathan Swift recognized: 'Satyr is a sort of *Glass*, wherein Beholders do generally discover every body's Face but their Own; which is the chief Reason for that kind of Reception it meets in the World, and that so very few are offended with it'.[2] Eavesdropping on interval conversations in established or subsidised theatres can be a depressing experience, as one discovers that right- and left-wing

209

audiences frequently demonstrate a complacency which is terrifying in its refusal to be punctured. And this depression and terror is at the heart of many political playwrights' relationships with their audiences, along with a violent urge to shatter somehow the veneer of 'decency, reasonableness, CULTURE' and produce an emotional and intellectual reaction through a statement that is uniquely resistant to reductivism, distancing or obstinate blindness. Shaw reveals this impulse when he writes: 'Capitalist mankind in the lump is detestable. . . . Both rich and poor are really hateful in themselves . . . I should despair if I did not know they will all die presently, and that there is no need on earth why they should be replaced by people like themselves', but adds 'And yet I am not in the least a misanthrope. I am a person of normal affections.'[3] Indeed, he is at least as normal as John Osborne, whose *A Sense of Detachment* represents this impulse at its most incoherent and counter-productive, and David Hare, who claims that the Portable Theatre company's disposition soured whenever their van approached a densely populated area.[4] Raymond Williams's identification of the Shavian 'twist' in the 'deeply humane man who hated what he called "capitalist mankind" ', could serve for many subsequent political dramatists committed to a generalized collective ideal of human perfectibility, but filled with a nauseous contempt for particular individual evidences of contemporary perverseness, frivolity and mindlessness. Shaw's own 'escape clause' of evolution as a social model became, as Williams writes, 'an evolution of humanity beyond man', but this does not diminish the fact that 'Shaw is always so articulate and penetrating that he remains a classical point to which we are bound, in wisdom, to refer'.[5] Williams intends this in a philosophical sense, but the statement remains even more relevant to drama. Shaw is a technically exemplary model, vital to his recognition that radical political commitment does not necessitate glib, simplistic, fundamentally sentimental plays which work on a stubborn belief in emotive passion and catch-phrase dogma as if these ingredients existed in some kind of vacuum. Instead, the more objections to its central thrust that a play can anticipate, contain, represent or express, then *overcome* within its own intrinsic framework, then the more convincing will be its eventual victory. The dramatic structures of several plays by David Edgar and Nigel Williams have benefited greatly from an awareness of this aspect of their craft, but the authors have not sacrificed or compromised the energy and political commitment of their writing in demonstrating such technical sophistication (a term which can denote a realistic wisdom in the ways of mankind, despite its more familiar connotations of bland slickness or refined speciousness).

I would further suggest to any budding (and some established) political playwrights that, at our present stage, unsentimental but assertive 'Scenes of Overcoming' such as those afforded by Barker's *No End of Blame* are doubtless difficult but also rare and valuable in a predominantly pessimistic, even nihilistic age; social and political tragedies are less helpful when one may feel only a few steps away from experiencing them first-hand, and even bleak forecasts, like Flannery's *Savage Amusement*, can contain a guarded but redemptive belief in human capability, humour and continued perseverance. Indeed, this note of existential affirmation in political drama might be productively examined and developed. It is certainly a constant consideration in the make-up of Shaw's higher evolutionary heroes and heroines, forging a future through the vague internal promptings of a force they have not always articulated, making their own individual contributions without an immediate sense of communal support – rather, working in an isolation relieved only by the unseen theatre audience, or meeting hostility from the contemporary forces of reactionism. The influence of Samuel Beckett on dramatists of the 1960's and 70's may be underrated compared to that of Brecht, but it is to some degree pervasive. The lives of a Susan Traherne, Bela Veracek or Albie Sachs may seem shapeless and futile to their protagonists, but they become exemplary, coherent self-definitions in the theatre, with all the potential inspiration this affords. In such cases, Hare, Barker and Edgar are not fundamentally attempting to vilify the values of an audience (except tangentially) so much as to offer an image of authenticity for their assimilation and self-comparison (which may, admittedly, be chastening to pride or complacency); the tone is closer to one of mutual existential challenge or validation. Compare Sartre's 'I cannot obtain any truth about myself, except through the mediation of another. The other is indispensable to my existence, and equally so to any knowledge I can have of myself'.[6] Audience and dramatic character both provide this 'other' which gives existence a sense of form and value, meeting each other half way, as it were, in a truly communal act. And once this 'meeting' is attained, identities merge in order to redefine themselves more truly and collectively: 'The moment I feel that my freedom is indissolubly linked with that of all other men, it cannot be demanded of me that I use it to approve the enslavement of a part of these men'.[7] Beckett, the most significant and concentrated existential playwright, shows in *Waiting for Godot* (1953) two tramps, isolated in a dark metaphysical void, but maintaining their resilience and existential dignity. The resilience of isolated characters is also offered for existential judgement in Wesker's *Caritas*, Barker's *No End of Blame* and *Pity in History*, Hare's *Plenty* and *Dreams of Leaving*, Edgar's *The Jail Diary of Albie Sachs*, Friel's *Volunteers* and Flannery's *Savage Amusement*, but the void of isolation, frequently unsympathetic or hostile, is defined in political, rather than metaphysical, terms, often through reference to history.[8]

A more aggressive attitude characterizes the playwright who faces the task of addressing an audience which constitutes or contains those he defines as his political enemies. Rather than offer a protagonist to an audience for mutual self-examination and co-operative self-definition, he will ideally make his protagonist's dramatic logic engage the audience's sympathies and turn them against their own customary values; or even simply attack audience surrogatges in a satirical manner. Again, Sartre is informative; when considering the work of negro author Richard Wright and its contrasting assimilation by two distinct sections of the public, he writes:

> Each of Wright's works contains what Baudelaire would have called 'a double simultaneous postulation'; each word refers to two contexts; two forces are applied simultaneously to each phrase and determine the incomparable tension of his tale. Had he spoken to the whites alone, he might have turned out to be more prolix, more didactic, and more abusive; to the negroes alone, still more elliptical, more of a confederate, and more elegiac. In the first case, his work might have come close to satire; in the second, to prophetic lamentations. . . . Wright, a writer for a split public, has been able to maintain and go beyond this split. He has made it the pretext for a work of art.[9]

The dynamics of this precarious balance have many parallels with the problem facing the political dramatist, but perhaps the kernel of its mood lies in the words 'incomparable tension'. Uncontainable, even self-destructive, nervous energy informs the work of writers most conscious of this split public, and some of the most powerful recent theatrical experiences have been created by playwrights who have managed to personify and articulate this tension, which has almost become a modern *cogito ergo sum*, in the voice of the volatile and violent modern malcontent, of which Griffiths's Gethin Price is the self-conscious and self-defining example *par excellence*. Correspondingly, a style of acting has recently evolved, or at least a distinct series of actors and actresses equipped and prepared to imbue such dislocated characters with a fierce, almost frenzied power (one thinks of Steven Berkoff, Patti Love, David Threlfall, Phil Daniels, Kate Nelligan and, particularly, Jonathan Pryce). This spirit of tension as an ideal is questioned, to some degree, by *Class Enemy* and other plays by Nigel Williams; but it is significant that no coherent or convincing alternative can be advanced unreservedly by these works.

The alienation available to political dramatists through use of historical settings has been reviewed in the previous chapter, but a final re-examination may be beneficial. The effective evocation of historical parallels which have pertinence to contemporary events is rarely as successfully managed as in Friel's *Translations*; more often, attempted illumination slides into unconvincing oversimplification, or vague statements of only tenuous relevance (The Industrial Revolution Peasant Uprising play, particularly, is hardening into a formal cliché). Re-examinations of more immediate, and therefore less 'official' recent history (as found in plays such as *Plenty*, *Mary Barnes*, *Maydays* and *Our Friends in the North*) can be considerably more productive and interesting. Speculative plays set in the future also need to remain in close touch with recognizable contemporary reality, or they risk degenerating into sterile fantasy. Again, plays which aim for a less distant setting, like Brenton's *Thirteenth Night*, have a better chance of maintaining their immediacy. As I write this, the 'expiry dates' of *The Churchill Play* and *Savage Amusement* (and, of course, Orwell's *1984*) have arrived, but then again, so have some of the social symptoms they predicted; what might have seemed alarmist fantasy to the initial audience – rioting, looting, swingeing cuts in public and educational expenditure, provisions for the use of army camps as overspill prisons – have already become chillingly recognizable. Of course, the dates on the plays' action

can always be changed should their prophecies remain unfulfil-
led, but even this hopeful notion highlights the political playwright's fundamental opposition to the critical temperament
which sees it as its duty to establish and promote a 'canon of
literature'. Many recent dramatists have felt increasingly drawn
to creating 'Short Sharp Shocks', immediate and topical, even
hopefully disposable, plays, such as one finds on an agitprop
circuit, although many of these writers are now working more
ambitiously towards more complex effects, more heterogeneous
audiences and the uncertain hope of a future. But their often
justifiable mistrust of literary institutionalization (with its threat
of ideological castration) persists, to the point where Howard
Brenton sees critical establishment values as an extension of the
other establishment values he opposes:

> Who stole Bert Brecht's corpse?
> An industry of critics
> Profiteering death[10]

Perhaps the dangers facing literary criticism and political drama
are surprisingly similar: external economic forces, and asphyxiat-
ing self-insulation. Any account of modern British and Irish
writing rejects what I propose to be its most urgent, powerful and
starkly original form if it dismisses, or treats insensitively, the
genre of political drama. Whilst modern political playwrights
must maintain a firm and realistic image, however disappointingly restrictive, of the predominantly middle-class audience
which they currently address through the legitimate theatre, in
order to expand, criticize or strengthen its various sections most
effectively. Sartre again:

> Whatever game [a writer] may want to play, he must play it on
> the basis of representation which others have of him. He may
> want to modify the character that one attributes to the man of
> letters in a given society; but in order to change it, he must first
> slip into it. Hence, the public intervenes, with its customs, its
> vision of the world, and its conceptions of society and literature
> within that society. It surrounds the writer, it hems him in, and
> its imperious or sly demands, its refusals and its flights, are the
> given facts on whose basis a work can be constructed.[11]

Having recourse to an unlikely religious metaphor, one might say that a political dramatist's audience individually constitute his personal cross; but collectively, they constitute his chance of shared authenticity and redemption. Dramatist and audience alike now face the difficulties of survival in an increasingly reactionary climate, and look forward to a perilous future from forces that have been sharpening their spears in readiness.

I did not leave the auditorium during the preview of *The Romans in Britain*: I stayed to the bitter end and witnessed the desultory and derisory applause . . .

I am not concerned with issues of artistic standards, obscenity, indecency or dramatic politicking in themselves. My purpose was to question whether any production so lacking in redeeming features (and grossly offensive to boot) ought to be staged at public expense.

It is clear beyond peradventure (and I have had a heavy postbag) that a large majority of the public is opposed to this use of public funds. Fashionable though it may be to pander to minority tastes and wishes, we still have not reached the stage in civic affairs where no account need be taken of widely-held views.

Accordingly it is inevitable that the GLC should consider its position. I doubt whether anyone would seriously suggest that one lapse of judgement should condemn the National Theatre to eternal financial limbo; but short rations often clear the head.

Sir Horace Cutler (Conservative Leader of the Greater London Council) in a letter to *The Times*, 28 October 1980.

I STIRRED THE POLICE, THEREFORE, I TOUCHED THE TRUTH.

No End of Blame

Notes

N.B.: Dates assigned to plays in the main text correspond to the date of first performance; in the notes, to the date of publication of the edition cited, unless otherwise stated. All works published in London unless otherwise stated.

INTRODUCTION

1. Peter Weiss, *Marat/Sade* (1965) p. 35.
2. George H. Szanto, *Theater and Propaganda* (Texas, 1978).
3. Ibid., p. 72.
4. Roger Hudson, 'Towards a Definition of People's Theatre', *Theatre Quarterly*, I, no. 4 (1971) p. 2.
5. Roland Barthes, *Mythologies* (1973) p. 146.
6. Peter Brook, *The Empty Space* (1968) p. 43.
7. Martin Esslin, *Brecht: A Choice of Evils* (1959, 1980) p. 117.
8. See J. W. Lever's *The Tragedy of State* (1971) for a particularly serious and sympathetic assessment of the Jacobean tragedy and its avenging malcontent in specifically political terms.
9. Edward Bond, Preface to *The Bundle* (1978) p. xiii.
10. Cited by Ronald Gray, *Brecht the Dramatist* (Cambridge, 1976) p. 77.
11. Ibid., pp. 74–6.
12. Jean-Paul Sartre, *What is Literature?* (1950) p. 60.
13. Brecht, quoted by John Willett, *The Theatre of Bertolt Brecht* (1959, 1977) p. 78.
14. Robert Brustein, *The Theatre of Revolt* (1965) p. 10.
15. Ronald Ayling, 'Sean O'Casey's Dublin Trilogy', in *Sean O'Casey: A Collection of Critical Essays*, ed. Thomas Kilroy (Englewood Cliffs, NJ, 1975) pp. 84, 88.
16. David Hare, 'A Lecture Given at King's College, Cambridge', in *Licking Hitler* (1976) p. 63.
17. David Edgar, 'Ten Years of Political Theatre, 1968–1978', in *Theatre Quarterly*, VII, no. 32 (Winter 1979) pp. 25–33 (32, 31).
18. Sandy Craig, 'Unmasking the Lie', in *Dreams and Deconstructions* (1980) pp. 30–1.
19. Brustein, op. cit., p. 13.

1 SOCIALIST SUPERMEN AND PILGRIMS' PROGRESS

1. Bernard Shaw, *The Revolutionist's Handbook* in Shaw's *Man and Superman* (1946), p. 213.

216

2. Bernard Shaw, *The Quintessence of Ibsenism* (1913) p. 205.
3. Bernard Shaw, *Three Plays for Puritans* (1946) pp. 13–14.
4. Bernard Shaw, *Plays Unpleasant* (1946) p. 27.
5. Ibid., pp. 61–2.
6. Ibid., pp. 86, 87.
7. *The Quintessence of Ibsenism*, p. 203.
8. *Plays Unpleasant*, p. 265.
9. Ibid., p. 286.
10. Ibid., p. 210.
11. Ibid., p. 26.
12. *Three Plays for Puritans*, p. 21.
13. *Man and Superman*, p. 10.
14. Ibid., p. 18.
15. Ibid., p. 17.
16. *Three Plays for Puritans*, p. 29.
17. *Man and Superman*, p. 22.
18. Ibid., pp. 227, 228.
19. Ibid., p. 216.
20. Ibid., p. 37.
21. Carl Levine, 'Social Criticism of Shaw and Nietzsche', *Shaw Review*, x, no. 1 (January 1967) pp. 9–17.
22. *Man and Superman*, p. 251.
23. Ibid., p. 169.
24. Bernard Shaw, *Saint Joan* (1946), p. 43. Maurice Valency's *The Cart and the Trumpet* (Oxford, 1973) develops this notion of Shavian historical tragedy as an expression of the 'cosmic dialectic'.
25. *Three Plays for Puritans*, pp. 129, 132, 134.
26. Bernard Shaw, *Back to Methuselah* (1939) pp. 9, 55.
27. Bernard Shaw, *Plays Pleasant* (1946) p. 8.
28. Bernard Shaw, *Major Barbara* (1960) p. 143.
29. Ibid., p. 124.
30. Ibid., p. 144.
31. Ibid., p. 141.
32. Ibid., p. 144.
33. Bertolt Brecht, *The Measures Taken*, tr. Carl R. Mueller (1977) p. 25.
34. *Major Barbara*, p. 152.
35. Bernard Shaw, *Heartbreak House* (1964) p. 7.
36. Ibid., p. 11.
37. *The Bodley Head Bernard Shaw Collected Plays*, iv (1972) p. 20.
38. Ibid., p. 142.
39. Ibid., p. 140.
40. Ibid., p. 182.
41. Ibid., p. 172.
42. Ibid., p. 201.
43. Ibid., pp. 214, 215.
44. Ibid., p. 248.
45. Ibid., p. 241.
46. *Back to Methuselah*, pp. 59–60.
47. *Heartbreak House*, pp. 8, 10.

48. Ibid., p. 55.
49. Ibid., pp. 86, 87.
50. Ibid., p. 152.
51. Ibid., p. 155.
52. Ibid., p. 156.
53. Ibid., p. 138.
54. Ibid., p. 160.
55. Bernard Shaw, *The Apple Cart* (1956) pp. 47–8.
56. Ibid., p. 105.
57. Ibid., p. 122.
58. Ibid. p. 9.
59. Bernard Shaw, *Plays Extravagant* (1981) p. 16.
60. Ibid. p. 14.
61. Ibid., p. 55.
62. Ibid., p. 59.
63. Ibid., p. 82.
64. Ibid., pp. 102, 103.
65. Ibid., pp. 120, 121.
66. Ibid., p. 116.
67. Ibid., p. 109.
68. Ibid., p. 122.
69. Ibid., pp. 107, 108.
70. *Too True to be Good, Village Wooing & On the Rocks. Three Plays by Bernard Shaw* (1934) pp. 199–200.
71. Ibid., p. 219.
72. Ibid., p. 272.
73. Ibid., p. 273.
74. Ibid., p. 274.
75. Bernard Shaw, *Everyone's Political What's What* (1944) p. 50.

2   KATHLEEN NI HOULIHAN'S OTHER ISLAND

1. Sean O'Casey, *Three More Plays by Sean O'Casey* (1965) pp. 286–7.
2. Bernard Shaw, Preface to the First Edition, *John Bull's Other Island with How He Lied to her Husband and Major Barbara* (1931) pp. 13–14.
3. *John Bull's Other Island*, p. 90.
4. Ibid., p. 15.
5. Ibid., pp. 174, 175.
6. Ibid. p. 176.
7. Ibid., p. 170.
8. Ibid., pp. 170–1.
9. Ibid., p. 92.
10. Sean O'Casey, *Three Plays by Sean O'Casey* (1957) pp. 110, 111.
11. Ibid., p. 27.
12. Bernard Benstock, *Paycocks and Others: Sean O'Casey's World* (Dublin, 1976) p. 11.
13. See David Krause, *Sean O'Casey: The Man and his Work* (1960, 1975) pp. 68–70.

14. *Three Plays by Sean O'Casey*, p. 45.
15. Ibid., p. 47.
16. Ibid. p. 50.
17. Ibid., p. 72.
18. Ibid., p. 204.
19. Ibid., pp. 208–9.
20. Ibid., p. 213.
21. Sean O'Casey, *Inishfallen Fare Thee Well* (1950) p. 186.
22. *Three More Plays by Sean O'Casey*, p. 51.
23. Ibid., p. 50.
24. Ibid., p. 54.
25. Sean O'Casey, *Collected Plays*, II (1950) p. 163.
26. Ibid., p. 182.
27. Ibid., p. 324.
28. Ibid., p. 320.
29. Ibid., p. 313.
30. Compare David Edgar's anti-fascist play *Destiny* (1976) which manages to move beyond political stock responses, engage the right-wing sympathies of potential audiences, then incite them to action against the implications of such sympathies.
31. *Three More Plays by Sean O'Casey*, p. 298.
32. Ibid., p. 310.
33. Ibid., p. 143.
34. Ibid., p. 170.
35. Ibid., p. 217. W. B. Yeats's one-act play *Cathleen ni Houlihan* (1902) is a similar excursion into mythological agitprop, in which the disguised figure of Cathleen herself intervenes to inspire the young man of a household to join the fight against the 'strangers' invading her house and connects sacrifice for the cause to a long, almost religious, tradition.
36. *Classic Irish Drama*, ed. W. A. Armstrong (1964) p. 220.
37. C. Desmond Greaves, *Sean O'Casey: Politics and Art* (1979) p. 190.
38. *The Sean O'Casey Reader*, ed. Brooks Atkinson (1968), pp. 584–5.

3   LEARN HOW TO SEE AND NOT TO GAPE

1. Bertolt Brecht, *The Exception and the rule*, tr. Ralph Manheim, in *The Measures Taken and other Lehrstücke* (1977) p. 37.
2. Erwin Piscator, *The Political Theatre*, tr. Hugh Rorrison (1980) p. vi.
3. Piscator writes elsewhere that 'Nietzsche, the scourge of the middle classes, and Wilde, the aesthete and snob, and all those in the last fifty years who ironized, attacked or interpreted this morbid bourgeois society helped me to escape from the middle classes, to shed my petty bourgeois background', ibid., p. 9.
4. Ibid., pp. 30, 33.
5. Ibid., p. 75.
6. Ibid., p. 134.
7. Ibid., p. 183.
8. Ibid., p. 173.

9. Ibid., pp. 186, 187.
10. Ibid., p. 326.
11. Ibid., p. 188.
12. See Ernest Schumacher, 'Piscator's Political Theater', in *Brecht: A Collection of Critical Essays*, ed. Peter Demetz (Englewood Cliffs, N.J., 1962) p. 92ff.
13. Bertolt Brecht, *The Messingkauf Dialogues*, tr. John Willett (1965) p. 69.
14. Bertolt Brecht, *Drums in the Night*, tr. John Willett, ed. Willett and Manheim (1980) p. 25.
15. Ibid., p. 53.
16. Notes to *Drums in the Night*, p. 71.
17. See David Bathrick, *The Dialectic and the Early Brecht* (Stuttgart, 1975).
18. Bertolt Brecht, quoted in notes to *Baal*, tr. Peter Tegel, ed. Willett and Manheim (1980) p. 66.
19. The potential of this scene was cleverly exploited in David Jones's production at The Other Place, Stratford, in 1979, by amending the scene to have Baal play to the theatre audience as nightclub audience, with invisible actors supplying catcalls from the audience area.
20. Bertolt Brecht, notes to *In the Jungle of Cities*, tr. Gerhard Nellhaus, ed. Willett and Manheim (1980) p. 72.
21. *In the Jungle of Cities*, p. 2.
22. Ibid., p. 13.
23. Ibid., p. 32.
24. Ibid., p. 20.
25. Ibid., pp. 26–7.
26. Ibid., p. 55.
27. Ibid., pp. 58–9.
28. Bertolt Brecht, *Man equals Man*, tr. Gerhard Nellhaus, ed. Willett and Manheim (1979) p. 42.
29. Ibid., p. 62.
30. Ibid., p. 76.
31. Ibid., notes, p. 100.
32. Bertolt Brecht, *Brecht on Theatre*, tr. John Willett (1964) p. 71.
33. Ibid., p. 86.
34. *The Measures Taken and other Lehrstücke*, p. 59.
35. Ibid., p. 60.
36. Ibid., pp. 32–3.
37. Ibid., p. 34.
38. Ibid., p. 25.
39. Jan Needle and Peter Thomson, *Brecht* (Oxford, 1981) p. 75.
40. Bertolt Brecht, *Mother Courage and her Children*, tr. Eric Bentley (1962) p. 5.
41. Ibid., p. 29.
42. Bertolt Brecht, *The Life of Galileo*, tr. Howard Brenton (1980) translator's note.
43. *The Life of Galileo*, p. 50.
44. Ibid., pp. 50, 51.
45. Ibid., p. 30.
46. Ibid., p. 85.
47. Bertolt Brecht, *The Good Person of Szechwan*, tr. John Willett (1965) p. 10.
48. Ibid., p. 23.
49. Ibid., p. 107.

50. Ibid., p. 109.
51. Bertolt Brecht, *Mr Puntila and his Man Matti*, tr. John Willett (1977) p. 76.
52. Ibid., p. 92. It is interesting to compare the drunken Puntila–Matti relationship with that of Louis Litvanov and his workers in Wesker's *The Wedding Feast* (1974), which ends on a similar note of abortive class contact. And the relationship between Eva and Matti has already been noted by Needle and Thomson as a comic echo of the mistress–servant confrontation in Strindberg's *Miss Julia*.

I would propose and welcome a revival of *Puntila* featuring George Cole in the title role and Dennis Waterman as Matti, in a revision of their *Minder* TV partnership. This would have the same effective manipulation of audience associations as the casting of Jimmy Jewel and Bill Fraser, the veteran comedians, as Eddie Waters in the 1975 Nottingham Playhouse and 1979 BBC TV productions of Griffiths's *Comedians*.
53. Bertolt Brecht, *The Resistible Rise of Arturo Ui*, tr. Ralph Manheim (1976) p. 8.
54. Ibid., p. 88.
55. Ibid., p. 94.
56. Ibid., p. 96.
57. *Brecht on Theatre*, p. 205.
58. *The Messingkauf Dialogues*, p. 94.

4   THE HIDDEN SITUATION

1. W. Somerset Maugham, *For Services Rendered* (1979) p. 53.
2. Katharine J. Worth, *Revolutions in Modern English Drama* (1972) pp. 7, 4.
3. John Galsworthy, *The Plays of John Galsworthy* (1929) p. 8.
4. Ibid., p. 35.
5. Ibid., p. 47.
6. Ibid., p. 139. A similar figure and final sentiment appears in Allan Monkhouse's *First Blood* (published 1924), in which the old worker Jabez Livesy criticizes his son Jack's militant sympathies, then loses his daughter Phyllis in a riot. *First Blood* features an eloquent and dramatically powerful shop steward Tom Eden, who recalls Galsworthy's Roberts and also loses control of his men, and a sympathetic go-between Lionel Stott, who together vie for Phyllis's affections. Like O'Casey's Minnie Powell, Phyllis sacrifices herself for Lionel, and the final tone of the play is condemnatory of violence whilst extending sympathy to the better representatives of both sides and their respective cases in the industrial dispute. In terms of plot and characterization, *First Blood* resembles a nineteenth-century industrial novel in dramatic form.
7. *The Plays of John Galsworthy*, p. 151.
8. Ibid., p. 476.
9. Ibid., pp. 473–4.
10. Ibid., p. 480.
11. Ibid., p. 481.
12. Ibid., p. 495.

13. Ibid., p. 500.
14. Ibid., pp. 504–5.
15. Ibid., p. 509.
16. Ibid., p. 510.
17. Ibid., p. 512.
18. C. K. Munro, *The Rumour* (1927) pp. 80–1.
19. Ibid., p. 107.
20. C. K. Munro, *Progress* (1924) p. 155.
21. Ibid., p. 158.
22. Ibid., p. 161. Harley Granville-Barker's *Waste* (written in 1907) is primarily the sexual tragedy of a Member of Parliament, but the mediocrity and self-interest demonstrated in the machinations of the new Prime Minister and his formulative cabinet give the play's political setting a flavour of expository scorn reminiscent of Munro's plays and Shaw's later extravaganzas.
23. *For Services Rendered*, pp. 52–3.
24. Ibid., pp. 53–4.
25. Ibid., p. 65. The climactic ironic use of the National Anthem predates the similar conclusion to Wesker's *Chips with Everything* (1962).
26. J. B. Priestley, *The Plays of J. B. Priestley*, iii (1950) p. 248.
27. Ibid., p. 289.
28. Ibid., p. 311. In my own production of the play for Stourbridge Youth Theatre in 1978, directed in conjunction with Nigel Price, we accentuated the expressionistic tendencies of the play and totally discarded the naturalistic status of this speech. Instead, a recording of the Inspector's voice with added echo and a simulated heartbeat was played whilst the actors were frozen in ensemble position by red spotlights.
29. Ibid., p. xi.
30. Ibid., p. 200–1.
31. Stephen Spender, *Trial of a Judge* (1938) p. 59.
32. Ibid., pp. 90, 92.
33. Ibid., pp. 94–5.
34. W. H. Auden and Christopher Isherwood, *The Dog Beneath the Skin* (1935) p. 40.
35. Ibid., p. 43.
36. Ibid., pp. 132–3.
37. Ibid., p. 146.
38. Ibid., pp. 155–6.
39. Ibid., p. 169.
40. Ibid., pp. 173–4.
41. Ibid., p. 179.
42. W. H. Auden and Christopher Isherwood, *The Ascent of F6 and On the Frontier* (1937) p. 64.
43. Ibid., p. 55.
44. Ibid., pp. 153, 155.
45. Ibid., p. 170.

5 ANONYMITY AND ANGER

1. John Osborne and Anthony Creighton, *Epitaph for George Dillon* (1958) pp. 56–7.
2. Alan Carter, *John Osborne* (Edinburgh, 1969, 1974) p. 191.
3. John Osborne, *T.V. Times*, vol. 102, no. 10 (26 February 1981) p. 3.
4. John Osborne, *Look Back in Anger* (1957) p. 19.
5. Ibid., p. 15.
6. Ibid., p. 59.
7. Ibid., p. 84.
8. Ibid., p. 93.
9. Ibid., p. 94.
10. Ibid., p. 43.
11. *Epitaph for George Dillon*, p. 60.
12. *Look Back in Anger*, p. 47.
13. Robert Wilcher, 'The Fool and his Techniques in the Contemporary Theatre', *Theatre Research International*, iv, no. 2 (February 1979) pp. 117–33 (123).
14. John Osborne, *The Entertainer* (1957) p. 71.
15. Ibid., p. 72.
16. Ibid., p. 89.
17. John Osborne, *A Subject of Scandal and Concern* (1961) pp. 46–7.
18. John Osborne, *Time Present and The Hotel in Amsterdam* (1968) p. 39.
19. John Osborne, *A Sense of Detachment* (1973) p. 24. It is remarkable that, to date, no critics have considered this play at any length; they generally prefer to skate over its relationship to Osborne's other work in a single dismissive sentence or ignore it completely, in apparent embarrassment.
20. Ibid., p. 13.
21. Ibid., p. 32.
22. Jean-Paul Sartre, *What is Literature?* (1950) p. 61.
23. Arnold Wesker, *The Wesker Trilogy* (1964) pp. 29–30.
24. Arnold Wesker, *Three Plays* (1976) p. 203.
25. Ibid., p. 185.
26. Arnold Wesker, *Play Volume Three* (1980) p. 106.
27. Arnold Wesker, *Plays Volume Four* (1980) pp. 178–9.
28. Brendan Behan, *The Complete Plays* (1978) p. 206.
29. Ibid., p. 204.
30. Ibid., p. 191.
31. Ibid., p. 217.
32. Ibid., p. 229.
33. Ibid., p. 237.
34. Arnold Wesker, *Three Plays*, p. 54.
35. Ibid., p. 69.
36. Ibid., p. 71.
37. Arnold Wesker, *Plays Volume Three*, p. 26.
38. Ibid., p. 33.
39. Ibid., pp. 46–7.
40. Brendan Behan, *The Complete Plays*, p. 103.
41. Ibid., pp. 113–14.

42. Tom McGrath and Jimmy Boyle, *The Hard Man* (1977) pp. 8–9.
43. Ibid., pp. 22–3.
44. Ibid., p. 33.
45. Ibid., p. 57.
46. Ibid., p. 63.
47. Ibid., p. 70.

6 BEYOND 'GOOD' AND 'EVIL'

1. Edward Bond, *The Activists Papers* in *The Worlds* (1980) p. 117.
2. John Russell Taylor, *Anger and After* (1962, 1969) p. 103.
3. John Arden, *Three Plays* (1964) p. 81.
4. Ibid., p. 96.
5. Ibid., p. 88.
6. Robert Wilcher, op. cit., p. 124.
7. John Arden, *Plays: One* (1977) p. 40.
8. Ibid., p. 42.
9. Ibid., p. 89.
10. Ibid., p. 93.
11. Ibid., p. 100.
12. In 1972, 7:84 Theatre Company presented a version of the play, *Serjeant Musgrave Dances On*, in which the historical parallels were made overt and Musgrave became a veteran of Derry's Bloody Sunday.
13. See Robert Wilcher, op. cit.
14. John Arden, *Plays: One*, p. 350.
15. Compare the painfully reluctant, but finally grim and uncompromising, order from Shogo to massacre the undifferentiated children in Bond's *Narrow Road to the Deep North*.
16. John Arden and Margaretta D'Arcy, *The Hero Rises Up* (1969) p. 76.
17. John Arden and Margaretta D'Arcy, *The Island of the Mighty* (1974) p. 12, Arden's Preface.
18. *The Island of the Mighty*, p. 79.
19. Ibid., p. 232.
20. John Arden, *Two Autobiographical Plays* (1971) p. 86.
21. John Arden, *Pearl* (1979) p. 26.
22. Ibid., p. 47.
23. Ibid., p. 61.
24. Malcolm Hay and Philip Roberts, *Bond: A Study of his Plays* (1980) pp. 116–17.
25. Edward Bond, *Lear* (1972) p. 45.
26. Ibid., pp. 79, 85.
27. Ibid., pp. 83–4.
28. Edward Bond, *Bingo* (1974) p. 7.
29. Ibid., p. 49.
30. Ibid., p. 17.
31. Malcolm Hay and Philip Roberts, op. cit., p. 199.
32. Edward Bond, *The Fool* (1976) p. 43.

33. Correspondence with Bond cited in Hay and Roberts, op. cit., p. 215.
34. Hay and Roberts, op. cit., p. 214.
35. Compare Robert Coover's handling of the Uncle Sam figure in his 1977 novel *The Public Burning*. Coover maintains the perverse vitality and moral repugnance of the character but also suggests his relationship to the popular imagination and the less extreme emotion on which he feeds.
36. *The Bundle* was in fact staged before *The Woman* although written later. This marginal sequential distortion may be confusing in terms of Bond's ideological development because of the differing weights of emphasis in the two plays' treatments of war. *The Woman* demonstrates the absurdity of imperialist warfare, whilst *The Bundle* urges the necessity of revolutionary warfare, a crucial distinction.
37. Edward Bond, *The Bundle* (1978) p. 46.
38. Ibid., p. 47.
39. Ibid., p. 54.
40. Ibid., p. 64.
41. Ibid., p. 78.
42. Hay and Roberts, op. cit., p. 280.
43. *The Bundle*, p. xiii.
44. Ibid., p. xiv.
45. *The Worlds*, p. 145.
46. See Introduction, p. 6.

7 HOME TRUTHS AND FOREIGN FREEDOMS

1. Tom Stoppard, *Every Good Boy Deserves Favour and Professional Foul* (1978) p. 55.
2. David Mercer, *Cousin Vladimir* (1978) p. 59.
3. Kenneth Tynan interestingly speculates that Brook was drawn to the possibilities of *US* for its potential for audience disruption and its Manichean philosophical bleakness rather than for any specific attack on American capitalist imperialism – see 'On the Moral Neutrality of Peter Brook' in *New Theatre Voices of the Seventies*, ed. Simon Trussler (1981) pp. 134–44.
4. Trevor Griffiths, *Occupations* (1972, 1980) p. 9.
5. Ibid., p. 8.
6. Arnold Wesker, *Fears of Fragmentation* (1970) p. 100.
7. *Occupations*, p. 46.
8. Ibid., p. 46.
9. Ibid., p. 60.
10. Trevor Griffiths, *The Party* (1974) pp. 9, 10.
11. Ibid., p. 49.
12. Ibid., p. 53.
13. Edward Braun, 'Trevor Griffiths' in *British Television Drama*, ed. George W. Brandt (Cambridge, 1981) p. 59.
14. Griffiths: 'I'll probably never complete a play in the formal sense. It has to be open at the end: people have to make choices, because if you're not making choices, you're not actually living'; Jonathon Croall, 'From House to House', *The Times Educational Supplement*, 25 June 1976, p. 19.

15. Edward Braun, op. cit., p. 67.
16. Tom Stoppard, *Every Good Boy Deserves Favour and Professional Foul*, p. 55.
17. Ibid., p. 91.
18. C. P. Taylor, *Good* (1982) p. 9.
19. Ibid., p. 43.
20. Ibid., p. 45.
21. Ibid., Author's Note, p. 7.
22. Christopher Hampton, *Savages* (1974) p. 30.
23. Ibid., pp. 64, 65.
24. Ibid., p. 81.
25. John Russell Taylor, *The Second Wave* (1971) p. 42.
26. David Mercer, *Cousin Vladimir*, p. 19.
27. Ibid., p. 31.
28. Ibid., p. 45.
29. Ibid., p. 59.
30. Ibid., p. 68.
31. Ibid., p. 83.
32. Ibid., p. 86.
33. Ibid., p. 87.
34. David Mercer, *The Monster of Karlovy Vary* (1979) p. 9.
35. Ibid., p. 13.
36. Ibid., pp. 16–17.
37. Ibid., p. 19.
38. Ibid., p. 41.
39. Ibid., p. 61.
40. Ibid., pp. 65–6.

8   CARTOON NIGHTMARES

1. Barrie Keeffe, *Sus* (1979) p. 26.
2. Howard Barker, *No End of Blame* (1981) p. 49.
3. Peter Ansorge, *Disrupting the Spectacle* (1975) p. 2.
4. Consider for example the confidences and cynical commentaries shared with the audience by Vindice in *The Revenger's Tragedy* (1605/6), Iago in Shakespeare's *Othello* (1603/4), Malevole in Marston's *The Malcontent* (1603/4) and Bosola in Webster's *The Duchess of Malfi* (1614). It is additionally interesting to compare critical reactions to Jacobean dramatists with critical reactions to the playwrights considered in this chapter, particularly in discussion of the dramatist's relation to his subject matter, which is often identified as sadistic, amoral or psychologically unbalanced (perhaps in order to insulate the critic and audience from the atmosphere of guilt the dramatists are attempting to fuel). Compare T. S. Eliot's view of Webster in the poem 'Whispers of Immortality' and his essay 'Four Elizabethan Dramatists' with Ronald Hayman's worried, uncomprehending reaction to modern writers in *British Theatre Since 1955* (Oxford, 1979), p. 126:

    Very often dramatized argument and analysis give way to entertaining but implausible violence in melodramatic climaxes, the underlying sentimentality being disguised by brutality. Catering for Victorian audiences, melodramatists coated the moralistic pill with sugar; contemporary melodramatists use viciousness. The *coups de théâtre* in the work of Bond, Brenton, Barker and Poliakoff are undeniably effective, but the recourse to violent killing serves almost every time as an alternative to continuing the thinking process.

On the other hand, J. W. Lever in *The Tragedy of State* criticizes Ian Jack's description of Webster as negative and unbalanced as follows:

> Had Webster's mind been properly balanced – that is to say, suitably conservative – he would, Jack implies, have seen the Renaissance world as a radiant vision of God-given harmonies. The facts of tyranny, intrigue, hypocrisy and violence would have been neatly conceptualized into an unhealthy 'Machiavellian ideal', before being banished from the writer's antiseptic brain. – Needless to say, no serious dramatist of the Jacobean age reacted in this manner (p. 80).

5. Sandy Craig, 'The Beginnings of the Fringe', *Dreams and Deconstructions*, p. 28.
6. Katharine J. Worth, op. cit., p. 143.
7. Ibid., p. 166.
8. William S. Burroughs, *The Ticket that Exploded* (1968) p. 151.
9. Katharine J. Worth, op. cit., p. 161ff.
10. Heathcote Williams, *AC/DC* (1972) p. 50.
11. Ibid., pp. 79, 80. Snoo Wilson, a Portable contemporary of Brenton and Hare, has several affinities with playwrights discussed in this chapter, particularly in his taste for black humour, shock, and fantastic invention, but is perhaps closest to the Williams of *AC/DC* or the Brenton of *Hitler Dances* in one of his more disciplined and political plays, *Vampire* (1972), which uses the similar theme of Burroughs-like 'vampirization' – the draining of psychic energy and terminal exploitation – to link the romantic mythology of war, modern pop star 'media turds' and a right-wing politician we also encounter in Barker's *The Loud Boy's Life*. Wilson's *Pignight* (1969) and *Blow Job* (1971) are less focussed or coherent excursions through characteristic Portable territory, anarchic accounts of slaughter at a pig farm and two skinhead hoodlums' backfiring attempt to blow a safe. Latterly, Wilson's impulse has tended more towards the fantastic, of which his most inventive realization is perhaps *The Glad Hand* (1978), a play of lighter texture showing the megalomaniac fascist Ritsaat's attempt to summon up and assassinate a Communist Antichrist – a plan abruptly halted when Ritsaat is killed in a revolt by the eccentric crew of his ship, who similarly wish to prove that 'reality' and 'history' can be altered by belief and decisive action.
12. Trevor Griffiths, *Comedians* (1976) p. 20.
13. Ibid., p. 23.
14. Ibid., p. 68.
15. Ibid., p. 50.
16. Ibid., p. 53.
17. Ibid., p. 52.

18. Ibid., pp. 65, 67.
19. Ibid., pp. 65, 64. Austin E. Quigley presents a careful and interesting reading of the theatrical effect of Price's act in 'Creativity and Commitment in Trevor Griffiths's *Comedians'*, *Modern Drama* XXIV no. 14 (Dec. 1981) pp. 404–23, also pointing out the discrepancy between Waters's rejection of the enforced cycle of hate and inaccuracy perpetuated by stereotypes, and Price's recognition and use of the emotional truths embodied in class stereotypes, where he sees no alternative to hate.
20. *Comedians*, pp. 67–8.
21. Trevor Griffiths, interviewed in *Gambit*, no. 29 (1976) p. 33.
22. David Hare, interviewed in *Plays and Players*, no. 221 (Feb. 1972); quoted by Ansorge, op. cit., p. 2.
23. Howard Brenton in interview, 'Petrol Bombs Through the Proscenium Arch', *Theatre Quarterly*, v, no. 17 (March–May 1975) pp. 4–20 (12).
24. Howard Brenton, *Magnificence* (1973, 1980) p. 39.
25. Ibid., p. 62.
26. Ibid., p. 70.
27. Howard Brenton, *Revenge* (1970) p. 51. Compare Jonson's *The Devil is an Ass* (1616) in which Pug, the demon, is appalled by the level of evil in London and longs to return to Hell to escape such depths of villainy.
28. Howard Brenton and David Hare, *Brassneck* (1974) p. 86.
29. Howard Brenton, *The Churchill Play* (1974) p. 51.
30. Ibid., p. 29.
31. Ibid., p. 27.
32. Ibid., pp. 86–7.
33. Ibid., p. 80.
34. Ibid., p. 65.
35. Howard Brenton, *Plays for the Poor Theatre* (1980) p. 23.
36. Howard Brenton, *Epsom Downs* (1977) p. 55.
37. Howard Brenton, *Thirteenth Night and A Short Sharp Shock!* (1981) p. 80.
38. John Arden and Margaretta D'Arcy, Preface to *The Hero Rises Up*, p. 5.
39. Howard Brenton, *The Romans in Britain* (1980) p. 77.
40. Ibid., p. 100.
41. *Thirteenth Night and A Short Sharp Shock!*, p. 39.
42. Howard Brenton, *The Genius* (1983) p. 39.
43. Howard Barker, *The Hang of the Gaol* (1982) p. 11.
44. Howard Barker, *On 'The Hang of the Gaol'* (RSC Warehouse Writers 1, 1978) p. 2.
45. Howard Barker, *Stripwell & Claw* (1977) p. 115.
46. Ibid., p. 204.
47. Ibid., p. 226.
48. Howard Barker, *Fair Slaughter* (1978) pp. 25–6. The inspired casting of music-hall comedian Max Wall as Old Gocher and John Thaw of *The Sweeney* fame as screw Leary in the original production is a fine example of manipulating popular public associations of actors in surprising new directions, as were the previously mentioned castings of Jimmy Jewel and Bill Fraser in *Comedians*.
49. *Fair Slaughter*, p. 27.
50. Ibid., p. 29.

51. Ibid., p. 44.
52. Ibid., p. 45.
53. Ibid., p. 40.
54. Ibid., p. 48.
55. Howard Barker, *On 'The Loud Boy's Life'* (RSC Warehouse Writers 9, 1980) p. 2.
56. *No End of Blame*, p. 2.
57. Ibid., p. 10.
58. Ibid., p. 11.
59. Ibid., p. 121.
60. Ibid., p. 25.
61. Ibid., p. 25.
62. Ibid., p. 32.
63. Ibid., p. 35.
64. Ibid., p. 38.
65. Ibid., p. 55.
66. Ibid., p. 55. However, I am informed that no audience member actually threw a pencil to Bela, at least on the play's run prior to London (although I was sorely tempted, only to have my impulse checked by an over-zealous lighting technician).
67. Barrie Keeffe, *Barbarians* (1978) p. 103.
68. Barrie Keeffe, interview with Catherine Itzin quoted in her *Stages in the Revolution* (1980) p. 247.
69. Barrie Keeffe, *Frozen Assets* (1978) p. 18.
70. Howard Barker, *On 'The Loud Boy's Life'*, p. 3.
71. Howard Barker, *That Good Between Us* (1980) p. 22.
72. *Stripwell and Claw*, p. 167.
73. Howard Barker, *On 'The Love of a Good Man'* (RSC Publications, 1980) p. 2.

9 EARNING A PLACE IN THE STORY

1. David Hare, *Plenty* (1978) p. 83.
2. David Edgar, *The Jail Diary of Albie Sachs* (1978) p. 46.
3. Howard Brenton, 'Petrol Bombs through the Proscenium Arch', p. 6.
4. David Hare, 'A Lecture', *Licking Hitler*, pp. 67, 69.
5. David Edgar, 'Address at Geissen Stadttheater, 30 September 1980'; made available and reproduced by kind permission of David Edgar.
6. 'A Lecture', *Licking Hitler*, p. 60.
7. Ibid., pp. 57–8.
8. a. David Edgar, 'Towards a Theatre of Dynamic Ambiguities', interview in *Theatre Quarterly*, IX, no. 33 (Spring 1979) p. 9.
   b. Ibid., p. 9.
9. David Hare, *Knuckle* (1974) p. 23.
10. Ibid., p. 27.
11. David Hare, *Fanshen* (1976) p. 7.
12. Ibid., p. 8.
13. Ibid., p. 15.

14. C. W. E. Bigsby, 'The Language of Crisis in British Theatre: The Drama of Cultural Pathology' in his selection of essays *Contemporary English Drama* (1981) p. 43.
15. Martin Esslin, *Brecht: A Choice of Evils* (1959, 1965, 1980).
16. *Fanshen*, pp. 24–5.
17. Ibid., pp. 67–8.
18. David Hare, interview with Ann McFerran, *Time Out*, no. 285, 29 August 1975; quoted by Steve Grant, 'Voicing the Protest', in *Dreams and Deconstructions*, ed. Craig, p. 117.
19. *Plenty*, p. 24.
20. Ibid., p. 40.
21. Ibid., p. 54.
22. Ibid., p. 78.
23. Ibid., p. 79.
24. Ibid., pp. 82–3.
25. Ibid., p. 83.
26. *Licking Hitler*, p. 36.
27. Ibid., p. 48.
28. a. Ibid., p. 54.
    b. Ibid., p. 54.
29. David Hare, *Dreams of Leaving* (1980) p. 35.
30. Ibid., p. 39.
31. David Edgar in interview with David Ian Rabey, 2 April 1981.
32. 'A Lecture', in *Licking Hitler*, p. 63.
33. David Edgar, 'Theatre, Politics and the Working Class', interview with Catherine Itzin, *Tribune*, 22 April 1977; quoted in *Stages in the Revolution*, pp. 147–8.
34. David Edgar, *Destiny* (1978) pp. 58–9.
35. David Edgar in interview with David Ian Rabey, 2 April 1981.
36. *Destiny*, p. 96. The Theatrescript edition (1976) features an earlier variation on the ending, in which the recognizable figure of Hitler emerged to speak the final words and concluded 'Told You'. Edgar says this device became rather cute and self-conscious in early performances, having been originally conceived as drawing the possibly expected parallel between British and German neo-Nazi movements in (by then) an unexpected way, but proving to be overly self-conscious in its anticipation of audience response.
37. Interview with Rabey, 2 April 1981.
38. Ibid.; compare Shaw on the Ibsenist art of 'sharpshooting at the audience': 'Never mislead an audience, was an old rule. But the new school will trick the spectator into forming a meanly false judgement, and then convict him of it in the next act, often to his grievous mortification' (*The Quintessence of Ibsenism*, p. 203).
39. David Edgar, *Teendreams* (1979) p. 45.
40. Ibid., p. 47.
41. Interview with Rabey, 2 April 1981.
42. David Edgar, *Mary Barnes* (1979) p. 23.
43. Ibid., p. 83.
44. Ibid., p. 87.
45. Ibid., p. 85.

46. *The Jail Diary of Albie Sachs*, p. 46.
47. Ibid., p. 8.
48. Ibid., p. 44.
49. Ibid., p. 78.
50. Ibid., p. 78.
51. Ibid., p. 79.
52. 'Address at Geissen Stadttheater'.
53. David Edgar, 'Adaptation as Art', *The Times*, 26 November 1980.
54. David Edgar, *Maydays* (1983) p. 63.
55. Ibid., p. 64.
56. Ibid., p. 65.
57. Ibid., p. 69.
58. Interview with Rabey, 2 April 1981.

10 PAST IMPERFECTS AND PRESENT INDICATIVES

1. Brian Friel, *Translations* (1981) p. 66.
2. Peter Flannery, *Savage Amusement* (1978) p. 60.
3. David Hare, 'A Lecture' in *Licking Hitler*, p. 70.
4. Brian Friel, *The Freedom of the City* (1974) p. 51.
5. Ibid., p. 21.
6. Ibid., p. 71.
7. Brian Friel, *Volunteers* (1974) p. 31.
8. Ibid., p. 26.
9. *Translations*, p. 64.
10. Ibid., p. 65.
11. Ibid., p. 68.
12. Peter Whelan, *Captain Swing* (1979) p. 95.
13. Caryl Churchill, *Light Shining in Buckinghamshire* (1978) Preface.
14. Caryl Churchill, *Softcops* (1984), Author's Note.
15. Ibid., p. 28.
16. Roland Barthes, *Mythologies* (1972), tr. Annette Lavers, p. 156.
17. Stephen Poliakoff, *Hitting Town and City Sugar* (1976, 1978) p. 132.
18. Stephen Poliakoff, *Strawberry Fields* (1977) p. 43.
19. Stephen Poliakoff, *Shout Across the River* (1979) p. 55.
20. Stephen Poliakoff, *The Summer Party* (1980) p. 44.
21. Ibid., p. 58.
22. *Savage Amusement*, p. 19.
23. Ibid., pp. 47–8.
24. Ibid., pp. 59–60.
25. *Strawberry Fields*, p. 35.
26. Nigel Williams, *Class Enemy* (1978) p. 9.
27. Ibid., p. 41.
28. Ibid., p. 35.
29. Nigel Williams, *Sugar and Spice & Trial Run* (1980) p. 46.
30. Ibid., p. 53.
31. Ibid., p. 52.
32. Ibid., p. 65.

33. Ibid., p. 68.
34. Nigel Williams, *Line 'Em* (1980) p. 26.
35. Ibid., p. 34.
36. Ibid., p. 40.
37. Ibid., p. 56.
38. Ibid., p. 57.
39. Ibid., p. 61.
40. *Sugar and Spice & Trial Run*, p. 15.
41. Ibid., p. 19.
42. Ibid., p. 20.
43. Ibid., p. 40.

CONCLUSIONS

1. Howard Barker, *That Good Between Us*, p. 49.
2. Jonathan Swift, Preface to 'The Battle of the Books', in *A Tale of a Tub and other Satires*, ed. Kathleen Williams (1975) p. 140.
3. Bernard Shaw, *The Intelligent Woman's Guide to Socialism and Capitalism* (1928) p. 219.
4. David Hare, 'Explorations: Portable Playwrights', interviews by Peter Ansorge, *Plays and Players*, ɪxx, no. 5 (Feb. 1972) pp. 14–23 (20).
5. Raymond Williams, *Culture and Society, 1780–1950* (1958) p. 187.
6. Jean-Paul Sartre, *Existentialism and Humanism* (1948), tr. Philip Mairet, p. 45. The note of existential challenge and affirmation which I identify in the works of Edgar, Barker, Hare, etc., is not to be identified with the heading of 'existential revolt' under which Robert Brustein classifies such authors as Beckett and Pirandello and even Ibsen as metaphysical rebels against universal alienation, with an almost absurdist view of man in a malevolent universe, akin to the philosophy of Artaud; I would claim Shaw and modern political dramatists proceed from a perception of immediate social alienation caused, and potentially healed, by distinctly political forces, and their heroes prove their integrity and authenticity by acting in relation to these forces, as posited in the philosophy of Sartre.
7. Jean-Paul Sartre, *What is Literature?*, p. 46.
8. As Howard Barker says of his own work: 'What I celebrate is energy and the small discovery of dignity. I think that is socialist. From confronting the pessimism comes the will to change. I think if my work does anything it forces a changed perception, even reluctantly. And it does this by refusing the expectation at every turn', *New Theatre Voices of the Seventies*, ed. Trussler, p. 196.
9. *What is Literature?* p. 59.
10. Howard Brenton, from 'Five on the Theatre', *Nail Poems: 32 Haiku* (RSC Publications, 1978) p. 2.
11. *What is Literature?*, pp. 56–7.

Index

233